Certifiable

Teaching, Learning, and National Board Certification

DAVID LUSTICK

ROWMAN & LITTLEFIELD EDUCATION
A Division of
ROWMAN & LITTLEFIELD PUBLISHERS, INC.
Lanham • New York • Toronto • Plymouth, UK

Published by Rowman & Littlefield Education
A division of Rowman & Littlefield Publishers, Inc.
A wholly owned subsidiary of The Rowman & Littlefield Publishing Group, Inc.
4501 Forbes Boulevard, Suite 200, Lanham, Maryland 20706
http://www.rowmaneducation.com

Estover Road, Plymouth PL6 7PY, United Kingdom

British Library Cataloguing in Publication Information Available

Library of Congress Cataloging-in-Publication Data

Lustick, David, 1962–
  Certifiable : teaching, learning, and National Board certification / David Lustick.
    p. cm.
  Includes bibliographical references.
  ISBN 978-1-60709-894-2 (cloth : alk. paper) — ISBN 978-1-60709-895-9 (pbk. : alk. paper) — ISBN 978-1-60709-896-6 (electronic)
  1. National Board for Professional Teaching Standards (U.S.) 2. Teachers—Certification--United States. I. Title.
  LB1771.L87 2009
  371.120973—dc22

                                                              2010034055

⊗™ The paper used in this publication meets the minimum requirements of American National Standard for Information Sciences—Permanence of Paper for Printed Library Materials, ANSI/NISO Z39.48-1992.

Printed in the United States of America

To my Mother and Father
who gave me a foundation
all the way down the line.

Contents

Preface

Some years ago, during an early phase of this work, my oldest son, Dakota, was a second grader. One cold winter evening around the dinner table, he shared a story with the whole family about what happened at school earlier in the day. He said they learned about the different types of jobs grown-ups have.

"When it was my turn, I told everyone that my Daddy is writing a book."

"I am?" I asked.

"Yes. You work downstairs every day writing your book."

"What kind of book?" I asked.

"It's your autobiography," he answered.

I had never considered the research and writing that occupied my time in my basement "office" as anything other than interesting work. But my son saw it as something more. To him, it was the story of my life. I was so struck with his perception of what "Daddy does" while pursuing a Ph.D. that the conversation has stayed with me.

This work in some respects is my "autobiography." It is the story of how a researcher tries to find an answer to a question that has both personal and professional value. In the most difficult and trying moments through this long process, my son's idea that it was a story helped me to stay on task to find an answer.

For me, teaching has always been part of how I define myself. Since elementary school, I worked to teach others. When teaching became my chosen career, the classroom was like a second home for me. Through the blur of day-to-day challenges trying to teach students about the world through the lens of science, I discovered the creative and often spontaneous power of purpose in the work of a teacher. I excelled at the practice. I pushed the boundaries of curriculum and technology. While preparing lessons, I would review textbooks and lab manuals to try to find the best vehicle for bringing about learning with my classes of students for that particular year. Often, I would think, "Is this the best way to teach this particular skill or concept?"

My dissatisfaction with the status quo curriculum or prepackaged labs resulted in my creating new approaches for my students. Sometimes they were successful and sometimes not. But with each attempt to improve, my reflective practice became richer in scope, more effective for my students, and, for a time, more interesting for me.

After seven years of this type of intensive teaching, I found myself getting stale, worn down, and maybe a little depressed. What had once been new had become tired. What was once a challenge had become routine. I was feeling the beginnings of the notorious "teacher burnout."

I had witnessed colleagues in New York City suffer for years with advanced stages of the affliction. One teacher in particular I remember used to come to work, walk into the teacher's lounge, and announce for all to hear: "673 days 15 hours until retirement." I knew I had to avoid this syndrome at all costs. With the threat of burnout hanging over my career, I heard President Clinton's State of the Union Address in 1997. It turned out to be a life-changing event.

During the speech, he said the following about teachers:

> To have the best schools, we must have the best teachers. Most of us in this chamber would not be here tonight without the help of those teachers. I know that I wouldn't be here. For years, many of our educators, led by North Carolina's Governor Jim Hunt and the National Board for Professional Teaching Standards, have worked very hard to establish nationally accepted credentials for excellence in teaching. Just 500 of these teachers have been certified since 1995. My budget will enable 100,000 more to seek national certification as master teachers. We should reward and recognize our best teachers. And as we reward them, we should quickly and fairly remove those few who don't measure up, and we should challenge more of our finest young people to consider teaching as a career.

His words rang in my head like a bell. "Reward and recognize our best teachers" and "credentials for excellence in teaching" piqued my interest and curiosity. What was the "National Board for Professional Teaching Standards"?

I took the president's words as a direct challenge to be one of those 100,000 teachers. In his plan to address the needs of schools, President Clinton described his ideas as a "Call to Action for American Education." I took that phrase in a literal sense: my president was calling on me to be one of those 100,000 master teachers. It was the first time in my life that a political figure had inspired me to do more with my life. I felt it was my duty as a good American to try to achieve what the President found important.

The next day I investigated the National Board for Professional Teaching Standards (NBPTS) through the brand new World Wide Web. I read the five core propositions and thought, "This is me. This is my kind of teaching." Within a month, I was preparing for certification and lobbying my administration for support. The next year, I successfully completed the certification process and became a National Board Certified Teacher in Adolescence and Young Adult Science.

The experience proved a high-water mark in my classroom teaching career. I put my entire heart, soul, and mind into it. I had the unusual experience of pursuing National Board certification while teaching at the American School in São Paulo, Brazil. Despite the intense isolation from others in my National Board certification cohort, I made connections with resource personnel on-line. In addition, I was able to solicit valuable assistance from some of my colleagues, students, and parents as I attempted to construct the entries of the portfolio. For the assessment center exercises, I had to fly from São Paulo to Miami, Florida, to take the two-day computerized assessment exercises.

After months of requests for financial assistance to cover the costs associated with National Board certification, my administration finally agreed to pay for half my travel expenses to Miami. All other costs associated with the certificate—the $300 registration fee, $1,700 certification fee, hotel, food, and so on—were my responsibility. I would also not enjoy any benefit to my salary or any financial gain if successful in my attempt to attain the coveted national certification.

For reasons that remain a mystery to me, my administration was not enthusiastic about my independent efforts to pursue the "new" form of certification. Likewise, my colleagues who were for the most part supportive and helpful, did not understand, appreciate, or necessarily approve of my ambitions. I felt that some of the teachers viewed National Board certification as a threat to the idea that, as teachers, we are all in it together. Trying to distinguish one's self from within this cultural value might have been perceived as an affront to what they viewed the teaching profession to be.

From their perspective, anyone who was "crazy" enough to pursue a career as a teacher should be given equal respect for the sacrifice. Whether they were effective in the classroom was secondary to the choice they made to dedicate their lives to helping young people learn. They were not in education for the money. They were not in education for the prestige. They were not teachers for the paperwork and requirements of the administration. All teachers are special because of what they sacrifice to work with learners.

National Board threatens this particular model of the teaching profession. It sends a message that deciding to be a teacher is not the distinguishing factor; rather, how effective one is at bringing about learning in the classroom becomes the primary consideration. In other words, some teachers may be better than others and National Board certification provided the first systematic means for verifying this assertion. Such an approach to the teaching profession is extremely threatening to a generation of educators raised under the auspices of the union-dominated, egalitarian view.

Teachers demonstrated this kind of apprehension by questioning why I was doing what I was doing. From their perspective, it seemed a little crazy to sacrifice so much for apparently so little. Why would anyone want to work so hard on something that seemed so unnecessary? Why would I want to prove that I was somehow better than everyone else? Why couldn't I be satisfied with the intrinsic rewards from the students I taught and their parents? Some teachers thought that they, too, could be successful with National Board certification if they wanted to work as much as it required and if they had the financial ability to cover all the costs.

Just because I was paying for this experience and committing extra hours of work after school and on weekends did not mean that I was a better teacher than someone who chose not to accept the extra responsibilities. For most of my colleagues at the time, National Board certification was an exercise in vanity. If I was successful, the experience would only benefit my ego and not translate into anything meaningful for the teacher, students, or the school as a whole.

I must admit that at the beginning of the experience, these ideas may very well have applied to me. I did want to prove to my community, as well as to myself, that I was an accomplished teacher as judged by an outside authority. Maybe I felt that I was not receiving the respect I felt I was due. Maybe the intrinsic rewards were not enough to validate the amount of work and time I put into my teaching. Maybe I was dissatisfied with the egalitarian model because it equated me with others who I was sure were far inferior to me at bringing about learning in the classroom.

I remember one teacher in particular who was an experienced teacher with a Ph.D. in chemistry. His content knowledge was far superior to mine in every respect, but he knew relatively little about how to teach that content to a diverse group of learners. It was true that for the high achievers, his traditional direct approach to instruction was quite effective as evidenced by the standardized test scores at the end of the year, but to the majority of average achievers, his pedagogy left much to be desired.[1] I knew this because many of them would come to my office hours for extra help because they knew I would employ different strategies and approaches to address their needs.

My colleague, though intelligent and experienced, was at a loss as to how to help these struggling students. To be fair, some of my higher-end students would seek him out during his office hours because I could not answer their advanced content questions to their satisfaction. However, we were hired to teach high school science, not college, and the needs of a secondary student go beyond just advanced content. I knew I was more effective than my traditional teaching counterpart at helping the majority of students not only appreciate and enjoy the experience of chemistry, but also succeed at learning the required concepts.

My knowledgeable colleague would probably find the National Board certification experience to consist of foreign ideas and silly tasks. He had little appreciation of the students as resources in the learning equation. He did not value the power of collaboration in learning nor in providing innovative and meaningful assessments. As is true with many traditional educators in science, he relied on lectures, note taking, didactic "discussions" (Q and A with the students asking questions and the teacher giving answers), and assessments based on memorization and problem-solving ability.

In many respects, I saw myself as a mirror opposite of this approach to teaching. For me, teaching and learning was a collaborative and evolving process. Assessment could involve memorization and problem solving, but it could also be open-ended and authentic. Students' ideas of natural phenomenon were assets to be mined in class, not obstacles to be overcome.

After reading the National Board's standards of accomplished science teaching, I knew that the standards described my approach to teaching and learning and not that of my esteemed colleague. The National Board's standards were the first documents to articulate and speak directly to my abilities and values as a science educator.

Faced with colleagues whose approach to instruction was traditional and who were not accepting of alternative pedagogies, I felt the teaching experience closing in on me in an unwelcome manner. National Board certification provided me with an opportunity to address this problem in an innovative and enticing way. Little did I know that its impact on me both professionally and personally would go far beyond these motivating factors.

If my decision to pursue National Board certification started out as an exercise in vanity, it ended as professional learning experience still impacting me to this day. The idea that the process would only benefit me and not my students was proved blatantly false. I knew that my intense and honest efforts at a critical self-reflection had changed some of my approaches to teaching and reaffirmed others.

For example, I gained a new appreciation for the learning experience as seen through the eyes of different students. For some, learning science was second nature and for others it was like pulling teeth. Appreciating how painful and difficult learning can sometimes be enabled me to anticipate problems with individual learners before they became big and weighty issues.

I also learned about the value of parents as a resource in a student's successful learning experience. Prior to certification, I mainly saw parents as a nuisance at their worst and as a hedge with student discipline problems at their best. However, after certification, I saw every parent as having a unique child with a different set of priorities and values. Addressing those differences allowed me to develop more prosperous and appreciably better relationships with those parents and their children.

I think I learned the most in my actual daily practice. After analyzing videotapes of my work, I quickly realized that I talked more than I listened. I missed important comments and questions between students. I was too easily drawn into the "sage on the stage" role of teaching. Finally, what I thought was "wait time" was really more like a one-second pause.

There is nothing more humbling than watching a video of one's teaching for the first time. The reality of the video confronts directly one's self-perception as a teacher. The disconnect between perception and reality can be quite disturbing. What I had thought was pretty good work proved to be awful, and what I had considered awful turned out to be not so bad. The video analysis forever changed me as a teacher and a person. Every time I stepped into a classroom, I was reminded of those horrible images I was forced to confront in the video. I was determined to address every identified weakness and turn it into strength.

After I achieved certification, I began thinking seriously about why I found the experience such a profound and productive professional development. When I arrived at Michigan State University to pursue a Ph.D. in Curriculum, Teaching & Educational Policy, I quickly discovered in the literature that there were many teachers who had had similar experiences with National Board certification and had written about it in journals and magazines.

An idea began to form that the mounting anecdotal evidence might constitute a legitimate phenomenon worthy of investigation. The literature had great breadth, but relatively little depth. When asked what they learned by going through National Board certification, the typical answer was an unfulfilling "I'm more reflective" type of response. Very few pieces went into any kind of detail about what "more reflective" might actually mean.

If I had been asked what I learned, I would have found it difficult to answer, too—not because I didn't learn anything, but because I had learned so much that it was impossible to sort out the complex nature of the outcomes and their respective influence upon my practice. I wanted to know what I and others learned from certification and the best way to find out was through research.

The study presented here is my attempt to answer the question, "What are teachers learning from the certification process?" The value of this research is not just for the educational policy community, classroom teachers, and the National Board, but for me. On a very personal level I wanted to understand the experience more thoroughly and be able to discuss learning outcomes beyond the "more reflective" rhetoric. If the research could answer some of my own questions, it might help other teachers decide whether to pursue Board certification and help other candidates understand their own experiences more thoroughly.

The decision to pursue an empirical approach to this question was based on two factors: (1) the policy community's desire for information based on empirical studies and (2) the unique opportunity to attempt to measure outcomes using the National Board's own rubrics and scoring procedures.[2] The idea to use the Board's own assessment tools to evaluate candidate learning from certification signifies the moment when this research became possible.

As I did this work on how and what others might be learning, I was constantly aware at every step what it was that I might be learning. I was conscious of my role in the process and how my ideas and perceptions were shaping and were shaped by the events I experienced. I approached this project with an intellectual curiosity and professional honesty. What, if anything, would the data reveal was learned from the process of certification? Was my experience common or uncommon? How would demonstrated professional knowledge among candidates change from before to after certification? When I began this investigation, I did not know the answers to these questions. Now I have a much better understanding. My learning is documented in this work.

As I reflect on this effort, two learning outcomes stand out. The first idea deals with the process of research in education and the other pertains to National Board. Before this investigative endeavor, I had no appreciation for the arduous work that goes into education research. Research was always something presented to me in its finished form that identified new knowledge or questioned existing consensus on one point or another. Now, I see it as a unique human endeavor prone to all the weaknesses and strengths of the people involved. Technology is a wonderful tool for conducting research, but in the end it is the investigator collaborating with a team of diverse individuals that makes a project come to life.

My other specific learning outcome is about the National Board. I went into this work with a rather naïve notion of the Board as a solitary institution dedicated solely to the identification and assessment of exceptional teachers. While I still think this is true, I now see the Board as an outsider; it is like a renegade entity fighting against ill-defined forces for a rightful and integrated position in American education. I have come to a point where I am both hopeful and apprehensive about the organization's prognosis.

National Board has been a central part of my life for the last twelve years. In 1998, I was part of the first cohort of Board-certified teachers in Adolescence and Young Adult Science. Later I served on the Board's committee to teach America about accomplished teaching. In preparation for this research, I also became an assessor during the summer for the Board scoring the Whole Class Discussion in Science entry in Pittsburgh, Pennsylvania.

In 2008 I successfully completed my Profile in Professional Growth as required to be recertified for another ten years. I have participated in many National Board–sponsored events at both the state and national levels. Through all this experience, I have come to know and admire many of the people who work tirelessly every day to make the work of the Board possible.

Because of my extensive experience with the National Board, I am susceptible to attacks of bias. In response, I approached this work from a critical disposition that manifests itself in both the rigor of my analysis and the presentation of possible implications of this work to prospective candidates, the National Board, and our educational system. In the words of Richard Feynman, I have "bent over backwards" to model "utter scientific integrity" about this work in an effort not to delude myself into discovering answers I wanted to find (1974, 12).

If some interpret this transparency as evidence of weakness, that is their prerogative. The harshest critics of the Board will find ideas in this book that, if taken out of context, will support their position. Those who blindly support anything the Board does will discover that an informed understanding is more effective than unquestioning loyalty. I am of the belief that total disclosure can only strengthen the important findings and implications associated with this work. The results are quite clear: National Board provides an excellent opportunity to become a more accomplished teacher.

National Board certification seems to accomplish the impossible. It identifies exceptional teachers while simultaneously fostering effective professional learning. For some, the idea that an assessment could also serve as an effective learning opportunity will go against their traditional conceptualization of each. Hopefully, this book will help such individuals come to a more integrated understanding of how teacher evaluation can lead to teacher learning. While I do not try to hide my affection for the organization or the promise it holds for exceptional educators both in the United States and around the world, I also see its weaknesses and liabilities.

The story told in this work began life as my dissertation at Michigan State University. In my efforts to adapt it for a more general audience, I bring to bear all my knowledge and experience with the Board to produce the highest quality discussion about teaching, professional learning, and National Board possible.[3]

If Boshier (1994, 73) is correct when he suggests that "good research emerges as the perfect intersection between socio-historical circumstances and one's own biography," then the chapters that follow tell a story worth sharing. If this is my autobiography, as my son suggests, then the work presented here represents only the first chapter. I consider my ongoing efforts to achieve knowledge and understanding as a "work in progress" requiring many more years and a career of study.

NOTES

1. Coincidentally, my students did just as well if not better on the same exams. So regardless of teaching philosophy, both teachers facilitated excellent test results, but the learning experiences for our respective students were quite different.

2. There is another important reason for this research. I submitted a proposal for research in response to a request for proposal from the NBPTS. After a thorough review of more than one hundred proposals submitted, the RAND Corporation recommended that my study be one of the twenty-one proposals selected for funding. While my budget of $187,000 was the smallest amount awarded by the Board during this particular round, it is hard to imagine anyone who was happier than me at the time. While I thank the RAND Corporation and NBPTS for giving me the opportunity to do research, I am quite cognizant of the appearance of bias this relationship might represent. My interactions with the NBPTS were always of the highest professional integrity. Never once did anyone ever ask me to alter, revise, or change anything about my results. My findings, whether flattering or problematic for the Board, were always received with great respect.

3. Portions of this work have previously been published in Lustick and Sykes, "National Board certification," 2006.

Acknowledgments

Though much of the work that goes into writing a book is done in seclusion and near isolation, I could not have initiated, worked through, and successfully completed this endeavor without an inspiring collective of friends and professionals from around the world. With far too many to name, I will do my best to focus on the individuals who were most important to the development of this project. The work that went into this book spans across my time at two different institutions. The initial research took place at Michigan State University (Go State!) while much of the writing took place at the University of Massachusetts Lowell (Go River Hawks!). Therefore, I find my acknowledgments divided between these two institutions.

First, I need to acknowledge the expertise and foresight of Tom Koerner, my editor at Rowman & Littlefield. Without Tom's encouragement, insightful comments, and understanding, I would not have been able to bring this work to completion. I will forever feel a debt of gratitude toward Tom and his staff for giving me this opportunity at the best possible moment.

My professors and friends at Michigan State University were an invaluable source of wisdom and guidance. It is a good thing that tuition covers the cost of an education, because if I had to give a nickel every time I sought out help or an answer to a question, I might have paid twice as much. From this perspective, my doctoral education at the Graduate School of Education was a bargain.

No other person has taught me more about excellence in teaching and scholarship than Gary Sykes. Gary is an intellectual force of nature. Our discussions about National Board and research were punctuated episodes of exhilaration. When confronted with a problem, Gary starts off slow and builds up a head of steam. Before long, he churns out ideas like a train chugging down the tracks. I left every one of our meetings literally shaking with energy and inspiration. I am forever in debt to the generosity of intellect, trust, and spirit he showed me as my chair, advisor, role model, and friend. An exceptional teacher, Gary's voice and perspective remain a permanent part of my psyche. If I could be a quarter the professor Gary is, I would be immensely satisfied.

Michigan State was an amazing place for me to learn and I need to thank Jim Gallagher and Bruce Burke who recognized the potential match and dragged me away from the classroom and into the world of academia. The quality of this study was greatly enhanced by the insightful and effective critiques provided by Mary Kennedy, Mark Reckase, and David Labaree. Their respective areas of expertise were a constant reminder of the level of excellence I continue to strive toward. A heartfelt thanks also to Susan Melnick, Bob Floden, and Yong Zhao for their consistent support, understanding, and wisdom. I am grateful for the assistance above and beyond the call of duty from Richard Houang who insisted that I slow down and think more about my work. He is not only a gifted statistician, but also a good friend.

At the University of Massachusetts Lowell, I want to thank Don Pierson who convinced me that UMass Lowell was the place for me to begin my academic career. He was right. The support and guidance given to me by my colleagues and the administration goes above and beyond my expectations. In particular, Anita Greenwood and Jay Simmons have been so helpful in their encouragement and open-door policies. It is an honor to have such personable and gifted colleagues who are always willing to listen and offer advice.

While my teachers taught me how to think about research in education, it was my friends who gave me the support and confidence to complete the task. Thanks to my very good friends, Cindy Kendall and Dan Copeland, who showed me what it means to be educated, intelligent, and caring. Their impact on me reverberates over time like thunder. And a heartfelt thanks to Joseph Flynn for listening when he didn't have to, talking when he needed to, and showing up whenever he wanted. My deepest gratitude goes to my colleague and friend, Jill Lohmeier, for her unwavering belief in my ability to succeed.

Thanks to Dean Grosshandler, Misty Sato, and my brother Ian for their willingness to provide honest feedback when it was most needed. They each went above and beyond in their respective ways to make this effort the best it could be. Friends and family like these are rare and precious. They have each enriched my life more than they will ever know, and to them all, I am grateful.

In addition to teachers and friends, individuals from across the country helped in ways too numerous to list. Thanks to all the teachers who gave their time and energy to discuss teaching and learning with me for this study. Thanks to the assessors who contributed their experience and expertise to the analysis of data and to the transcribers, secretaries, and support personnel who improved the quality of my work through their individual efforts and professionalism. It has been my pleasure to collaborate with such a talented group of professionals. I am humbled and honored by the awesome commitment to excellence that they shared with me.

In the last few months, Brandis Kelly has worked as my copy editor for this book. Like an angel, she appeared at my office willing and able to provide the critical eye of an English major. For the many hours she spent pouring over drafts and finding mistakes I am most appreciative and grateful.

When I think of exceptional classroom teaching, Mrs. Slocum, my fifth grade teacher comes to mind. Back at Wiley Elementary School in Watertown, New York, she showed me what it means to focus on the whole child and not just the outcomes. Without her insight and skill, I might never have found my way back to the way of learning.

Last, but certainly not least, I wish to thank my family. My wife, Doreen, has been a constant source of encouragement and understanding that has made my work possible. Her love, beauty, and unending patience have enriched my life immeasurably. Our three children, Dakota, Avalon, and Troy, never made me feel too guilty about sacrificing time together for time on this book. The days and months spent completing this work have made me cherish their company even more.

Foreword

GARY SYKES

This volume comes at a welcome time in our nation's continuing efforts to improve teaching and learning in the schools, and to build a teaching corps with the needed knowledge and skills to face the demands and challenges of the twenty-first century. By some accounts, we are on the verge of transformational changes in education, ushered in via technology, charter schools, and new accountability arrangements. Perhaps schools will disappear in the face of online teaching, districts will wither in the face of assemblies of independent chartered schools, education schools will be challenged by a medley of alternative providers, and teachers will be held accountable for their students' learning as measured by new tests and assessments.

Perhaps. But any reading in the history of educational reform gives pause to some of the more audacious claims made by the current round of reformers. These new developments and more are likely to unfold in the coming decades, but it seems unlikely that they will replace traditional schools, districts, education schools, or teachers; it is equally unlikely that the reforms will fully realize their ambitions while steering clear of a range of unanticipated and adverse consequences.

One current reform, however, has navigated the tricky waters of change to produce some widespread and positive results. Launched in 1986, the National Board for Professional Teaching Standards (NBPTS) will soon celebrate its twenty-fifth anniversary, a quarter decade of substantial achievements. What is most striking about the National Board is its insistence that good teaching is the heart of the matter, that it can be identified, and, as a result, that good teachers can both be "found" and "made." Board certification may simply draw highly qualified teachers to its ranks, in which case certification simply signals competence; or the process of certification may itself constitute a form of professional development that actually cultivates and enhances teaching. It is undeniable that Board certification is a rigorous and demanding course of examination and study that constitutes a mark of distinction among teachers.

In his splendid study, David Lustick explores the meaning of accomplished teaching in some depth, providing rich cases to consider together with evidence on the question of Board certification as professional development. As with almost all of the many studies accumulating about Board certification, the evidence is mixed, but in the numbers and the narrative may be discerned positive indications that teachers learned from the process itself on at least some important dimensions of teaching.

The volume constitutes a reflection on three matters that are central to the debates today about teaching. One is the nature of teaching itself: Is this a complex practice? Can it be easily routinized? Is teacher planning and decision making important and do teachers differ from each other in the ways they go about their work? And most important, are there dimensions of good teaching that are not easily captured either in standard evaluation protocols or in attention just to the value added by teachers to student achievement? Lustick supplies thoughtful commentary on these questions, generally noting the subtleties and complexities in discerning aspects of good teaching.

A second issue of note concerns how to study teaching in order to get at its qualities and its effects. The book may be read as a cautionary tale about the difficulties in the conduct of such investigations, taking the reader behind the scenes in ways that most studies fail to do. What we can conclude from this excursion into the frailties of the research process is that no single study can be definitive on the important issues because all such studies are flawed, even the most rigorously designed field experiments. In this case, a cunning quasiexperimental design was employed (meaning that there was not random assignment of teachers to the "intervention" being studied, nor use of fully constituted control groups), but a variety of practical problems emerged to challenge the findings.

One argument might be that these problems constituted fatal flaws to the study. Another argument, one that comes closer to the truth of inquiry, is that all such studies contain these difficulties, but few investigators fully reveal them. This volume, then, serves as a valuable contribution to the literature on the conduct of inquiry on teaching. Originating as a doctoral dissertation, this volume's account of the inquiry itself will make valuable reading for graduate students who are learning the research process.

Finally, the latter chapters of the volume take up the future of the National Board itself, considering a range of options to ensure its continuing vitality and relevancy to American education. The theme of professionalism in teaching that emerged in the 1980s and 1990s has been eclipsed by a new set of reforms that pay scant attention to teaching itself, preferring to concentrate just on outcomes as measured by tests. What is needed is better balance between efforts to cultivate the teaching profession as well as holding it to reasonable account.

The reform pendulum continues to swing, in the midst of which the National Board is an indispensable reform because it maintains focus on qualities of "good to great" teaching at a time when such emphasis is missing in the dominant reforms of the day. Considering the role of the National Board in the future of the teaching occupation is of central importance, and the NBPTS continues to fight the good fight in keeping teaching central in the mission of education. Lustick's thoughts on these matters are carefully considered and worth attending.

In sum, this volume makes a fine contribution to the literature on one of the most significant reforms in American education. Board certification has become part of the institutional fabric of the education system, with influence that extends beyond the growth in numbers of Board-certified teachers. State and local policy makers are weaving National Board certification into new roles for teachers, pay for performance, schoolwide initiatives, and others. Lustick's study helps us understand in detail the nature of this reform and its implications for the future. It deserves wide and close reading.

Introduction

This book will mean different things to different groups of people. First and foremost, this book illustrates why National Board certification represents such a significant achievement for each of the 80,000-plus candidates who were successful. For the other 60,000 or so candidates who were not successful, this book explores why the experience may still have been worth the effort. For every teacher who thinks National Board certification might be in their future, this book addresses some of the fundamental questions regarding the kinds of practice and types of evidence that reflect well upon a candidate.

While the book examines the experiences of secondary science teachers, most of the ideas and insights shared will be relevant to any K–12 educator interested in learning about practice. Finally, for those educators who are unfamiliar with the National Board, the discussion presented here provides an overview and sense of the potential certification offers the individual and the profession.

For educational researchers, the book is a detailed account of a sophisticated investigation into a meaningful question. What are teachers learning from National Board certification? The narrative compares the ideal intentions of a study with the actual products of research. Research involving human behavior is rarely neat and tidy. Any principal investigator who claims otherwise should be approached with a healthy dose of skepticism.

The story of research in these pages is one of planning, unexpected obstacles, and innovative compromises that move the effort forward toward finding an answer. For education researchers who face a serious challenge (either methodological or theoretical), the accounts of both quantitative and qualitative methodologies may provide insight, solace, and hope during those moments when all efforts teeter on the brink of failure. Mistakes, errors, and unanticipated events are part of the research experience. It is how they are dealt with that marks one's skill as a researcher. With a little luck, they can become opportunities rather than barriers to excellence.

Lastly, for education policy makers who look at the Board as an intriguing and potentially meaningful reform to improve the quality of teaching and learning in schools, this book offers suggestions on how to move forward. The educational system faces great challenges ahead. From ensuring equitable learning opportunities for all to making public education a valued and respected institution, the problems are significant.

National Board represents one small step toward a system that acknowledges the complexity and richness of exceptional teaching. Policy makers, educational leaders, and politicians can learn from this book that accomplished teaching is more than simply improving student achievement. To acknowledge and reward the very best teachers is to point a way forward to a future that benefits teachers, parents, and their children. The real issue is how one defines "best."

Great teaching is about the positive ways teachers impact the lives of students. Talented teachers foster understanding of content and mastery of skills with learners in ways that are meaningful to both the individual and the community. Because it involves so many facets of human experience, exceptional teaching is difficult to define. Because the outcomes of exceptional teaching are not always explicit or immediate, it is a real challenge to accurately evaluate. And because a sense of the mysterious is associated with this kind of practice, it is not easy for most teachers to achieve this level of effectiveness.

National Board represents the best effort to date for defining, identifying, and fostering accomplished teaching. At an immediate level, this book is about the learning candidates for National Board experience. From a big-picture perspective, this book explores what it means to be a professional educator in a world where expertise is defined by those who do not teach. While this book is more analytical than persuasive, it is hard to avoid the potential solutions the Board offers for some real and meaningful problems in schools.

The National Board faces an uncertain future. After a brief childhood and an abbreviated adolescence, it is time for the National Board to become an adult. No longer can it depend upon government funds to underwrite its efforts. No longer can its annual survival depend solely upon the actions of state legislatures. The Board must figure out how to be an asset for the work of all teachers and a valued resource for schools. By carving out a purpose for itself as a reform that solves important problems, the National Board for Professional Teaching Standards (NBPTS) may someday reach its full potential. If in some small way this book helps facilitate the Board's maturation process, then it will have been a success.

OVERVIEW

This book is a means of addressing a few central questions about teaching and learning for a generation of educational stakeholders wanting to provide a quality educational experience for all learners. What is exceptional teaching? How might it be defined and assessed? How can the assessment of accomplished teaching actually foster improvements to teacher quality?

The important findings from this research are presented in an accessible style for a diverse audience of educational stakeholders. From parents to policy makers, educators faced with issues about exceptional teaching and professional learning should find the discussion relevant.

The research reported on here comes out of a national study completed in 2006 that examined candidates for National Board certification in Adolescence and Young Adult Science. More specifically, the project asked the question, "What are candidates learning from National Board certification?" To determine possible answers, a quasiexperimental investigation with 140 secondary science teachers from forty-two states was conducted.

The presentation is divided into three parts aligned with each aspect of the book's secondary title: *Teaching, Learning,* and *National Board Certification* respectively. Each part is further divided into three supporting chapters. Part I provides context and raises questions, and Part II describes the methods used and the answers found. Part III looks at how the findings from this investigation might impact the quality of teaching, certification, and the future of the National Board.

Part I: *Teaching* considers the problem with exceptional teaching and identifies the major concepts examined in the book's argument. While defining, assessing, and fostering great teaching might appear like a reasonable endeavor, education has been slow to adopt reforms that challenge the egalitarian ideal that all teachers are good in their own ways.

After chapter 1 presents three key assumptions upon which National Board certification rests, chapter 2 presents five candidates' descriptions of a successful lesson. They all try to teach the same objective, but their styles, approaches, and beliefs cover a wide range. Using standards of performance to make evidence-based judgments regarding a teacher's classification as "accomplished" or "not accomplished" illustrates both the difficulty and necessity of a robust teacher assessment process.

While not always clear or pretty, the example represents a radically new way to gauge the quality of teaching and learning. The five science teachers presented in chapter 2 provide an opportunity to appreciate and understand the difficult tasks associated with both the work of the Board and the investigation into candidate learning.

Chapter 3 outlines the work of the Board, including the development of the five core propositions, standards, assessments, and evaluative procedures. By developing valid and reliable assessment instruments, rubrics, and procedures, the National Board effectively compares a teacher's work against a set of professional standards in order to arrive at a meaningful measure of quality. This process is central to understanding the data presented and discussed in the next three chapters.

Part II: *Learning* describes the research that identified, quantified, and substantiated what candidates learn from the certification process. Chapter 4 outlines the design and procedures used to collect data. To make precise and accurate measurements of teacher learning, the procedures and protocols used by the Board to evaluate accomplished teaching were adapted to measure changes in teachers' understanding about individual standards. By comparing what teachers know before and after certification, significant changes become observable learning outcomes.

Chapter 5 presents the results of the pre- and postcertification comparisons. The strategies for analysis that resulted in the identification of specific learning outcomes are discussed. Observed gains at the overall-, set-, and individual-standard levels identified assessment of student learning, reflective abilities, and the use of inquiry to promote in-depth understanding as the three standards associated with the most candidate learning. The limitations of these findings are also discussed within the challenges faced by such a complex investigation.

Chapter 6 examines the rich and abundant qualitative data to further substantiate the observed learning outcomes. The chapter considers the evidence for learning associated with assessment, reflection, and inquiry through candidate comments and responses to specific interview prompts. The curriculum and resources available to candidates are then considered to see how certification might foster professional learning in these specific areas.

Part III examines National Board certification from several perspectives informed by this investigation. It considers how the conclusions might impact teacher quality, the certification process, and the future work of the Board. Does teacher learning from certification translate into improved classroom instruction? How might the conclusions inform and improve the certification process? What lessons can the National Board take away from this work that could improve its relevancy as a significant and lasting education reform?

Chapter 7 considers the possible connections between observed teacher learning and changes to teacher quality. Understanding how Board certification may possibly impact the classroom teaching of candidates informs public discourse around issues of teacher quality and the ways professional development might be leveraged to produced desired changes.

Just because National Board candidates acquire new knowledge and skills does not necessarily translate into changes in practice. From this position, "learning" is not of much value if it fails to improve the quality of teaching and learning in the classroom.

By grouping candidates from this study into "dynamic," "technical," and "deferred" categories of learning, a proposed relationship between the certification experience and its impact upon the quality of practice is described. Roughly half of all candidates make immediate changes to their teaching based upon what they learn (dynamic) while the other half direct their learning toward becoming better candidates for certification (technical). Interestingly, the observed learning outcomes and possible impacts on practice apply both to candidates who were successful and to those who were not successful at achieving Board certification.

Chapter 8 considers how the findings from this research may impact the work of the National Board. The chapter develops suggestions regarding how to improve the quality of the Board's assessment process and the viability of the organization in the face of significant challenges from both within and outside the education community.

The book closes with a final commentary that ties the results of this investigation to the future of the National Board. This investigation offers many insights into how the Board might adapt to a changing policy environment and the dangers it must avoid. After almost two decades and the certification of nearly one hundred thousand teachers, the National Board finds itself at a crossroad. The future of the Board may rest on the relationship it establishes with the broader community of teachers. For teachers, administrators, and policy personnel, this concluding chapter may help stimulate discussion regarding innovative and sustainable means of maintaining the NBPTS.

If this book helps the reader develop a more thorough understanding of the National Board, the certification process, and what candidates learn from the experience, then it will have achieved its primary explicit goals. However, the argument laid out in these chapters also makes the case for a richer vision of what accomplished teaching means in an era of high-stakes accountability. This more implicit point has implications that reach far beyond the National Board and go to the heart of the character and quality of this nation's educational system.

As this book goes to press, states across the country are implementing or considering measures that would significantly change their support for National Board certification. In Florida, the state with the second most National Board–certified teachers, the Legislature is considering a bill that would end yearly bonuses for Board-certified teachers and institute a merit-pay initiative based on student test scores.

Ohio has ended its yearly bonus program for Board-certified teachers, but made National Board an option for teachers to obtain their highest-level professional license. Legislation at the state level pays for most of the costs of certification and the yearly bonuses enjoyed by successful candidates. These fiscal commitments function as the lifeblood for the Board's mission. Without this support, the future of the National Board is uncertain.

Ironically, this change in the policy environment comes at a time when the value of certification as an effective professional development is just being established. This book argues for a vision of teaching and learning that has become overshadowed by a myopic obsession with education based solely on improving student achievement. While the two may not be mutually exclusive, policy discourse tends to polarize the issue.

The states' diminished ability to support National Board is not necessarily a bad thing. In state budgets, the line item dedicated to Board incentives does just as much to provoke animosity among taxpayers as it does attract teachers into certification. As states search for ways to integrate National Board certification into their licensure systems, the teaching community can decide whether the National Board represents the knowledge and skills of their most accomplished members. The future of the Board may depend on the degree to which all teachers wish to support its mission of defining, assessing, and fostering accomplished practice.

I

TEACHING

The Problem with Exceptional Teaching

The United States faces a serious problem in the way it identifies and promotes exceptional teaching.[1] While most of the public's attention is on low-performing schools, little consideration is given to the effective teachers who work to foster students' learning. Absent the glare of the media spotlight, these teachers receive a subtle, but mixed, message.

On the one hand, policy makers wax poetic about what it means to be a high-quality teacher with words like "commitment," "compassion," "courage," and "content." On the other hand, districts reward teachers based primarily upon issues unrelated to the quality of instruction. Teachers' compensation is usually determined by their years of service and accumulated graduate credits. Compared to how new teachers are educated, observed, tested, and licensed prior to entering the classroom, experienced teachers have precious few options for distinguishing themselves from colleagues.

Reasons for this situation are both historical and complex, but suffice it to say that it is much easier to define, discuss, and enforce the basic requirements a teacher should have upon entering the classroom than it is to promote improvement and evaluate effectiveness later in a career. Too many poor or adequate teachers are grouped together through common compensation structures with effective and accomplished teachers. Such a uniform view of pedagogical quality is unfair to teachers and damaging to the system.[2]

How can schools improve if mediocrity and exceptional performance are treated equally? Furthermore, how can teachers learn to be accomplished within a system that does not effectively distinguish between varying degrees of quality?

To illustrate this problem, consider the following story of two chemistry teachers named Dan and Rich. Dan and Rich work at the same school with equivalent education credentials and the same number of years of experience. Dan implements an impressive class project about the periodic table while Rich covers the topic with a lecture- and worksheet-based lesson. In Dan's approach, individual students research an assigned element in depth using their textbook, online resources, and print documents from the media center.

Dan provides guidance as each student creates a poster that visually conveys some important property of the element and presents his or her findings to the class. The posters contain basic information such as atomic mass, atomic weight, name, and symbol, but are also visually attractive and engaging. Students use their posters to collectively construct a life size periodic table in the hallway outside of class, which serves as a science exhibit for the entire school community.[3]

Dan receives accolades and commendations from parents and administrators regarding the project. It is even written up in the school paper. Because of both the intrinsic rewards (professional kudos and community recognition) as well as the extrinsic rewards (demonstrated student learning, increased student engagement and interest in science), Dan is encouraged to pursue similar strategies in the future.

In contrast, Rich briefly lectures about the periodic table, pointing to a wall chart and using his white board to write notes. He also hands out a worksheet for the students to complete individually during class time. Students are assigned a chapter of reading from the textbook and questions to answer about the periodic table. They go over these questions the next day before moving on to another topic. Rich's students listen to his presentation and occasionally a select few students raise hands to ask questions, which Rich is more than happy to answer. Rich's students are not particularly interested in chemistry and would best be described as "going through the motions" of learning, rather than actively engaging with content.

Interestingly, students of both Dan and Rich perform equally well on a common assessment that asks questions about the periodic table. However, a survey of student attitudes reveals that Dan's students have a significantly more positive attitude toward school and toward science in particular. The survey results also indicate that Dan's students are more likely to pursue further studies in science at both the secondary and postsecondary levels.

Are Dan and Rich equivalent educators? In the current system, they are treated the same even though they are qualitatively different in their approach to practice and the kinds of outcomes they solicit from learners. The fact that Dan consistently engages, empowers, and inspires students to learn while Rich only meets minimum expectations does not have any bearing on the official label associated with each teacher; both are considered highly qualified. Should Rich and Dan be considered equally effective? Should they receive equal compensation? Is Dan a better teacher than Rich? If so, should Rich be encouraged to make his teaching more engaging and interesting to students in a manner similar to Dan's?

Current systems of teacher evaluation and promotion consider educators like Dan and Rich to be the same. In a system based primarily on administrative observations, years of employment, and graduate credits earned, teachers tend to move through the system in an orderly and predictable fashion. As long as work is deemed "satisfactory," teachers continue to progress step by step, year after year, through the district's career ladder. This approach has proven effective at maintaining the egalitarian ideal that all teachers are equally good in their respective disciplines and specialties.

The policy also sends the message that areas of specialization (i.e., elementary generalist, history, secondary calculus) are equally valued within a district. However, a heavy price is paid for maintaining the status quo and ignoring the rich amalgam of skills and knowledge that goes into exceptional practice and the valuable spectrum of student outcomes it can produce. Such tactics tend to promote passable instruction at the expense of exceptional teaching. Why should a teacher invest the additional time and effort to be extraordinary if average performance will garner the same rewards?

By ignoring the varying degrees of "satisfactory" instruction from the promotion and compensation of teachers, the system ensures a population of educators that gravitate toward the median, and where mediocrity becomes the norm. Rather than using the evaluation of teachers to promote improvements in teaching that make tangible differences in the lives of students, current policies work to stifle innovation, professional growth, and excellence.

The current laws and reform efforts focus attention and resources upon the lowest-performing schools. While this is a completely understandable priority, it does lead many to neglect the other end of the quality spectrum. Many education stakeholders would be thrilled if teacher quality gravitated toward the median. For half of the teaching workforce below the median, this means improvement. However, for those who are already effective in the classroom, there is a sense of abandonment and neglect. How can the best teachers in both successful and failing schools be supported in their efforts to provide effective instruction and grow professionally?

Even if a district wanted to change its evaluative procedures so as to identify different grades of performance, it would be unlikely to do so successfully. The risk (or even the appearance) of bias and the general disruption to the community that could result from errors in judgment are just too high. If removing the incompetent teacher is a challenge, differentiating between satisfactory and exceptional teachers could draw much public antagonism from those who might see the distinctions as little more than a popularity contest.

Districts are ill prepared and ill positioned to develop the standards and corresponding set of valid, reliable, and transparent assessment instruments needed to avoid the problem of subjectivity. The problem with exceptional teaching lies in the local community's lack of tools necessary to identify, assess, and reward it. The job is just too big.

Today, advanced-level teaching assessments give districts real power in identifying and rewarding teachers like Dan while simultaneously offering the Riches of the world an opportunity to become better educators.

The most successful advanced teacher assessment program is offered through the National Board for Professional Teaching Standards (NBPTS). NBPTS (hereafter referred to as *the Board, National Board,* or *NBPTS*) offers local districts an effective means of differentiating between good and exceptional teaching.

For more than two decades, the NBPTS has taken on three monumental tasks. First, the NBPTS drew upon teachers, scholars, and research to define "accomplished teaching" across different disciplines and student age groups. Second, the Board (in collaboration with Educational Testing Services)[4] developed a research-based innovative approach to assessing teachers against these standards of accomplished teaching.[5] And third, the Board set out to make the certification process not only valid and reliable, but also a worthwhile professional learning opportunity for the teaching candidate.

It is the professional-development aspect of the National Board process that serves as the focus of this book. Is National Board certification a good opportunity for teachers to learn and grow professionally? If so, what are teachers learning from their National Board experience? If Rich and Dan were candidates for Board certification, what would they learn about their teaching and how might their respective practices change? Even if they were unsuccessful at achieving National Board certification, would they learn to be better teachers?

In education, successful efforts to improve teaching and learning in a meaningful manner demand in-depth analysis and dissemination among educational constituents. The National Board for Professional Teaching Standards presents the classrooms of this nation with the valuable promise of promoting the kinds of teaching and learning that parents, administrators, and policy makers can embrace knowing that students and society are the long-term beneficiaries of these important efforts.

THREE KEY ASSUMPTIONS

Before delving into the process of National Board certification and the research that examines what teachers learn from the experience, it is prudent to discuss three basic assumptions with which a national assessment system for identifying exceptional teachers must contend. The first assumption deals with the nature of teaching and learning as a complex cognitive endeavor. Teaching is an intellectual activity that requires an individual to think critically about effects of professional decisions upon others.

The second assumption states that complex teaching requires an equally complex means of assessment. Simply using student test scores (or any other single "objective" output measure) as a means of identifying excellence in teaching runs the risk of misidentifying exceptional teaching. The obsession with achievement may actually harm the quality of instruction by promoting a very limited vision of learning outcomes.

Finally, the third assumption states that exceptional teachers can foster student learning even in the most challenging of school contexts. In other words, just because a school may not have the best resources, most involved parents, or best prepared students, exceptional teachers can still foster significant learning. The discussion that follows further explains the importance of each assumption and its relevancy to the study of National Board certification.

Assumption #1: Teaching and Learning is Complex

The Board's efforts to describe, assess, and identify accomplished teaching takes place within a maelstrom of divergent ideas and approaches to education. For some, teaching is the straightforward process of one person helping another person to understand something he or she did not previously comprehend. For others, teaching is a complex human activity that integrates a multitude of disciplines, skill sets, and specialized knowledge.

The straightforward view of teaching gains support from the routine instruction people provide one another every day. We help strangers who are lost to find their destination. We provide a definition when asked about the meaning of a word. We question how to make the best chocolate chip cookies, and, hopefully, we find a tasty answer from someone willing to share a secret recipe. It is therefore not surprising that some believe successful teaching is an easy matter of matching someone who understands and is willing to share with those who do not know and want to learn.

Unfortunately, teachers do not always know everything that they should about a topic, and students do not always want to learn about said topic. The classroom is rich with diverse beliefs, understandings, and experiences regarding any one particular idea or issue. Some students are ready and eager to learn, while others are not. Some teachers think they know enough, while others see every day as a learning opportunity. While the straightforward view of teaching may be helpful in a pragmatic approach to education, it is insufficient at best and insulting at its worst.

The insidious problem with such a superficial understanding of effective teaching is that it undermines the complexity, subtlety, and nuance inherent in the goal of human improvement. Teaching is the process of one human being working to improve some aspect of another human being. Ignoring the intricacies of practice shows no appreciation for the significant knowledge, skills, and dispositions that effective teachers bring to bear in their efforts to foster understanding in all learners. The issue, therefore, is to identify and define the knowledge base that constitutes effective or accomplished teaching.[6]

Accomplished teaching begins with strong content knowledge and a disposition to work with others; however, these are but two dimensions of many that describe successful teaching and learning. The accomplished teacher appreciates content and its relevance to the lives of the students. Why do students need to know this particular learning objective? Why should they care? To help students make a connection between content and their world, teachers need to know something about student interests, abilities, understandings, skills, and life experiences. Knowing who students are as learners and individuals is but one critical step toward effective teaching. Other aspects include the ability of a teacher to:

- Ensure an equitable experience for all learners
- Employ effective assessment practices
- Understand diverse learners
- Evaluate and use quality curriculum
- Appreciate how specific concepts pose particular challenges for students
- Create a positive learning environment
- Leverage the relationships between teachers, colleagues, and community
- Reflect critically upon one's practice
- Learn from experience and diverse sources of information

A complex view of teaching sees all facets of teaching as vital to a successful classroom learning experience, and appreciates that in different school contexts, different dimensions might take on greater significance. From this view, teaching can be thought of as the ultimate multitasking dynamic endeavor.

Formalizing the parameters of accomplished teaching so that they are clearly understood by educational stakeholders is a huge undertaking. While definitions and principles of great teaching are available, they tend to be not much more than the opinion of a small group of individuals.[7] In order to be embraced by the teaching profession, standards of exceptional teaching should emerge from an amalgam of teacher expertise, research findings, and scholarly literature from multiple domains (e.g., psychology, metrics, sociology, education, and content areas).

A standards document that defines and explains exceptional teaching must clearly address the multiple dimensions of effective teaching and the respective indicators associated with each dimension. These standards of ideal teaching must be specific enough to describe the observable evidence that indicate a particular standard of practice being met, yet vague enough that they do not dictate a specific approach to teaching and learning.

This is a difficult balancing act. Teachers are not all the same. They demonstrate different strengths, weaknesses, preferences, beliefs, and philosophies. If the standards are too inclined toward one specific approach or style, then they run the risk of losing validity among teachers who do not align their practice to the preferred approach. On the other hand, if the document is so vague as to promote an "anything goes" agenda, it will fail to gain respect and legitimacy among the educators who make use of the process.

The National Board tackled this problem with a few very innovative strategies. First, it placed practicing classroom teachers in the center of the process. Along with education scholars, policy makers, and administrators, outstanding classroom teachers were recruited to serve both on the Board and on the standards committees. The National Board operated from a position that for professional standards of teaching to be accepted by the community of teachers, it must come from within and not be imposed from above.

Therefore, the products of the Board represent a consensus view regarding what accomplished teaching entails for each area of certification. A consensus approach to knowledge building infers that knowledge might change as the community evolves and faces unforeseen challenges. Because standards are seen as a dynamic statement of accomplished teaching, the Board's bylaws require it to revisit and revise standards as needed on a regular basis.

Second, the Board asked two critically important questions: (1) What timeless qualities of accomplished teaching can apply to all teachers regardless of age level or discipline taught? And (2) what does accomplished teaching look like for each of the different areas of specialization within the spectrum of K–12 classrooms? The Board realized that the standards that describe what a first grade teacher should know and be able to do will look very different from the standards that describe a secondary science teacher's practice. Yet, there should be aspects that both accomplished teachers have in common.

To the first question, the Board developed its five core propositions.[8] According to the Board, all accomplished teachers abide by the following assertions:

1. Teachers are committed to students and their learning.
2. Teachers know the subjects they teach and how to teach those subjects to students.

3. Teachers are responsible for managing and monitoring student learning.
4. Teachers think systematically about their practice and learn from experience.
5. Teachers are members of learning communities.

The five propositions were one of the Board's first publications, and they have remained unchanged. They represent a significant achievement, since they are both powerful in meaning and attractive to a wide audience of educators. Who is going to argue with the idea that teachers are committed to student learning? Furthermore, the propositions originate from the work of practicing classroom teachers and not from a particular special interest group, political party, or organization with business interests. The motivation is one of professional sincerity.

The next big step for the Board was to define accomplished practice one specialty at a time. Beginning with the Elementary Generalist, the Board again brought together committees of educators from different parts of the system and asked them to identify and define the standards of practice associated with the specific responsibilities of the identified specialty and age level. The only requirement insisted upon by the Board was that every standard developed must support one of the five core propositions.

Standards committees met repeatedly over the course of a year. Members would return to their respective communities and solicit feedback from colleagues about their work to develop standards. Committee members would then share their learning regarding what standards worked or what ideas needed further refinement. Finally, after multiple opportunities for public review, the standards were published and ready for assessment. This process has repeated itself for each of the twenty-seven different areas of certification.[9]

The Board's vision of accomplished teaching is multidimensional and requires more energy and time to understand, assess, and appreciate than simpler conceptions of good teaching. The straightforward view of teaching and learning is attractive because it requires so little effort to determine performance. It is easy, relatively inexpensive, and readily accessible to use test scores as a measure of quality. Evidence for this seductive view of teaching and learning can be seen in the increasing emphasis on standardized test scores over the last decade.

If a state or district reports that scores are up, then things are good. If scores are flat or down, then things are bad. Test scores provide an easily understood yardstick for judging the quality of instruction and make for effective headlines in the news media. Educational outsiders such as real estate agents, journalists, and politicians use test scores to sell a property, write a headline, or attract voters, respectively. Causal reference to test scores does not require much thought on the part of the consumer and promotes a conception of teaching that is linear and uncomplicated. The heavy reliance on standardized test scores as an objective measure of teacher quality is an illusion at best and damaging to students at worst.

Teaching and learning exudes complexity and richness of experience. Using test scores as a measure of quality is like measuring athleticism using the 100-yard dash. Sure, nearly everyone can do it and maybe even improve their times, but is it an adequate reflection of the quality of an athlete? Gymnasts, swimmers, or divers may be quite slow, but they are still accomplished athletes. Using a singular dimensional measure to describe a multidimensional endeavor is not only inadequate, but dangerously misleading.

While student achievement on a standardized test is one important indicator of quality and a potential resource for improving a teacher's efforts to foster learning, it is insufficient as a basis for judging the quality of instruction. In fact, test scores used as high-stakes indicators of quality actually corrupts the process by disproportionately overshadowing other important indicators such as attitudes, creativity, and collaborative problem solving.

Placing too much emphasis on only one measure promotes a shallow type of pedagogy that sees the test as the lone and final authority. If exceptional teachers like Dan with his periodic table project are to be distinguished from adequate teachers like Rich, then a more meaningful approach to assessment is needed.

Assumption #2: Complex Teaching Requires Complex Assessments

Ask members of any school community to identify the best teachers in the school, and it is likely that the lists will be highly congruent. Though precise, such local consensus defies validity because the evidence upon which individuals probably make judgments is less than empirical. Local attitudes toward teachers could be the result of popularity and charisma just as often as they are the result of meaningful learning in the classroom. These informal distinctions within a community remain unofficial, nonbinding, and unsubstantiated.

The identification of exceptional teaching is usually approached from a subjective perspective. While members of a community are likely to agree upon a list of the best teachers in a school, they may not have the same reasons. Ask ten different people about the characteristics needed to be a great teacher and you are likely to get ten different answers—or ten answers that are so vague as to render the answers of little value.

For example, when a group of undergraduate students were asked to define a quality teacher, almost everyone identified "nice," "fun," "inspiring," and "good with children." While these characteristics are positive and play a vital role in effective teaching, they are highly subjective. How does one measure "nice" or "fun"?

Teacher tests, state certification requirements, honors and achievements, principal evaluations, and years of experience are all currently used to measure and describe teacher quality. Each piece contributes something important to the overall evaluation of an individual teacher. However, the teacher's practice in the classroom remains noticeably absent.

An individual can have the best credentials, the most impressive resume, great recommendations, and still be an ineffectual teacher. Research has shown teacher performance on tests such as the National Teacher Exam is a poor indicator of future performance in the classroom.[10] While teachers commit considerable time and effort to ensure they remain certified and qualified to teach, little evidence exists that these efforts are successful at differentiating teachers who demonstrate a range of instructional quality.

Consider an ideal teacher assessment situation. In a perfect school, a team of perhaps three individuals armed with comprehensive and clearly defined standards of accomplished teaching would spend a month or two shadowing and studying a teacher's work in school. The teacher being assessed would understand the standards and work to align practice accordingly.

The team would observe every class, document every teacher decision, record the consequences of teacher actions, record video of classroom proceedings, and take notes regarding the nature of teacher interactions with colleagues and community members, including parents. The team would monitor student learning over the course of a unit using both formal and informal assessments noting the development of learning in relation to instruction.

After an exhaustive effort to collect assessment data, the team would compare the evidence against the defined benchmarks and determine the extent to which individual aspects (standards) of practice are met or not met. They would consider all the standards and make an informed judgment regarding the preponderance of evidence collected (including evidence of what students learned or did not learn).

Individually, each team member would write a report that would make the case for a teacher's status as "exceptional" or "not exceptional" according to the evidence held up against the agreed-upon standards. In the last step, the three individuals present their conclusions to each other in order to arrive at a final evaluative outcome. The final result, all supporting evidence, and written analyses would then be presented to the teacher and openly discussed over a series of meetings.

Such an ideal evaluative process might be highly effective at identifying and fostering accomplished teaching. However, the rigor, level of human involvement, and expense would make such an approach completely impractical. For example, a highly trained and qualified team of three evaluators working full time would be a bargain at $3,000 per week. Over a minimum of a month, the cost of this approach could easily exceed $12,000. No district in the country could afford such an extravagant approach to teacher evaluation. Is there a way to incorporate aspects of the ideal teacher assessment into a more efficient yet effective approach?

Such a method of evaluating teaching must address three significant challenges. First, the evaluation process must be transparent. The means by which decisions are arrived at must be visible to all interested parties. Second, a robust evaluation system for accomplished teaching must be fair, precise, and accurate. In this context, "fair" refers to the level of objectivity necessary to ensure equal treatment of individual teachers throughout the assessment process. A successful evaluation should not be influenced by a teacher's race, ethnicity, gender, or age. All candidates must be held up and compared solely on the merits of the evidence they present.

Precision refers to the assessment instruments examining the desired phenomenon (or in this case the quality of teaching and learning). In the case of accomplished teaching, the phenomenon is the degree to which a teacher's practice aligns with the standards that define exceptional work. If the assessment process is influenced by factors beyond the standards, it loses its validity. Instruments and procedures may appear robust and precise, but if they end up examining something unrelated to the desired phenomenon (e.g., the quality of the school's physical plant), then their value as a tool of differentiation is minimal.

Accuracy pertains to the degree an evaluative process can effectively differentiate between good and great teaching. Without accuracy and reliability, the instruments suffer. Reliability refers to the consistency of results over time. All the candidates identified as "accomplished" must be qualitatively different from the teachers identified as "not accomplished" regardless of when they were evaluated or who evaluated them. Finally, the validity of the evaluation process rests on the final product. Is the process of assessment successful in differentiating between teachers who meet the standards and those who do not?

The third challenge faced by a robust advanced certificate assessment system concerns the professional value of the process to the individual teacher. In other words, teachers being assessed should actually learn how to be better teachers as a result of the process. Such an outcome would make the assessment experience an effective professional development method.

Since a comprehensive evaluation process is far more than a one-time observation or computerized exam, teachers must invest significant time and energy toward the collection of evidence that describes their practice in light of the standards.[11] If the process is embedded in the day-to-day practice of teaching and focused upon student learning, then teachers become students of their own profession—learning about how their work compares to an ideal.

The process of National Board certification addresses these challenges in an effective and efficient manner. Certification is a two-pronged approach to teacher assessment that has all the theoretical advantages of the idealized approach to assessment described earlier and the practical advantages of being affordable, accurate, and meaningful to the candidate. Certification encompasses building a structured portfolio and a computerized content exam. As is discussed in chapter 3, both parts of certification represent rigorous challenges for candidates who are required to analyze and substantiate how their teaching impacts student learning.

Assumption #3: Cross-Context Validity

Schooling overflows with nuances and contextual variables that influence the final outcome of a teacher's year with a group of students. Variables such as literacy skills, transience, absenteeism, tardiness, emotional health, physical health, previous classroom learning experiences, level of support from family, home environment, learning disabilities, life experiences, type of curriculum, resources available, the physical condition of the school, and involvement of local community are but a few of the variables beyond the control of the teacher that influence a student's academic performance.

Within the milieu of school, teachers learn to control certain aspects of their work. For example, teachers adapt to conditions and develop resources from what the environment has to offer. A teaching context defines the available resources, the historical involvement of the community, the values and attitudes toward learning, and the curriculum that is taught. Each piece of the contextual puzzle contributes to a community's expectations of "exceptional" teaching.

The inequities present in public education presents special challenges to the assessment of exceptional teaching. While some teachers work with students who are well prepared and motivated to learn, others struggle to maintain a safe learning environment. While some teachers have the advantage of teaching science in state-of-the-art facilities with nearly limitless resources, others must make do with rooms that may not even be equipped with safety equipment or running water. When teachers work in dramatically different environments with dramatically different students, how can they all be held up to the same standards of accomplished teaching?

The diverse range of schools poses a special challenge for any national system to differentiate teacher quality. The standards of accomplished teaching and the assessment instruments used to determine the level of teacher excellence must be equally valid, accessible, and meaningful to all kinds of teachers, regardless of the educational resources available or the kinds of students taught. It must bring educators from extreme contexts or communities together around issues of quality.

Exceptional teaching occurs in all kinds of classrooms. Just as excellent facilities and abundant resources are not a guarantee of accomplished teaching, difficult conditions do not prohibit exceptional instruction. Exceptional teaching can occur under all conditions. In the end, it is about what a teacher knows and is able to do that determines the quality of his or her efforts to bring about understanding with learners.

Of all three assumptions, this one is most problematic. The Board faces an ongoing challenge to improve its ability to assess accomplished teaching equally in both affluent and impoverished schools. To address this problem, National Board assessors go through a three-day bias training program so as to be prepared to focus on evidence and not appearances.

SUMMARY

The National Board holds the promise of helping communities transform their classrooms from exercises in the mundane to realms of understanding, inspiration, and expression. The Board is not a silver bullet to the challenges faced by education, but it does offer a vision and a process for identifying accomplished teachers while providing a rich professional learning opportunity. For states, districts, and teachers struggling with both of these issues, the National Board provides an effective and efficient option to the chronic problem of differentiating teachers of varying abilities.

A quality system of teacher assessment faces the three awesome challenges of defining, identifying, and fostering accomplished teaching. While quite considerable in scope, they are not insurmountable. The NBPTS addresses all three of these challenges in its process of certification.

The Board's standards provide the form and shape that allows evidence to be examined, quantified, and assessed. The final decision regarding a teacher's status as accomplished or not accomplished remains a mediated human judgment informed by evidence. It is not perfect, but it is the best that exists for identifying the most significant teachers in the classroom.

What is exceptional teaching? If the question is reworded to ask, "What is exceptional teaching according the National Board for Professional Teaching Standards?" then the range of answers narrows considerably. Understanding the Board's vision of "exceptional" teaching, how it goes about identifying "great" teaching, and the ways in which it may or may not foster improved practice among those teachers who become candidates is the focus of this book.

NOTES

1. "Exceptional teaching" is my way of describing effective practice. The National Board uses the phrase "accomplished teaching" to refer to its view of effective practice. While these two views are very similar, it is important to point out that they are not synonymous. "Exceptional" is reserved for a more general definition of what great teaching might be and "accomplished" is used for instances that specifically refer to National Board's conception.

2. See Weisberg et al., *The widget effect,* 2009, for a description of research and detailed discussion about the broken teacher evaluation system in the United States.

3. See Lustick, "Elemental design," 1997, for images and full description of a similar periodic table project.

4. Educational Testing Services, *Technical analysis report,* 1999.

5. The National Board did not invent the use of portfolios to assess teacher quality. Shulman, *Mentoring teachers,* 1991, demonstrated the value of a portfolio as a means of documenting evidence of effective teaching in the Teacher Assessment Project.

6. An important step toward this body of specialized knowledge in teaching can be traced back to Lee Shulman's (1987) description of pedagogical content knowledge (PCK). Shulman and Sykes (1986) demonstrated how PCK could serve as the starting point for a bold national standard of excellence in teaching.

7. See Pratt and Collins, "Summary of five perspectives," 2001, for the Teaching Perspectives Inventory as an example of an unsubstantiated vision of great teaching. The American Board for Certification of Teacher Excellence (2005) provides a simplified vision of teaching excellence.

8. See National Board for Professional Teaching Standards (2002) for a thorough description of the five core propositions of accomplished teaching.

9. Currently, the Board only offers twenty-four different certificate areas.

10. See the National Research Council's 2001 report, *Testing teacher candidates: The role of licensure tests in improving teacher quality,* for a discussion on teacher tests and a predictive factor of teacher quality.

11. According to Baratz-Snowden (2007), the National Board developed its own list of criteria for a system to assess advanced teaching. The list is known by the mnemonic "APPLE." The system must be "administratively feasible, professionally acceptable, publicly credible, legally defensible, and economically affordable" (2). While these are very important characteristics, they do not specifically address the goal of effective learning.

Five Descriptions of Successful Teaching

It is one thing to discuss the need for complex assessments to identify exceptional teaching, but it is something entirely different to actually apply such evaluative practices to real teachers working with actual students. The classroom overflows with potential data regarding the quality of teaching.

Every decision made, every word spoken, and every action taken reveals something explicit about the quality of the teaching and learning experience. For any given example of teaching, it is imperative to sift through the mounds of possible information and target only the evidence that has bearing upon a specific question or issue. How does one know what is and is not evidence? How does one differentiate between signal and noise?

A framework can greatly refine this process and allow for a much more efficient and purposeful evaluation of evidence. Using theoretical constructs to both observe and quantify professional behavior and its possible impact upon learners may sound good on paper, but in practice, it is a difficult task. The National Board's five core propositions provide a good case in point. While all five appear self-evident at first glance, a few of the propositions are easier to observe and document than others.

A teacher's understanding of content can be evaluated by the number of accurate versus inaccurate statements about any specific phenomenon made during a given period. A teacher's ability to manage behavior can be assessed by the number of times student behavior requires a corrective intervention during a class meeting. However, some propositions are more problematic. How does one gauge a teacher's commitment to students? How is a teacher's understanding of pedagogy assessed? To what degree does a teacher employ effective assessment practices?

Further complicating these questions is the fact that evidence is not always explicit. Sometimes the work of teachers is unobservable. For example, a teacher may be monitoring student learning by listening to students' questions or comments through informal assessment strategies. For the observer, nothing appears to be happening. Yet the teacher may be processing information and making meaningful determinations about how best to proceed later in the lesson or further along in the unit.

Observation alone is insufficient for accurately evaluating the quality of a teacher's work in the classroom. The only way an observer may gain access to implicit forms of evidence is through either written or verbal communication from the teacher. As a teacher addresses specific questions while debriefing someone not directly involved with a classroom lesson, additional evidence may surface and be recognized.

Therefore, the process of reflecting on one's practice becomes a key component to understanding the quality of a teacher's work. What a teacher decides to share, emphasize, or question during the reflective process becomes a strong indicator of a teacher's priorities, skills, and understanding about practice. This is the foundation upon which the National Board's assessment procedures stand.[1]

In the preceding chapter, descriptions of Dan and Rich helped to illustrate the problem with identifying exceptional teaching. To the outsider, Dan seemed to engage learners to a greater degree than Rich. What would happen if Dan and Rich both became candidates for National Board certification? How might their own respective analysis of events in the classroom impact an observer's perception of quality?

In this chapter, five candidates' for National Board certification share descriptions of a "successful" lesson. All five teachers chose independently to describe a lesson that addresses a common goal: namely, understanding of electron configuration and the periodic table in chemistry.

Anyone who has entered a science classroom will remember the ubiquitous presence of the periodic table on the wall or in the textbook. It is the unusual chart made up of lots of letters and numbers describing the known elements' mass, number of protons, and electrons. Its arrangement reflects important knowledge about the chemical behavior of an element and its number of valence electrons.

Understanding the periodic table is a central tenet of any secondary chemistry or physical science course. It is also one of the most challenging objectives of teaching science since it combines both concrete information (physical characteristics of elements) and abstract ideas (energy, reactivity, and subatomic structure).

Comparing these five candidates' descriptions reveals a level of implicit evidence that may not have been available through direct observation. The five descriptions of successful instruction illustrate how a framework for accomplished teaching can make the difficult challenges associated with assessing exceptional practice more manageable.

The candidate descriptions represent only one small piece of the much larger document presented to the Board. While decisions about the overall quality of practice should not be made based upon such a narrow slice of practice, the responses do provide a taste of the kind of work an assessor must do before making a standards-based judgment about the quality of instruction.

To the uninitiated observer, all five teachers seem like good people who enjoy working with students. They all appear to understand enough science to teach this particular lesson, though the depth of that understanding may vary. All these teachers appear to manage their classrooms effectively and fairly. All identify evidence of their success at fostering student understanding. However, they differ in significant ways.

Consider the placement of the learner in each teacher's approach to instruction. Does the learner occupy a central position in the approach to instruction? Or is the learner more tangential to the teacher's work? Are students viewed as active participants in the education process? Or are students assumed to be more passive as they accept content knowledge from the teacher? To what degree are students actively engaged in learning? Using the Board's five core propositions as a starting point, other questions to consider while reading these descriptions might include:

1. To what extent is the teacher committed to students?
2. How well does the teacher understand his or her subject matter?
3. To what extent does the teacher manage and monitor student learning?

4. Does the teacher think systematically about his or her practice?
5. To what degree is the teacher a member of the learning community?
6. What evidence is presented that might answer these questions?

These five examples of teaching originated from interviews with candidates conducted as part of the study described in chapter 4. Each teacher was presented with the same series of questions in the same order. The first five questions address the context of learning and the learning goals for the lesson. Questions six and seven allow the teachers to describe the successful lesson in detail. Questions eight, nine, and ten provide teachers an opportunity to share any significant characteristics of the students that may have helped or hindered this particular lesson. Finally, the last question asks teachers to articulate how the experience may shape their future work with this topic. The questions asked were:

1. Please describe for me the setting for the class you will share.
2. How many students were in the class and what grade levels were represented?
3. What were the student learning goals for this lesson?
4. Why were these goals important for these students?
5. How did these goals fit into your overall goals for the year?
6. What about this particular lesson is most significant to you?
7. What specific evidence helped you determine that you were successful at achieving the identified learning goals with your students?
8. Were there any ethnic, cultural, or linguistic diversity circumstances you considered in the planning or teaching of this class?
9. Did the range of abilities of the students (e.g., exceptional needs, cognitive, social and behavioral, sensory, or physical challenges) or the personality of the class affect your planning? If so, how?
10. In the teaching of this lesson, did spontaneity play a role in the success of this class? If so, how?
11. What (if anything) would you do differently if you had the opportunity to pursue this lesson in the future? Why?

The answers to these questions were edited into the narratives presented here. While the editing process improved the appearance and readability of each teacher's description, the meaning and intent of what the teachers said remains unchanged.

FIVE TEACHERS

Lidia, Robert, Elaine, Patricia, and Anita all teach secondary science and all were candidates for National Board certification. While candidates, some were interviewed before they began the certification process, and some were interviewed after they completed the process. Though they work in different settings with different populations of students, they are all dedicated to fostering understanding of scientific concepts and skills.

Each candidate was asked to describe a "successful lesson." Specifically they were told, "Take a moment and think of a recent class that was memorable because of the student learning that you believe took place." Each of these five experienced teachers was a "highly qualified teacher" according to the criteria established by the No Child Left Behind Act of 2002. Each teacher was certified in the area that they taught.

Prior to each teacher's answer, a brief context is provided that describes some very basic characteristics of the teacher and the class of learners. Following each teacher's narrative, some analysis as might be provided by an assessor for National Board is presented. The purpose of the sample analysis is not to be complete or robust, but rather to model for the reader examples of what might serve as evidence to address the five core propositions.

Of the five teachers presented here, two were identified as accomplished by achieving National Board certification. The other three were unsuccessful. Which examples of teaching better represent accomplished practice? Was it Lidia's focus on making the learning experience "enjoyable"? Was it Robert's request to have students stand and identify patterns? Does Elaine's crossword puzzle and theatrical approach to practice provide evidence of accomplished teaching? Did Patricia's use of exploratory investigations and student-to-student interactions prove to be the key? Or did Anita's coloring activity and high regard for following directions hold more weight with the assessors? The answer may be surprising.

1. Lidia

Lidia is a science teacher from a suburban district in Virginia with seven years of teaching experience. She chose to share a lesson from a chemistry

class of twenty-four juniors and seniors that she describes as "average" in ability. Lidia was interviewed before going through National Board certification,
and shared the following thoughts:

> The goals for these students in this lesson were to understand how to use the
> periodic table in order to determine the number of protons, neutrons, and elec-
> trons in a given element—ion or isotope. These goals are important because in
> chemistry class it's important to be able to understand and be able to read the
> periodic table and gather information for future lessons or for future activities
> such as writing chemical formulas, writing ions, and chemical reactions. So it's
> something that is a basic thing that will be built upon and utilized throughout
> the school year.
>
> The most significant aspect of this lesson is the variety of students at differ-
> ent levels. Some students can pick up on things very quickly. And others tend
> to struggle with it. And a lot of times you can verbally say something, and they
> can look at the periodic table and identify these things that you are asking them
> to do. But not everyone gets it, so we worked through it visually as well. And by
> the end of the class I had everybody at the same point. They fully understood
> what it was they needed to do.
>
> I have one young man in my class who I think sometimes tends to second
> guess himself. He never thinks that he has the correct answer or never fully
> understands what it is that he's doing. He tends to just call out answers. And a
> lot of times, I'll say "You have given me the number 'twenty' for the last three
> answers. Now everything can't have twenty protons?!"
>
> Little things like that—being able to let him know that I want him to be
> successful. I want him to succeed—shows the other students that I'm not just
> standing in front of the class. I think for me that's more on a personal level.
> Yes, I'm their teacher; but I'm there to help them to learn and also to make it
> enjoyable. It's not just I'm the teacher and you're the student and this is what I
> need to teach you. I think some degree of spontaneity, humor, kind of adds to
> the class and makes it more enjoyable.
>
> To determine my success at achieving the identified learning goals with these
> students, I gave them a quiz the next day and they were able to do exactly what
> we had worked on the previous day.
>
> If I had the opportunity to pursue this lesson again in the future, there are
> things I would probably change. I feel like sometimes I'm giving them informa-
> tion or helping them walk through it. However, I think that it's important for

them to work together. Students who catch on very quickly can work with other students to help them through it.

If they are effective, then they don't need me as the speaker in front of the class. I think it's a very easy concept once kids work through it and realize exactly what they need to do to determine the different things. But I think sometimes they have more of a sense of pride and a sense of ownership in the class and what they are learning if they can help each other and work together. If I had more time, I'd probably let them do that.

Lidia appears to care about her students. She is sensitive to their different needs and adjusts her teaching to accommodate "verbal" and "visual" learners, but she does not provide any specific examples of how these needs were met. Lidia seems to understand the science content she is teaching, though she only gives the briefest descriptions of subatomic particles.

She manages her students and uses humor to make learning more "enjoyable"; however, the humor might be interpreted as ridicule by some. Lidia would like more time to explore this topic. In this description, Lidia does not mention her colleagues or any outside influences in her teaching.

Most strikingly absent from Lidia's description is any detail about what actually transpired. Lidia never mentions what she or the students actually did during this lesson. As readers, we are left wondering if the focus of the lesson was on peer-coaching or lecturing and notes. According to this lesson description, does Lidia present enough evidence to be identified as accomplished?

2. Robert

Robert is a chemistry teacher from Georgia, also with seven years of experience. He describes his students as "high achievers" and describes his school as being in an urban setting. For his choice of a successful lesson, he chose a ninety-minute class meeting made up of twenty-five juniors and one sophomore. Robert was interviewed after going through the certification process and describes his successful teaching as follows:

My goal was for the students to basically understand the organization of the periodic table including the placement of metals, nonmetals, and semimetals, as well as the role of the valance electron, the energy levels, and the different sublevels s, p, d, and f (orbitals). All these things tie into and relate to the organization of the periodic table.

These learning goals are important to these students so that they will be better able to interpret data on the periodic table and be able to gain more information from the table itself. In terms of my course objectives, all of these goals—especially the role of the electrons—are significant in chemistry and chemical changes and chemical properties. So in order to have a good understanding of that, they have to understand the role of the electron and how to get it from the periodic table.

Why was this lesson significant? Basically it went from a situation where students saw a periodic table with a bunch of numbers and letters on it to within one class period being able to take a particular element on the periodic table and understanding why it's located exactly where it is, how many electrons are there without having to do any work. They could determine very easily how many electrons there are, what kind of charge it would have, and how it would bond. Basically, the reason I picked this lesson is because it takes so many different things they learn and ties it back to the periodic table within one class meeting.

The first thing I did was—and this is something that I've modified every year for the past three or four years and it's gotten better every time—the first thing basically I ask them is to describe an electronic figuration for a different particular element that I assign to each student. And then once they have done that I ask them to look up in their book and find answers to a whole bunch of different questions about that element.

For instance, how many valence electrons does it have? What sublevel is it in? What energy level are the valance electrons in? There are a number of different questions about that particular element. Each student works on only one element and everybody works alone. Then, once they have this information filled out, I asked them for answers.

For example, I would ask the class, "anybody who has two valence electrons please stand up and identify your element." Students stand up and say the name of their element: "magnesium," "calcium," "strontium," "barium," The rest of class can see that all the people that are standing up have something in common. They make the connection that everyone standing up represents elements located in the alkali earth metals column, group, or family of the periodic table.

And then I do the same thing with different groups of elements. How many people are nonmetals? And students who did an electron figuration for oxygen, carbon, and iodine stand up. Students take note that "Hey, all these people are located on the right side of the periodic table."

It's just like I can pick out any particular trend in the periodic table and they can all of a sudden make a connection between what they did to the whole periodic table. They gain an understanding of how the whole thing is organized. So it's a pretty in-depth lesson; but it just very much seems to come to life and make a whole lot of sense for them.

The evidence that informs me of my success at fostering learning is kind of informal. At the end of class, I pick an element that they've never done before—something weird like molybdenum and I can come up with 20 different questions about the element molybdenum—and I can go around the room and I can ask each person one different question about that one particular element. What energy level is it in? What sublevel is it in? How many valence electrons does it have? Is it a metal, metalloid, or nonmetal?

I can go around the room and within one or two elements I can basically ask every single person in the room a different type of question and the thing that shows me that they really understood it was that out of those twenty-six students, I only had three or four that didn't answer their question correctly. And so it's very rewarding and that all of a sudden, you know, they understood so much out of that table in such a short time.

The class was predominantly white and predominantly college-bound students. I think I had six African American students in the class. I would say that the one thing that did affect the lesson would be the dynamic of the class itself. This class asked more questions throughout the semester than almost any other class that I had. They seemed very engaged as far as wanting to learn more. And so basically I tried, specifically for this lesson, to leave enough time for them to ask those higher-level thinking type of questions.

Three or four years ago when I did the lesson the first time—it was just something that was very spontaneous. I didn't have anything planned. The next time I had a worksheet planned as far as "hey, do this first, then we are going to ask questions later." The next time that I did it, I incorporated more things into it. However, I cannot tell you what kinds of things that I'm going to add to it next year when I do it, but I generally add to it every time.

Based on the questions from students and the organization of the questions: When do I ask this question, first, second, third, or fourth? Switching those questions around really does help student understanding of the material. The biggest thing I think I've learned from this lesson is the organization of the questions. I mean I might have fifteen questions listed, but it might be easier if question thirteen were right next to question six. And so I'll go back and tweak that a little bit.

Robert reveals quite a bit about his teaching through this description. He is sensitive to his students as evidenced by his decision to "leave more time for higher order questions," because this group "asked more questions throughout the semester than almost any other class that I had." He also seems to be quite comfortable with the complex content inherent in the periodic table such as trends, energy levels, orbitals, and valence electrons. Because of Robert's effective classroom management, students can express their ideas through actions rather than just words as indicated by being asked to stand as a means of answering questions.

Robert also demonstrates the habits of mind that are associated with reflective practice by recalling how the lesson has developed and might evolve in the future. He seems to work in isolation, never mentioning the influence of colleagues on this example of teaching and learning. According to this lesson description, does Robert present enough evidence to be identified as accomplished?

3. Elaine

Elaine teaches secondary science in California. She has five years of experience and describes her students as having "varied" abilities. Her school serves a primarily suburban community. For her successful lesson, Elaine chose to discuss the fifty-minute lesson she conducted with twenty-eight freshmen from an "Integrated Science I" course. Integrated Science is very similar to an introductory physical or general science class, except that it is followed in the sophomore year by Integrated Science II. The two-year course provides a "spiral" styled curriculum where ideas are revisited in greater depth from one year to the next. Elaine was interviewed just as she began the certification process.

> We had just started a unit on the natural resource of air. Basically, we look at the unit topic from all different perspectives—earth science, geology, biology, and chemistry. We were looking at what gases make up the atmosphere and then we were looking at even more detail about kinds of atoms in those gases. So we started looking at the periodic tables and at elements. We looked at what is an atom and got into its basic atomic structure.
>
> The day before this lesson, we started talking about atoms in terms of matter and looking at the periodic table to get a grasp of how it's arranged in terms

of reactivity and halogens and nonmetals and metals, and then the next day we went into more detail about each individual box and what they tell us. By the end of the next lesson, students will learn to read the periodic table, and understand what information is contained in atomic mass and atomic number and be able to identify elements according to atomic mass and atomic number.

These goals are important for students to learn because of several reasons. In Integrated Science II, they go into bonding of atoms. And basically how atoms bond and make up compounds that we see every day and also in terms of understanding the difference between ionic and covalent, so they need to know the atomic structure of an atom. And then just getting into the idea that it's important to understand that everything around them is made up of atoms and those atoms are made of smaller sub particles. And how to figure out the sub particles—the number of sub particles in each atom.

The goals for the year are to teach any required California standards for freshman science. And so they are in the state standards for chemistry. My year-long goal for any of my courses is also to help students apply what we are learning in class to their real life so that they understand its importance.

So what I told them in terms of this lesson was that we are looking at the building blocks that basically put everything together. So it's important to start at the smallest part of matter and then see how it all builds up to make the things that you see everyday—whether it's a table or your bike or your skateboard and that type of thing.

I have five Spanish-speaking students and I have to plan with their needs in mind. So, sometimes I'll help translate different activities—but for class activities I have one student who speaks both English and Spanish. We work together to help the students understand what the objective is for the activity and to help to lead them through some of the questions until they get the patterns as well.

I think there is not as much of a language barrier with science like the periodic table, because there are numbers involved. Spanish is actually pretty similar to the English in terms of atomic particles. So I did take that into consideration because I always try and make sure that, whatever we are doing, I'll be able to work with the paraprofessional who helps me translate or explain the activity to my Spanish speakers.

I also consider the range of abilities in my planning for this lesson. I make my seating charts for every unit. Students who might need some extra help, I'll try and place them with a student who seems to learn a little easier. By pairing students like this, the student who picks up things quicker can help tutor the student who takes a little bit longer to learn a concept.

And I always continually tell the students that it will click with you—it might take a little longer but it's going to work. And constantly encourage them in that way. And then the students who have more behavior issues in terms of their social interactions and not being able to sit in one place that type of thing—I also try and place them in the room where I can get to them pretty quickly and help refocus their energies on their work rather than on their buddy at the next table.

I think in most of my classes, I don't plan out minute by minute what I'm going to say but I always do have a plan. I always think of my teaching as a theatrical performance every day. I need to hook the kids in grasping the information. So I have some anecdotes about what we are dong that day or get really excited about the topic. I make sure that they understand how it connects to their real life.

I teach the same lesson four times during the day so it definitely changes in how I approach the information after I've taught it one time or two times or even three times. My class is always a little different. I definitely have to change during the day, which also makes it enjoyable cause you learn that one thing that you thought might work doesn't really work. So you have got to change it before the next class period and think of a better way to explain, introduce, or reinforce it or any of those types or things.

We went through the basic information about what the atomic numbers tell us, what the atomic mass tells us. And then did some examples together. And then I had created a crossword puzzle where they had to apply the knowledge that they had to identify different elements according to their atomic number or how many protons they have or how many neutrons or how many electrons they have.

In order to get the answers to the crossword, they had to apply what they had learned from our class discussion to their individual work. And they had to use a tool, the periodic table, to figure it out. So, they had to do several things. They had to use a tool. They had to use the scientific skills that we had learned together as a class and basically combine those to complete this activity.

And most of the kids, I would say almost 95% of the kids, really—it started to click with them and they just said, "Oh, this is so easy!" At the beginning of the class period, they were hesitant about looking at numbers in science. I have found that students are always very hesitant to connect science and math and the two subjects are very, very, thoroughly connected. But to actually see that math and science are connected scares a lot of students.

So this was using math but it wasn't scaring them and they were understanding it and they were able to complete the activity without much help from me—

even though I was circulating around. As soon as they started to see patterns, they were able to apply those patterns to the questions.

To further assess their learning, the next day I started class with a short little pop quiz where I put on the overhead two boxes from the periodic table representing different elements and they had to tell me information. I had some set questions and they had to write down the information. Or write down the answers to the questions according to what they saw on the overhead. So it was a double-check in terms of that.

If I were to teach this lesson again, I think what I'd like to do is maybe have the students pick a particular element and go out and look at not only what the numbers tell us but also how we use it in daily life. So it could be looking at gold and going into a bit of history about gold by doing a little research project in the library. So, again, I was trying to connect basic atomic chemistry to their lives.

Elaine has a strong sense of who her students are and what their needs might be. She makes extensive accommodations for her English language learners and describes strategies for effectively managing student behavior, including her priority for making every lesson a "theatrical performance." However, it is important to note that Elaine's repeated use of the first person plural "we" as in "we discussed," "we talked about," and "we went through" might very well mean "I" with few contributions from learners.

She does not share many student comments or questions as part of her description. Elaine shows an appreciation for the interconnectedness of science with other subjects, but the depth of her understanding is not clear. In her repeated implementation of the same lesson, she demonstrates some of the habits of mind consistent with reflective practice.

Elaine seems to work in isolation because she does not mention any influence from her colleagues except for a bilingual paraprofessional. How does Elaine's lesson description compare with Robert's or Lidia's? Is her use of a crossword puzzle congruent with Robert's standing activity or Lidia's classroom discourse? Based on this description, is the teaching and learning experience that Elaine describes indicative of accomplished teaching?

4. Patricia

Patricia has been teaching secondary science for twenty-seven years. By any definition, she is a veteran teacher. She teaches in an urban district in a southern state, and describes her students as below-average achievers. Patricia chose to share a successful lesson from a lower level sophomore chemistry class. She teaches twenty-eight students during the fifty-five minute lesson she describes here. Patricia was interviewed after she completed the certification process.

The student learning goals were to look at elements and decide whether they were metals, nonmetals, or metalloids based on what they had read in their textbook. Metals have certain uses that you want to be able to pick out. I do know that they need to be able to recognize these properties for the test that we give in our state in order for them to graduate from high school. To explore this concept, I used an inquiry-based approach that fits within our year-long emphasis on inquiry as a means of learning science.

What was most significant or memorable about this lesson was that I think that they found out that there were so many elements that were like "crossovers." Elements had properties of metals and they had properties of nonmetals. This was very interesting to them because my students have always been brought up in an environment where everything is black or white. It either was a metal or was a nonmetal. And there is no crossover and that it was very easy to tell the difference between the two. And so I think that really amazed them that you could have this knowledge, you could have read this knowledge, and that it was still difficult.

In the lesson, I gave them some pieces of equipment and we had talked about which were metals, what were properties of metals and properties of nonmetals—they had brought those up in class. And so I said, "So, you have ten elements. Perform whatever tests you think are necessary to determine if they are metals or nonmetals." And some of them wanted to make a judgment call right off—"Oh, it's shiny, it must be a metal." I left them to do as many tests or as few tests that they needed. And so a lot of them found out that making the judgment call right off just didn't do it for them. They needed a little more information on it.

I did not have to consider any language problems. All of my students are minority students. The biggest challenge I have is that the students come from middle schools and high schools—or middle schools and elementary schools where science is never taught. And up until probably the ninth grade, that's the big challenge. So using pieces of equipment, trying to make a decision, trying to come up with a hypothesis or doing inquiry-based lessons are extremely difficult for them, since they have very little experience with it.

I had to consider the range of abilities of these students in my planning. We have a class of twenty-eight tenth graders and the majority of them are males—one needs to be very busy all the time—and know that you are going to have outbursts and constantly—a lot of arguing over whether it was a metal or whether it wasn't a metal—

"Why didn't you argue?"

"Why didn't you do this test?"

"Well, I got the results from this test and you're wrong."

That will always happen. But I think those are very important things for them to see that we don't all have to agree. How we are looking at something has a lot to do with what the answer is going to be.

You always have to plan things out in a lesson; but I think we are always surprised sometimes with who can come up with an answer. I was kind of surprised once in a while when I would have a student who would say, "Well, I know you got this and I got this, but we can't just rely on one test—we've got to look at three out of five tests in order to do this." It wasn't always the students that you expected to come up with that statement.

My assessment evidence was basically informal. I had a lot of students who said to me, "I always thought it was very easy to tell the difference. Teachers have always told us that this is a metal, this is a nonmetal. So we thought it was easy all the time to tell. You just looked things up on the periodic tables to tell a metal for a nonmetal." They had always assumed that it was easy to look at something and tell it was a metal. When I heard these kinds of sentiments from the students, I felt like they had gotten the idea that in science you—it's not always easy to get an answer. And you may get some things that cloud the issues before you ever get to the answer.

If I were to teach this lesson again, I think I might not give them the reading assignment to start with; but just ask the question. And then let them investigate more on their own.

Patricia demonstrates both a strong understanding of the nature of science, and a desire to use inquiry in her approach to teaching and learning science— as evidenced by her "black and white" comment. In addition, the open nature of her exploratory activity and the encouragement of student-to-student interactions are evidence of her promotion of learning through inquiry.

She seems to understand her students—she describes their lack of experience or current conceptions as important considerations in her planning and teaching. She also identifies her place as a member of a professional community when she says, "I used an inquiry-based approach that fits within our year-long emphasis on inquiry." Her use of "our" reflects a dimension of professional collaboration not seen in the other descriptions.

Though Patricia displays a sharp understanding of both her students and her place in the teaching community, it is unclear how much she understands about atomic structure as it relates to the periodic table. How does Patricia's description compare and contrast with the other descriptions of successful lessons? According to this lesson description, does Patricia present evidence of accomplished teaching?

5. Anita

Anita is also a veteran teacher with more than sixteen years of experience teaching secondary science. She teaches physical science in a rural district of a southeastern state and describes her students as being average in ability. Anita chose to share a ninety-minute lesson during which she taught twenty students from grades nine through twelve. Anita was interviewed after completing the certification process.

For this lesson, I wanted them to understand the layout of the periodic table. Students should be able to use the periodic table to pull information and understand things like the numbering of the families using the new International Union PAC [Pure and Applied Chemistry] method and the ACS [American Chemical Society] System.

Students should also know the common names. They should be able to look at the table and tell where the metals, nonmetals, and the metalloids are located. Students need to look at the periodic table and tell me how many valence electrons something has or how many total electrons and protons it has.

These goals are important because I'm getting ready to move into chemical bonding. And in order for them to understand why the formula for calcium chloride is "$CaCl_2$," they need to understand valence electrons. The students want to know, "Why do you have to have that two subscript with the chlorine? Why isn't it with the calcium?" So being able to get them to understand how many valence electrons each atom has just by looking it up on the periodic table helps them to understand why we have the formulas that we do.

In terms of the course goals, one big thing is they need to understand why certain compounds are formed. They need to understand—first of all it's part of my curriculum for our state's End of Course Test; but I feel that it's important for them to understand why certain things react more readily than other things do. I'm trying to get them to think analytically—critical thinking skills and to think for themselves and getting them to understand the basic layout of the periodic table and teaching them some reasoning steps is what I'm going thru with them utilizing the periodic table.

The kids really seemed to understand—they got excited about it. They are like "Oh, that's what that table means. I never understood what that thing was for before." So they now see the periodic table as a tool. Each student was given a periodic table containing only the element symbols and their atomic number.

I then gave each student a box of colored pencils. And we went through and we talked about how the notes they took the day prior connected to the basic layout. So what I was doing was making it visual for them. We went through and we labeled the families according to the International Units system, one through eighteen. Then we labeled them according to the ACS system the 1A, 2A B groups, 3A thru 8A. Then we went through and gave each family a name.

I feel that it's important that they know the alkaline metals, the alkaline earth to transitions, the halogens, and the noble gases, and where the lanthanide and actinide series are. We went through and drew the line in that separates the metal from the nonmetal. And then recognized the metalloids and discussed what a period is. And we went through, and I would tell them "Okay, color the alkaline a certain color." They were sitting there and saying "alkaline metal, alkaline metal, alkaline metal" the whole time they were coloring alkaline metals.

The next day they were given a quiz where I gave them a reduced version of the same periodic table and the same colored pencils. And I had written out the names of the colored pencils—that's what I wanted them to color. We also went through and talked about how you can look at the periodic table, look at it and just by an elements position know how many valence electrons it's got. We also talked about atomic size and how you can use the chart to relate or compare sizes of atoms.

I know that they understand the layout. For example, if I ask them about sodium's valiance electrons, then they have got to know that sodium is in Group 1A and because it is in Group 1A it has one valence electron. They should be able to just look at the group and answer the question. I also went around looking at what they were doing. Glancing at their quizzes, they were all colored the same. So they were able to follow the directions.

I've got three Hispanic students in that class, one of whom is very weak in her English. So I had her paired with another Hispanic student who is pretty strong.

But I would go through and make sure that I was pointing and looking right at her, when I was going through and giving the directions and making sure that she could show me what was going on. I also have color blind males.

So I make sure that I use the family names that are written on the colored pencils. I knew that this would be something that everybody could do. I knew that this would be a good lesson since everybody loves to color.

If I were to do this lesson again with these learners, I would have it typed out instead of relying on verbal instructions, which is difficult for my visual kids. So I feel like I hit my tactile kids, I hit my auditory kids, and I hit the visual—I hit all three in that activity. But it would have been better had I had it typed out for my visual people. Instead of just saying what I wanted them to do.

Anita demonstrates a good understanding of the concrete aspects of the periodic table. She expresses a preference for students to understand (or at least remember) the names and locations of different groups of elements. However, an underlying concept as to why elements are grouped the way they are is not mentioned.

Anita places a high emphasis on her coloring activity and students' ability to "follow directions." She also checks to see if all her students are "getting it," especially when she discusses the Hispanic girl. Her assessment appears to be based on the degree of similarity between students' coloring of the periodic table. She also seems aware of the different learning styles students might have, but she does not identify any specific students who prefer one approach over another.

There is a sense that Anita uses a shotgun approach by addressing content from a variety of directions (tactile, auditory, visual) in the hope that something will work. How does Anita's lesson compare with the previous four descriptions? How does her use of the coloring activity differ from Robert's standing approach, Elaine's crossword puzzle, or Patricia's inquiry approach? According to this lesson description, does Anita present enough evidence to be identified as accomplished?

SUMMARY

While it would not be possible to make a valid and reliable judgment of teacher quality based on only a brief description of one lesson, the exercise does provide the opportunity to experience the challenges associated with identifying evidence in support of exceptional teaching. Which of the five teachers was successful at achieving National Board certification?

Robert (students stand in response to questions) and Patricia (focus on inquiry learning) achieved National Board certification while the other three did not. Why were these two teachers successful? Was there something different in their descriptions that might provide an inkling of a rationale? Were their lessons qualitatively different than their colleagues' lessons?

One possible difference can be found in the way these five teachers approach the students' role in the learning process. Lidia, Elaine, and Anita tended to see the students as primarily passive learners. In their descriptions, the teacher knows the content and the students do not. The goal of the students is to acquire the understanding that the teacher currently possesses. The main strategy for reaching this goal is for the teacher to tell and the students to listen and do what the teacher tells them to do.

Within this approach, Elaine and Anita employed a "fun" or "enjoyable" activity (crossword puzzle and coloring, respectively). However, "fun" does not necessarily mean active learning. Students may be engaged in an activity, but their minds are only superficially involved. In education terms, these are commonly referred to as "hands on" versus "minds on" activities. All three teachers provide very little description of students thinking independently, critically, or analytically about the content being presented.

Robert and Patricia are different. In their descriptions, students have an important role in defining the knowledge to be learned. Students are called upon to examine evidence, draw conclusions, and look for patterns. For example, Robert asked students to stand if their element had a certain characteristic. The class was then asked to analyze the result and figure out the connection between the students standing and the periodic table. So, if all the students with two valence electrons (electrons in the highest energy level) stand, the class might conclude that this group of elements makes up the second column of the periodic table.

Though not an exceedingly difficult task, the process is substantially different from informing the students that elements with two electrons are placed in the second column—which is basically what Lidia, Elaine, and Anita did.

Patricia offers a more extreme example of this approach. Patricia demonstrates a very high regard for student ownership over the learning process. She presents them with a challenge, and with the tools necessary for reaching that challenge. Patricia leaves the procedure and choices up to the students, and promotes a free-flowing yet disciplined discourse between learners.

For anyone without first-hand experience teaching, this is a remarkable pedagogical strategy. Successfully achieving a more open-ended inquiry approach to learning requires a teacher to relinquish a significant degree of control over the proceedings. In order to share the power over classroom discourse, a strong dimension of trust must exist between teacher and students. Without this trust, no inquiry activity is possible.

Such a level of mutual trust and respect may only develop after experiences that teach students about how inquiry can succeed and how it can fail. It is highly unlikely that Patricia's lesson was a one-time event. It is probably a common occurrence in her classroom. Because her lesson was inquiry-based does not imply that all her lessons are inquiry-based. She may very well use direct instruction to disseminate information on a regular basis. Similarly, the unsuccessful teachers may use inquiry from time to time. However, an assessor of teacher quality must examine the evidence presented and not speculate about what might be the case.

In these examples, these teachers chose to address the same question with very different assumptions. Their answers reflect different conceptualizations of what is means to be "successful." While all five talked about students' learning as important to the success of their respective lessons, Robert and Patricia apparently achieved their goal in a more engaging fashion.

This brief exercise makes three very different points. First, it illustrates the difficulty of assessing teacher quality based on only a single observation. The single annual observation used by administrators across the country provides only limited access to the full spectrum of parameters pertinent to assessing the quality of the teacher.

Any high-stakes consequences based on only a brief interaction with a teacher and his or her students is likely to result in mistakes where exceptional teachers are identified as average and average teachers are identified as exceptional. Its reliability or consistency of results is highly suspect, especially when administrator turnover is so common; one set of expectations for excellence is replaced by another. This series of lesson descriptions highlights the need for a more robust approach to assessing teacher quality.

Second, the examples shared here illustrate the need for an acceptable vision of exceptional teaching against which teachers are measured. Such a vision is then defined by standards that dictate observable and accessible criteria. Both the teacher and the evaluator are drawing at straws with regard to what should be emphasized, what form evidence should take, and the relative value of specific pedagogical decisions. Just as student performance on a single test cannot serve as the sole indicator of quality, the work and thought that goes into the process of fostering understanding must also be considered.

The five teachers whose lessons on the periodic table are shared here each have strengths and weaknesses. The question remains: What are the standards of accomplished teaching and how can they be used to identify teachers who meet those standards?

Third, the exercise raises the possibility that clear expectations and an in-depth assessment system might help teachers to improve their work with students. For example, the preceding exercise raises the issue of the relationship between teaching and learning. How do teachers know that students are learning and how do they represent that learning? Is it possible that an evaluative process for measuring teacher quality might help practitioners develop answers to these questions?

Could the teachers in this chapter learn to improve the quality of their instruction as a result of the assessment process? After experiencing a rigorous reflective analysis based on outside criteria, are they likely to teach this topic the same way? Or might they learn something from the experience that motivates them to try something different? Is it possible for a procedure designed to identify accomplished teaching to serve double duty, and also be an effective professional learning experience?

In other words, might Lidia and Elaine's descriptions of successful lessons change as a result of going through National Board certification? Is it possible that Robert and Patricia's lesson descriptions were better because of their experience with the certification process? The goal of the research presented in part II is to answer these types of questions.

All five teacher descriptions illustrate the wealth of information available to the teacher when confronted with the challenge of reflective analysis. Deciding what to talk about and what not to talk about is a real issue for most candidates. To make a reflection both efficient and effective, it becomes imperative to sift through the mounds of possible information and target only the evidence that has bearing on a specific question or issue. How does one know what information is evidence and what information is not? How does one differentiate between signal and noise?

In this chapter, the five core propositions served as a preliminary guide to interpret the lesson descriptions. However, they remain insufficient to conduct a detailed analysis. More specific standards and indicators of accomplished teaching are required. In chapter 3, the Board's framework for accomplished teaching (standards and assessments) will provide the needed lens for collecting and evaluating available evidence for accomplished teaching.

NOTE

1. While the role of reflection in teaching has been around since the time of John Dewey, Donald Schön (1983) makes a powerful case for the role of reflection in today's classrooms. The influence of this work upon the creation of the National Board is substantial.

3

The Work of the National Board

The way an individual teaches is dependent upon the totality of their formal and informal experiences. From what Lortie calls their "apprenticeship of observation" (1975, 61) as students, to the way a relative taught them to fish or play basketball, every learning experience represents a thread in the tapestry that results in classroom teaching. From this view, the more significant the experience, the more likely it will impact an individual's practice. Military service, business training provider, and (hopefully) teacher education programs are common examples of important experiences that influence an individual's approach to teaching.

For some teachers, National Board certification represents a profound and meaningful learning experience. As Cindi Rigsbee (a 2009 Teacher of the Year finalist and National Board–certified teacher) explains, "The process made me push myself to work harder and smarter than ever before. Every day I ask myself, 'How can I make this lesson better? How can I ensure that I am providing the best instruction possible for my students?' Simply put, the National Board Certification process made me a better teacher."[1]

For others, Board certification represents a rigorous experience, the impact of which is less understood. When a recent successful candidate, Mr. Rosenfeld, was asked, "Did it [National Board certification] make you a better teacher?" the candidate responded, "I think I'll have to think on that some more. I'm a different man in the classroom than I was then, but I'm not sure how much of that I would attribute solely to 'The Very Hard Test.' To me, teaching has always been a process of evolution. One thing I can't deny is that 'Natty' Boards are now a part of the journey, for better or worse."[2]

Rosenfeld's observation that his Board experience is "now part of the journey" is consistent with that of many other candidates. While some candidates exposit on the virtues of Board certification, other candidates either cannot describe its impact, or focus solely on the tedious technical requirements.

Different anecdotal accounts about National Board certification lead one to ask interesting research questions. Do teachers become better teachers as a result of certification? Or do they learn how to be better candidates for National Board, which may or may not impact classroom teaching? If improvements to teaching begin with a teacher acquiring new knowledge, skills, or habits of mind, then identifying the specific learning outcomes from professional development becomes a necessary step to understanding how certification may impact classroom work. What are teachers learning from National Board certification? Before addressing these questions, it is critical to understand the nature of the National Board's work with teachers.

This chapter is divided into three sections. The first section presents a brief history of the Board's development and its mission to define, identify, and foster accomplished teaching. The second section describes the standards for accomplished teaching in Adolescence and Young Adult Science (AYA Science).

AYA Science candidates represent the target population for the investigation presented in part II. Therefore, understanding the AYA Science standards of accomplished teaching serves as a starting point for appreciating what candidates may or may not be learning. Finally, the third section describes the complex assessment process employed by the Board to evaluate the work of candidates. The work of both candidates and assessors is fundamental to the investigation's design and strategy for measuring learning outcomes.

A BRIEF HISTORY OF THE NATIONAL BOARD

In 1983, the National Commission on Excellence in Education (NCEE) released *A Nation at Risk: The Imperative for Education Reform*. The report brought the crisis in education to the forefront of the national agenda and confirmed what many people already knew: schools were failing to adequately prepare students. The situation was considered so dire that the security of the country lay in the balance. The NCEE described quite clearly the possible options: (1) continue with education as usual and jeopardize the future of the nation or (2) develop reforms that would dramatically improve achievement and secure America's economic competitiveness with the rest of the world. One area targeted for needed reform was the teaching profession.

A Nation at Risk concluded that "the professional working life of teachers is on the whole unacceptable" (p. 20). How could the professional working life of teachers be improved? How might the status of the teaching profession be elevated to attract more capable individuals into education? In 1986, the Carnegie Task Force on Teaching as a Profession developed a proposal for reform that would address both of these questions.

Their report, *A Nation Prepared: Teachers for the 21st Century*, outlined the purpose and organization of a National Board for Professional Teaching Standards. The Task Force recommended that in order for teachers to improve their professional status, the knowledge and skills associated with exceptional teaching needed to be codified through standards. Furthermore, a valid and reliable means of assessing a teacher's practice against such standards needed to be developed.

To accomplish these goals, the Carnegie Task Force looked to the medical profession for an organizational model. Doctors have enjoyed a respected position in society and have consistently attracted some of the most qualified individuals into their ranks. What might education learn from this profession that might improve the quality and stature of teachers?

In 1910, Abraham Flexner completed a report for the Carnegie Foundation that described a strategy to improve the process by which medical doctors were prepared and certified for practice. As a result of the Flexner Report, the National Board for Medical Examiners (NBME) was established in 1915. The NBME is made up of members of the medical community with expertise in different areas of medicine. The NBME determines what doctors should know and be able to do for each of the different areas of specialization.

Interestingly, the medical exams offered by the NBME were not accepted by most states until after World War II. After completing medical school, doctors need to pass the appropriate examinations in order to be "board certified" and begin practicing medicine. By creating an organization to assess doctor quality, the medical profession maintained authority over their domain regarding definitions of required knowledge and skills. Though there might be input from outsiders, the final decisions regarding what doctors should know and be able to do, as well as the means of evaluating individuals against such criteria, was kept within the medical community.

Using NBME as a model, the Carnegie Task Force recommended that a diverse group of educators come together to define and assess teacher quality. It was proposed that such a centralized effort would have several outcomes. First, by creating a comprehensive series of standards tailored to specific teaching responsibilities (e.g., teaching assignments based on the age levels of learners and content-area expertise), the NBPTS would provide a consensus view of a knowledge base for teaching.

Second, teachers could voluntarily enter into the assessment process and achieve a credential of professional distinction. Such an accomplishment might help to raise the stature of teaching and attract more highly qualified individuals into the field. Third, a national set of education exams would provide an alternative means for teacher compensation. Rather than paying teachers according to how many years they have been teaching and the number of credit hours earned, a national board–type exam would give administrators an additional tool for differentiating compensation among educators.

Unlike merit pay, a national exam would assess a teacher's ability to foster learning and to reflect analytically upon practice. Regardless of the school or students, a teacher could present evidence from his or her work that demonstrated how closely his or her teaching (and the documented learning outcomes) aligned with the standards defined by the National Board. Finally, acknowledging that the creation of a National Board of Professional Teaching Standards would be expensive, the Carnegie Task Force envisioned that states could use the Board's standards and assessments to replace their own licensure procedures and thus make the entire system more efficient.

In 1987, the National Board for Professional Teaching Standards was established as a nonprofit, nonpartisan, and nongovernmental organization through a grant from the Carnegie Foundation of New York. The Board is composed of twenty-six educators. Most Board members are current or former classroom teachers and the rest represent other educational stakeholders such as scholars, researchers, union leaders, policy makers, and administrators. The Board's work began with developing the five propositions of accomplished teaching. Once refined and accepted in 1991, NBPTS began the process of defining the standards for specific certificate areas, beginning with English Language Arts/Early Adolescence and Generalist/Early Adolescence.[3]

In parallel with the development of standards, the Board built its assessment system upon the work of Lee Shulman's groundbreaking research on portfolio construction and pedagogical content knowledge.[4] Certification requires a candidate to complete a number of distinct entries that comprise a portfolio of practice and a content-specific examination. The candidate's work is then assessed by a panel of peers using specific rubrics and procedures.

After seven years of development, the NBPTS certified its first teacher in 1994. For almost a decade, the number of candidates grew at an exponential rate, doubling from one year to the next. Around 2003, the rate of growth leveled off with approximately fifteen to twenty thousand teachers entering into the certification process each year. Currently, more than eighty-two thousand teachers representing twenty-seven different areas of specialization have achieved National Board certification.

With an overall passing rate close to 50 percent more than 160,000 teachers have been candidates for the accomplished teaching certificate. National Board certification is valid for ten years from the time it is issued. Prior to the certificate's expiration, the teacher has the option of applying for renewal of the credential by completing a Profile of Professional Growth, which is focused more on professional rather than student learning.

National Board certification costs $2,565 per candidate.[5] Each candidate is required to pay a nonrefundable $500 deposit to become an official candidate, a $65 administrative processing fee, and the remaining balance must be paid in full prior to completion. However, very few teachers pay this fee out of pocket.

Most candidates obtain funds to cover certification from local, state, or federal sources. Funding for the NBPTS is a mix of public and private funds and is heavily dependent on state and federal legislation. While the Board continues to develop, adapt, and adjust to a volatile educational reform environment, its basic mission of defining, assessing, and fostering accomplished teaching remains intact.

THE WORK OF THE NATIONAL BOARD

The NBPTS identified three responsibilities around its system of certification: (1) standards (establishing, reviewing, and refining standards of accomplished teaching through consensus about what teachers should know and be able to do), (2) assessment (providing a valid and accessible means to evaluate teachers against the standards), and (3) professional development (providing teachers with the opportunity to strengthen their practice through self-examination).[6] All standards, assessments, and scoring rubrics are based on the five core propositions of accomplished teaching. The five core propositions (introduced in chapter 1) are repeated here for the reader's convenience:

1. Teachers are committed to students and their learning.
2. Teachers know the subjects they teach and how to teach those subjects to students.
3. Teachers are responsible for managing and monitoring student learning.
4. Teachers think systematically about their practice and learn from experience.
5. Teachers are members of learning communities.

The core propositions represent a meaningful achievement in education. Teachers are often seen as a community representing a wide range of beliefs, dispositions, values, and knowledge regarding effective practice. The goal of the core propositions is to create agreement among all kinds of teachers regarding what the profession should aspire to and what it should promote within the ranks. Whether one teaches first grade or high school physics, the core propositions are designed to be self-evident, meaningful, and indicative of the best teachers.

To be successful, the vast majority of teachers should agree with the propositions. Otherwise, the Board is not working on behalf of all teachers and students, but only a small minority. In other words, the teaching profession as a whole should be able to look at the core propositions and say, "We embrace these ideas and strive to fulfill them every day."

A quick review of the propositions reveals the National Board's vision of accomplished teaching as a fairly well-rounded endeavor. Proposition 1 places students and student learning at the forefront of teacher work. In some respects, the following four propositions are all supportive of the goal to foster student learning.

Proposition 2 makes it clear that teachers are not only purveyors of knowledge, but that accomplished teachers understand the pedagogical challenges and strategies associated with students understanding specific aspects of content. For example, a first grade teacher will anticipate the difficulty some students will experience differentiating between "b" and "d" and will plan accordingly.

Proposition 3 emphasizes two important aspects of practice: behavior management and assessment. Learning will not take place in an environment that is chaotic or where feedback about learning is not accurate, timely, and meaningful. Proposition 4 refers to the reflective process of evaluating one's work with learners. Accomplished teachers engage in a regular process of self-evaluation and make changes to improve the quality of work.

Finally, proposition 5 promotes the idea that accomplished teachers see themselves as members of several different communities. Because teachers are members of the school, local, state, and national communities, they may access the expertise and resources available from these communities to improve the quality of learning in their classrooms. The core propositions are important because they outline the areas for specific standards, and the standards shape the assessments for comparing a candidate's evidence against the ideal.[7]

It is fair to say that most of the Board's work has been divided between the development of standards and the complex assessments for measuring practice against those standards. While both are difficult challenges, developing valid and reliable assessments proved to be the most challenging. The year-long certification process for teachers has two main components: the construction of a detailed, reflective, and analytical portfolio over a four-to-six month time span, and the completion of a rigorous four-hour computerized assessment that measures a candidate's understanding of content knowledge.[8]

Unlike other professional teaching exams (i.e., the Praxis) or the medical boards, National Board certification is designed to assess experienced state-certified practitioners, rather than serve as a gateway to the classroom. The Praxis exams are designed for individuals just beginning their careers. Most states require a teacher to pass the Praxis (or something equivalent) before they can be licensed to teach. The doctor must pass the medical exam as part of a state's licensing process before he or she may begin practicing medicine.

Organizations like the American Board of Medical Specialties (ABMS) provide doctors the opportunity to become "boarded" in a particular specialization within the field of medicine. Like ABMS, National Board offers teachers a voluntarily means of distinguishing, affirming, or developing their practice.

National Board certification is also unique because it encourages teachers to work together on issues related to portfolio construction. Teachers routinely share and discuss their work, evidence, and reflections so as to help and learn from each other. In the end, all work submitted by a candidate must be his or her own, but it is likely that teachers helped each other understand the issues presented in different entries.[9]

The four-hour assessment center exam is not collaborative, and is administered to individual candidates. Though candidates may set up study groups to prepare for the content knowledge exam, each person takes the exam alone.

It is important to note that National Board assessments are purposely rigorous so that candidates are challenged to put forth their best evidence for the Board's assessors to consider. The portfolio represents a candidate's conception of accomplished teaching. By specifically asking for the "best" evidence possible, the Board is able to determine what a candidate's understanding of "best" is in relation to the pertinent set of standards. Candidates are free to make videos of as many lessons as they wish before choosing one to submit as evidence.

Because of limitations enforced on number of pages of analysis and amounts of evidence presented, teachers with much to say and present are forced to efficiently and effectively prioritize their work.[10] Choosing what evidence to include is one of the most difficult aspects of constructing the portfolio. Requiring teachers to make the comparison between the ideal (standards) and the actual (evidence presented) is an effective way of learning about the standards of accomplished teaching.

Completing the portfolio is a demanding and at times tedious process embedded in the day-to-day work of teachers. One teacher in this study, Andrea from Virginia, said, "I think if I had to go back and get a Ph.D. or have triplets, I would do that before I'd go through National Board again." Another teacher, Robert from Colorado said, "I thought the National Board Portfolio was the most difficult thing that I'd ever done in my entire career. I consider getting National Board Certification far greater than getting my masters' degree or anything else. I thought it was just an enormous project and very worthwhile."

Other teachers in this study used such descriptions as "absolutely overwhelming," "massively significant," and "highly stressful experience." Not one of the 120 teachers interviewed for this study described the experience as being "easy," "simple," or "dull."

The heart and soul of the certification experience is represented by the construction of a portfolio. *Portfolio* here has a meaning different than how most teachers, teacher educators, and lay persons tend to define the term. For example, a common conception of the portfolio is a beautifully presented collection of accomplishments bound in a special folder or case. Whether in art, journalism, education, or architecture, a portfolio is a kind of visually based professional resume that is representative of a person's work.

In the Board's idea of a portfolio, the emphasis is on how a teacher thinks about his or her work to foster learning in students. It is not about its aesthetics or style of presentation. In the context of National Board certification, the portfolio is a highly structured template that must be used in precisely the same manner by all candidates. When complete, the "portfolio" is a collection of written analyses, student learning artifacts, documented accomplishments, videos of teaching, and administrative documents.

The current version of the portfolio is divided into four sections. Each section addresses a different group of standards. The first section focuses on a teacher's ability to assess learning of diverse students through the analysis of planning, student written work, and feedback. The next two sections require an audiovisual sample that shows the candidate teaching and working with students to accomplish specific goals. The fourth section asks the candidate to analyze his or her work in both the professional and local communities. More specifically, the candidates are asked to document their intentional efforts to partner with families of their students. For each of these portfolio sections, there are two parts: (1) the presentation of evidence and (2) an analysis of the evidence as it relates to the relevant standards. The following section provides an overview of the work needed to complete a portfolio for AYA Science.

CONSTRUCTING THE ADOLESCENCE
AND YOUNG ADULT SCIENCE PORTFOLIO

The portfolio for AYA Science addresses thirteen standards grouped together into four categories.[11] Figure 3.1 summarizes the AYA Science standards.[12] The first group of standards pertains to what teachers need to know and be able to do when preparing for student learning. Knowledge of

I. Preparing the Way for Productive Student Learning		
	1. Understanding Students	
	2. Knowledge of Science	
	3. Instructional Resources	
II. Advancing Student Learning		
	4. Science Inquiry	
	5. Goals & Conceptual Understanding	
	6. Contexts of Science	
III. Establishing Favorable Context Learning		
	7. Engagement	
	8. Equitable Participation	
	9. Learning Environment	
IV. Supporting Teaching and Learning		
	10. Family & Community Outreach	
	11. Assessment	
	12. Reflection	
	13. Collegiality & Leadership	

FIGURE 3.1
Overview of Standards for AYA Science

scientific content, understanding students, and utilizing available resources are all necessary precursors to effective instruction.

The second group of standards addresses how accomplished teachers actively promote scientific learning with students. Teachers are expected to promote specific learning outcomes, help students understand the importance of those outcomes, and effectively use an inquiry approach to instruction.

The third set focuses on the learning environment created by the teacher. Accomplished teachers are expected to be equitable, fair, and respectful to all learners while providing meaningful opportunities to develop scientific understanding.

Finally, the fourth set of standards addresses teaching activities that tend to take place outside of the classroom. Accomplished teachers are expected to effectively assess student work and to use the data to reflect upon the strengths and weaknesses of a particular lesson, strategy, or pedagogical decision. In addition, accomplished teachers are expected to think about ways to collaborate with colleagues, family, and community to improve the learning experiences for all students.

While the standards and the portfolio are both divided up into four parts, they are not congruent. Evidence from any of the four portfolio entries might be used to support any of the thirteen standards. Entry 1 does not exclusively address the first set of standards about preparing the way for learning. However, as can be seen in the entry descriptions that follow, some standards are more closely aligned with specific entries. The four portfolio entries in AYA Science are "Teaching a Major Idea over Time," "Active Scientific Inquiry," "Whole-Class Discussion in Science," and "Documented Accomplishments: Contributions to Student Learning."[13]

Using videos (entries two and three), examples of student work, and artifacts representing professional accomplishments, teachers address questions in each section of the portfolio while constructing a presentation of their best practice. The final submitted product serves as evidence demonstrating the teacher's impact upon classroom environment, student learning, and the school community.

A teacher does not become an official candidate for National Board certification until the $500 assessment fee deposit is paid. Once this nonrefundable fee is received, the candidate receives a detailed 150-page guide for how to construct the portfolio and present the evidence. The portfolio guide provides step-by-step instructions, guidelines for self-evaluation, checklists for required tasks and materials, and the set of questions each candidate is expected to answer within a limited amount of space.[14]

Decisions regarding how to approach all four entries within a particular time frame, teaching assignments, and academic calendar are left to the candidate. For example, a candidate might begin keeping a communication log with parents for entry 4 while simultaneously planning the unit for entry 1 with colleagues.

Entry 1 (Teaching a Major Idea Over Time) focuses on curriculum planning, student engagement, and assessment of learning. In science (like other disciplines), teaching students about "big ideas" (e.g., conservation of energy, atomic theory, natural selection) requires repeated exposure from different perspectives in order to foster deep student understanding. Entry 1 requires the candidate to plan a unit of learning over an extended period. Teachers are encouraged to effectively align assignments, activities, and instruction with the identified learning goals. Data for this entry takes the form of the documented lesson plans and examples of student work (with and without teacher feedback) from homework, quizzes, activities, and tests.

Candidates are asked to identify two different students based on their level of achievement, and follow their learning over three assignments. The analysis is represented by the candidates' written responses to the predetermined prompts. The prompts for entry 1 are divided into three sections: "Overview & Context," "Analysis of Instruction and Student Work," and "Reflection." Here are the questions for each of these sections[15]:

Instructional Context

1. What are the number, age(s), and grade(s) of the students in the class featured in this entry, and the title and subject matter of the class?
2. What are the relevant features of your teaching context (school, class, students, community) that were influential in developing your response to this entry?
3. What is the major idea in science that you have chosen as the focus of your response to this entry?
4. What were your goals for student learning in connection to the major idea during this period of instruction?
5. Why do you consider this major idea in science and these goals to be important and appropriate for your students to learn?
6. What were the activities you and your students engaged in, and how were they sequenced and organized to build on students' interests, prior knowledge, and developing understandings as the sequence unfolded?
7. What challenges are inherent in teaching this major idea to your students? How is your instruction designed to meet these challenges? Did you modify your planned instruction in any way to meet these challenges?

Analysis of Instruction and Student Work

8. What are specific examples of ways the three activities worked together to further your students' understanding of the selected major idea in science?
9. What are specific examples of ways you provided students with a context for the science featured in this sequence by establishing connections to students' backgrounds, experiences, and interests and/or to other areas of study? How do you help students make meaning of science and internalize its relevance?
10. What are specific examples of ways you make good use of instructional resources to support your teaching and extend student learning? Based on your students and your teaching context, why did you select these instructional resources to support your teaching?

11. What are the educationally important characteristics of each of the three pieces of work? What does the work tell you about the students' growth in understanding of the major idea in science? What does the work tell you about any challenges or misunderstandings this student is experiencing?

Reflection

12. How successful was the instructional sequence in advancing student understanding of the major idea?
13. What would you do differently if given the opportunity to teach this sequence with these students again?

The answers to these questions are limited to ten double-spaced, typed pages with one-inch margins in a font no smaller than ten-point.[16] In addition, thirty-nine pages of required supporting materials are compiled, described, and included in the entry. All four entries require candidates to keep within strictly enforced space limitations. Anything that goes over the space allotment will not be considered in the assessment process.

A review of the prompts reveals two distinct areas of focus: what candidates planned to do and how instruction fostered student learning. To substantiate a teacher's assertions, the prompts repeatedly require the use of "specific examples" to serve as evidence. The emphasis on an evidence-based analysis of teaching and learning is a common theme across all four entries. Entry 1 ends like each of the other entries, with some reflective questions that ask the candidate to form summative conclusions and articulate their own professional learning.

The ten-page limit for answering these questions provides an added challenge for all types of candidates. For those candidates who embrace the opportunity to reflect and think about their teaching, keeping responses within the length limitations is a real test of their abilities to communicate professionally. It means this group of candidates must scrutinize their work to include those items and points that are most relevant and important to a given prompt.

They cannot use everything; therefore, they must prioritize and include the most important evidence. A candidate with the ability to efficiently use language has a big advantage over candidates whose communication skills are not as developed. For candidates unaccustomed to thinking and writing about their practice, the challenge is to develop enough ideas to fill up ten pages. To a teacher who is not practiced in thinking about the complexity of his or her work with learners, ten pages can seem like a lot of space to fill.

Entry 2 (Active Scientific Inquiry) examines a teacher's conception of how students make meaning from an inquiry experience. Candidates are instructed to avoid "cookbook" investigations, laboratory skill activities, and teacher-centered demonstration events. At the heart of entry 2 is a twenty-minute video tape divided into three sections.

Section one demonstrates how a teacher introduces an inquiry based activity. Section two of the video illustrates how the teacher interacts with students during the investigation. Finally, section three provides insight into how a teacher brings closure to lesson. Within audiovisual requirements (i.e., twenty minutes from one class meeting and no more than three edits), teachers are free to choose how long to make each of the three sections, and to identify the activity that lends itself most effectively to the goals of the entry. The prompts for entry 2 follow a very similar pattern to entry 1:

Instructional Context

1. What are the number, ages, and grades of the students in the class featured in this entry, and what is the subject matter of the class?
2. What are the relevant characteristics of this class that influenced your instructional strategies for this instructional sequence: ethnic, cultural, and linguistic diversity; the range of abilities of the students; the personality of the class?
3. What are the relevant characteristics of the students with exceptional needs and abilities that influenced your planning for this instruction? Give any other information that might help the assessor "see" this class.
4. What are the relevant features of your teaching context that influenced the selection of this inquiry lesson? This might include other realities of the social and physical teaching context.

Planning

5. What are your goals for this investigation, including concepts, attitudes, processes, and skills you want students to develop? Why are these important learning goals for these students?
6. How do these goals fit into your overall goals for the year?

7. How are the use of scientific inquiry and this investigation appropriate for addressing your goals for these students?

8. What are the central features of the three segments selected for the video recording? Explain how the three segments support different aspects of the inquiry process.

Video Recording Analysis

9. Citing specific evidence from the first segment of the video recording, how did you support student inquiry in order to conceptualize the primary questions and/or methodology of the investigation?

10. Citing specific evidence from the second segment of the video recording, how did you support student inquiry during the collection and processing of data during the investigation?

11. Citing specific evidence from the third segment of the video recording, how did you support student inquiry as they analyzed, considered, and evaluated the final results of the investigation?

12. How well were the learning goals for this inquiry investigation achieved?

13. Cite one interaction on the video recording that shows a student and/or students learning to engage in scientific inquiry.

14. How did you make use of available resources to promote student learning and inquiry?

15. Describe a specific example from this lesson as seen on the video recording that shows how you ensure fairness, equity, and access for students in your class.

Reflection

16. As you review the video recording, what parts of the investigation were particularly effective in terms of reaching your goals with this group of students? Why do you think so?

17. What would you do differently if you had the opportunity to pursue this investigation in the future with a different class? Why?

Entry 2 continues the process of asking candidates to use specific evidence to support their assertions. Unlike entry 1, entry 2 emphasizes evidence from the video of the candidate's work with learners. The prompts also demonstrate how some standards are overlapping while others might stand alone. For example, prompt 7 specifically asks the candidate to describe how issues of equity were addressed in the video, which directly addresses standard 8 (Equitable Participation). In comparison, the analysis prompts 1–3 each provide an opportunity for a candidate to be evaluated on standard 11 (assessment), standard 1 (understanding students), and standard 2 (knowledge of content).

Entry 3 (Whole Class Discussion about Science) provides an opportunity for a teacher to showcase his or her skills at fostering scientific discourse among students. According to the Board's standards for accomplished teaching, teachers are effective at fostering learning communities in which ideas and evidence are discussed according to the criteria of science. Students are encouraged to engage in an evidence-based scientific discourse. Students may point out weaknesses in other students' theories according to available evidence, or offer alternative explanations based on a different interpretation of the data.

Entry 3 provides a window into a teacher's knowledge of the nature of science and conception of the learning environment. Do students feel comfortable sharing ideas? To what extent do students participate? Are ideas supported by evidence?

For candidates who rely heavily on direct instruction and lecture to teach science, entry 3 is probably the most challenging part of the portfolio. When a good twenty-minute unedited discussion is captured on video, it is rarely a one-time affair. Rather, it is the product of a concentrated, long-term effort on the part of the teacher to foster whole-class discussions. For teachers who do not employ the regular use of whole-class discussions, trying to do it "for the portfolio" is difficult to complete successfully.

Effective whole-class discussions require skills and a level of trust that cannot be assumed to exist. How to participate, behave, and trust one's peers are all learned qualities. To be successful, a teacher needs to begin teaching these skills early in the school year so that students are comfortable and confident when the cameras are rolling. Since most teachers see themselves primarily as the "sage on the stage," transferring the nexus of communication from the teacher to the students is often a difficult task. Entry 3 asks the candidate to answer the following questions:

Instructional Context

1. What are the number, ages, and grades of the students in the class featured in this entry and subject matter of the class?

2. What are the relevant characteristics of this class that influenced your instructional strategies for this instructional sequence: ethnic, cultural, and linguistic diversity; the range of abilities of the students; the personality of the class?

3. What are the relevant characteristics of the students with exceptional needs and abilities that influenced your planning for this instruction? Give any other information that might help the assessor "see" this class.

4. What are the relevant features of your teaching context that influenced the selection of this whole-class science discussion? This might include other realities of the social and physical teaching context that are relevant to your response.

Planning

5. What are your goals for this lesson, including concepts, attitudes, processes, and skills you want students to develop? Why are these important learning goals for these students?

6. How do these goals fit into your overall goals for the year?

7. Why is discussion a particularly useful teaching approach for addressing your goals for this lesson?

Video Recording Analysis

8. How does what we see in the video recording fit into the lesson as a whole? Provide information that assessors would need to understand the video recording.

9. How well were the learning goals for the lesson achieved? What is the evidence for your answer?

10. How did your design and execution of this lesson affect the achievement of your instructional goals?

11. What interactions on the video recording show a student and/or students learning to reason and think scientifically and to communicate that reasoning and thinking?

12. How do interactions in the video recording illustrate your ability to help students explore and understand the scientific concept(s) being discussed?

13. Describe a specific example from this lesson as seen on the video recording that shows how you ensure fairness, equity, and access for students in your class.

Reflection

14. As you review the video recording, what parts of the discussion were particularly effective in terms of reaching your goals with this group of students? Why?

15. What would you do differently if you had the opportunity to pursue this discussion in the future with a different class? Why?

It is often quite amazing to see how certain science teachers conceptualize the concept of "whole-class discussion." Some candidates interpret it as an engaging lecture where students spend all their time listening attentively. Some videos show candidates lecturing for twenty minutes with the occasional student question and teacher answer. On the rare occasion, candidates may script the discussion.

In this approach, candidates write out comments and questions on index cards that are numbered in a specific order. The index cards are handed out to students who then read their cards in turn to the rest of the class. In this example, the candidate clearly does not comprehend what is meant by a whole-class discussion. When a video shows a group of learners actively listening and talking to each other about science, it is clear that the candidate is presenting strong evidence of their accomplished practice.

Finally, entry 4 (Documented Accomplishments) considers how a candidate's work with families, colleagues, and the local community supports the goal of student learning. This is the only entry that does not depend upon student work. Instead, entry 4 utilizes a candidate's documented evidence of involvement with the previously mentioned groups.

The entry is similar to the kinds of evidence traditionally collected for the distinction of "teacher of the year" or the types of artifacts one might expect to see in a traditional portfolio. It's the candidate's opportunity to demonstrate how his or her involvement with various communities contributes to the quality of classroom learning.

Every accomplishment or piece of evidence must be accompanied by a verification form signed by a third party that confirms the accuracy of the teacher's claim. In addition, the candidate must explain how a particular accomplishment impacted his or her ability to foster improved learning in the classroom. These brief analyses force the candidate to evaluate each activity on its merits to improve teaching.

Teachers are limited to accomplishments achieved during the last five years. For involvement with parents, candidates are encouraged to maintain a contact log that identifies every parent interaction, reason for interaction, mode of interaction, and the duration of each interaction. Candidates are limited to a maximum number of accomplishments for both their professional and local communities, and are also limited as to the number of pages that discuss each accomplishment's connection to fostering student learning.

Evidence can be as dramatic as a "Teacher of the Year" award or as simple as a thank-you note from a parent. For most candidates, entry 4 is probably the easiest to assemble and complete. It is the only entry that does not ask the candidate to describe the context. Since different assessors see different entries, candidates are encouraged to provide the necessary details within their descriptions so that assessors can appreciate the significance of each accomplishment. Here are the questions for entry 4:

Description and Analysis

1. What is the nature of this accomplishment? Be very specific. Remember that the assessor will know nothing about you or your teaching context.
2. Why is this accomplishment significant? To be significant, the accomplishment must be an important effort or achievement that demonstrates your work as a partner with students' families and their community; as a learner; and as a leader and/or collaborator with colleagues or other professionals.
3. How has what you have described had an impact on students' learning? You need to connect your accomplishment to the learning of your students or the students of your colleagues. Where appropriate, cite specific examples.

Reflective Summary

4. In your work outside of the classroom (beyond explicit student instruction), what was most effective in impacting student learning? Why?
5. Considering the patterns evident in all of your accomplishments taken together, what is your plan to further impact student learning in the future?

The AYA Science portfolio is shared here as the example of National Board certification, and the other certificate areas are equally challenging and similarly organized. The differences pertain mainly to entries 2 and 3, which can be tailored to address the unique instructional requirements of a particular content area or age group of learner. Portfolios for all certificate areas are closely aligned with the set of standards that describe a candidate's specialization.

Viewed in its totality, the portfolio represents an enormous undertaking for a teacher who is already over-worked, underpaid, and feeling squeezed. Yet it is the most promising method available to evaluate a teacher's ability to think about the complex parameters of accomplished teaching and how instructional decisions directly (or indirectly) impact students' learning experiences. If planned out and addressed regularly, the extra work a candidate needs to take on is manageable—as evidenced by the approximately twenty thousand candidates who complete the process every year.

Because the portfolio tasks are embedded in the daily work of candidates, its construction is not an exercise in the abstract. Rather, it is anchored in the real kind of instructional work necessary to foster learning with a specific group of students. Therefore, it is possible that in the process of putting one's instructional work with learners under such close scrutiny and examination, candidates might learn something that makes them more effective.

After all four entries are completed and organized into their labeled, barcoded, and sealed packets, the candidate puts all required evidence in "the box" to be shipped to the NBPTS offices in Texas for evaluation. The day the candidate ships that box off is usually a day of great relief and celebration. The time and effort required to organize so many files, forms, and artifacts is significant. However, while the candidate may not completely understand the necessity of the various forms and attention to technical detail, the work of the National Board assessors depends on it. In the next section, the work of the assessors is described.

ASSESSING THE PORTFOLIO

Once a candidate's "box" of evidence is received by NBPTS in mid-June, the assessment process begins—although from the outside, the "process" seems mysterious. Candidates submit their portfolios and six months later the outcomes are announced. Most candidates are probably unaware of the detailed procedures and significant professional efforts that go into a portfolio's assessment; yet what happens after portfolio submission is just as important as the candidates' work to create the portfolio. As this section demonstrates, the process of evaluating a candidate's evidence represents a significant organizational and evaluative achievement.

Ironically, after the candidate has carefully constructed and organized the box of evidence according to the detailed and explicit instructions, NBPTS begins the assessment process by dismantling a candidate's portfolio. Entries 1 through 4 are removed from the candidates' boxes and grouped accordingly with all the other entries from that particular certificate cohort.

When completed, all materials for entry 1 are boxed up and made ready for shipping to a designated city. The same process happens for the other entries, with each set of entries destined for a different city. The process of dismantling and shipping the entries to their respective cities takes about a month. These procedures are repeated for each of the two dozen or so different certificates offered each year.

Meanwhile, long before the candidates complete their portfolios, NBPTS recruits individuals to serve as assessors during the summer.[17] Assessors must hold a Bachelor's degree and a valid teaching license in the state where they reside. Individuals must have at least three years' teaching experience and be working currently at least half-time in the certificate area for which they are applying to be an assessor. No current candidate or former unsuccessful candidate may be an assessor. Different requirements are stipulated for retired teachers, National Board–certified teachers, and returning assessors.

The assessment process is labor-intensive and requires extensive assessor training. Each entry must be scored by at least two different assessors. On average an entry can take anywhere from thirty to ninety minutes to fully evaluate. Assessors are given a modest honorarium at the rate of $18.75 an hour. Considering that eighty hours of work over a two-week period is required, an assessor can make upwards of $1,500; however, they may need to use this money to cover the costs of transportation and lodging if they do not live nearby.

The number of assessors needed depends on the number of candidates for any particular certificate. For example, if the average assessor scores nine entries a day and there are five hundred entries, then approximately sixteen assessors should be able to complete the task in two weeks. However, due to attrition and dismissal because of bias, the Board tries to err on the side of caution: too many assessors are better than too few.

Assessors for a given entry are organized into teams of approximately ten individuals. Each team is run by a lead assessor. The lead assessor has experience as an assessor, plus additional training in leading the group and resolving assessment issues. The lead assessor is responsible for training assessors on all aspects of their work—from bias awareness, to using the NBPTS scoring system. It takes a couple days for an assessor to understand the score scale, rubrics, benchmarks, and other tools and procedures associated with assessing entries. In total, about one-third of an assessor's time is dedicated to learning about and practicing the assessment process.

A key goal of the training process is to identify any possible biases a potential assessor might have. Before an assessor gets the opportunity to score a "live" entry, he or she must first demonstrate to the lead assessor the ability to recognize any bias he or she might have and an understanding of the assessment protocols. Potential biases include gender, age, race, religion, and regional biases. Assessors who do not succeed in the bias training are dismissed.

The remaining assessors then learn how to read the evidence of a portfolio through the lens of the Board's standards for accomplished teaching. Understanding the Board's perspective on teaching remains the vital step to ensuring validity. Since every portfolio is assessed by a minimum of two individuals, the degree to which the two assessors concur on the evaluation of the evidence greatly affects the reliability of the process.

In instances where raters disagree by more than 1.25 points on a 4-point scale, a third assessor (usually the lead assessor) is brought in to resolve the incongruity. Obviously, when this discrepancy straddles the "accomplished" versus "unaccomplished" line, the third set of eyes becomes very important. Because two sets of eyes are needed to score every entry, assessors are forbidden to discuss entries with anyone other than the lead assessor.[18]

Portfolios are assessed based on the preponderance of evidence provided by the candidate. For each standard in a given certificate, assessors identify and record specific evidence that supports the standard. For example, as evidence of "Knowledge of Students," an assessor might note that a teacher refers to each student by name. As evidence of "Instructional Resources," an assessor might point out that the teacher provided sufficient supplies for all students to participate in a given activity.

After reviewing the evidence presented by a candidate, the assessor makes a final judgment on a 4-point scale. This judgment is the crucial step that essentially converts a collection of qualitative pieces of information into a quantitative measurement. Therefore, the crux of the assessor training focuses on understanding the benchmark examples of a portfolio entry characterized as a 1, 2, 3, or 4 where 1 and 2 represent unaccomplished teaching, and 3 and 4 represent accomplished teaching.

The goal of the assessor is to make a determination based on the preponderance of evidence as to whether an entry represents accomplished or unaccomplished teaching. After the assessor makes the overall determination of an entry's quality, he or she then specifically determines the final score.

In the case of accomplished work, the issue is whether or not it meets the standards ("3") or significantly exceeds them ("4"). In the case of unaccomplished work, the assessor determines if it is close to accomplished ("2") or significantly deficient by the Board's standards ("1"). At this second juncture, assessors can further refine their assessment to the closest tenth or quarter point (e.g., 2.25 or 3.75) on the four point scale.

In order to make these judgments in a precise and accurate manner, assessors need to fully understand the Board's vision of accomplished teaching and apply the framework toward the evaluation of evidence presented by candidates. To accomplish this goal, assessors who pass bias screening move on to explore the business of portfolio evaluation through a series of exemplar entries. For the purposes of the discussion here, entry 3 (Whole-Class Discussion about Science) is used as the example.

The training program begins by presenting an entry that qualifies as a 3 ("accomplished"). Assessors-in-training follow along with the lead assessor as the candidates' written responses to prompts are reviewed. Examples of evidence that support specific standards are discussed. When it is time to evaluate the video, assessors-in-training watch it only once and take notes. They are not allowed to go back and review any portion of the recording.

Following the 3, trainees examine the exemplar for a 2 or "unaccomplished teaching," and then a 1 or "severely unaccomplished teaching." Each of these first three exemplars providing a progressively weaker example of evidence for accomplished teaching. Each exemplar is followed by an in-depth discussion regarding the nature of the evidence, the standard that is addressed (or isn't addressed) and any questions trainees might have about a particular exemplar.

Finally, the group of trainees reviews an example of a 4 or "highly accomplished teaching." Once the four possibilities are introduced, discussed, and understood, trainees go through multiple practice entries to determine if they can score them accurately. When they achieve a high rate of agreement (usually by the third or fourth day), assessors are ready for "live" entries.

When all entries are scored by the end of two weeks, the assessors' work is complete. Since assessors who score one entry have no knowledge of the other components of the candidate's portfolio, assessors are left wondering which of the candidates reviewed will achieve National Board certification. Just because a teacher scored very well on one entry is no guarantee that he or she will score equally well on the other three entries.

Once the assessment centers close, the National Board begins the process of gathering all data for each and every candidate, and determining a final score. The portfolio is reconstructed, and a weighted score is computed from the four sections of the portfolio plus the assessment center exam.[19] If a candidate achieves a final score of 2.70 or greater out of 4.0, then he or she is awarded National Board Certification.

It takes the Board a few months to complete and tabulate the assessment results for each candidate. Between Thanksgiving and Christmas, the Board announces the names of all candidates who have been identified as accomplished. For those who were not identified as accomplished, the option of "banking" the good scores and redoing one or more of the unsatisfactory parts of their submission is available. Individuals who choose to redo portions of their portfolio have three years to complete the process, and are charged an assessment fee based on the number of entries they resubmit.

For the Board, the evaluation of portfolio entries is where the rubber meets the road. The validity of the process rests on the quality of the bias and assessor training. Strong and effective training increases the level of inter-rater reliability, or the degree to which two or more individuals agree that they are observing the same phenomenon.

The level of confidence in the accuracy of the results is directly dependent on the inter-rater reliability. Assessor training remains a vital component of the assessment process and one of the reasons why National Board certification costs more than $2,500. Much of that money pays for the significant human labor involved to ensure an equitable and reliable outcome.

SUMMARY

Part I of this book explored the issues associated with defining, identifying, and fostering exceptional teaching. These three chapters provide the necessary context and information to appreciate and understand the complex investigation that is presented in part II. Chapter 1 described the challenges associated with distinguishing exceptional teachers from their peers, and introduced the National Board as a viable means of addressing the issue. Chapter 2 provided an opportunity to experience the challenges associated with describing and measuring exceptional teaching by presenting the work of five chemistry teachers.

This chapter explored the work of the Board to create a system for promoting and evaluating accomplished teaching. From the development of the five propositions of accomplished teaching to the presentation of the derived standards for specific certificates, the work of the Board is comprehensive. If defining accomplished teaching is a significant achievement, the robust and rigorous assessment process represents a monumental improvement in the science of professional measurement. The Board's use of a portfolio and assessment center exam represents the kind of quality evaluation that exceptional teaching deserves.

Overall, the process of completing the portfolio and assessment center exams represents an important professional learning opportunity for the candidates. Once a teacher decides to pursue National Board certification by paying their $500 certification deposit fee, it is likely they will live with the process for at least one academic year, if not more.

While the Board has made the certification schedule much more flexible, the process can still be conceptualized as a twelve-month process. During the first six months, candidates familiarize themselves with the requirements of the portfolio. The second six months is dedicated to the intensive analysis of student learning in relation to the candidate's teaching. This analysis serves as the focused activity during the construction of the portfolio. Finally, after completing the portfolio at the end of the year, the candidate must also arrange to take the four-hour exam on relevant content knowledge.

This kind of work is very time consuming and exhausting. To finish and submit the portfolio on time, a candidate can spend 150 to 300 hours or more developing the portfolio. In terms of graduate education, National Board certification is equivalent to approximately two master's-level courses. However, most candidates would say that certification is far more difficult. It is the candidate's sustained attention to teaching and learning within the framework of the National Board's standards that makes the certification process an effective professional learning opportunity. What skills and knowledge do candidates learn from this intense experience? In part II, the strategy and rationale for investigating this question, as well as the significant findings, is presented.

NOTES

1. National Board for Professional Teaching Standards (NBPTS) Teacher of the Year Finalist, 2009.

2. Rosenfeld, *Eduholic,* 2008.

3. For a comprehensive discussion of how the Board developed, tested, and validated both the standards of accomplished teaching and the assessments to measure teachers against those standards see Ingvarson and Hattie (2008). Ingvarson and Hattie's editorial work on this volume stand as the most thorough discussion about the National Board to date.

4. Because of Lee Shulman's fundamental contributions to both the idea of a National Board for Professional Teaching Standards and the assessment system that would make it work, he is often referred to as the "father" of the National Board.

5. The cost of certification has changed. In 1998, the cost was $2,000. Then the price went up to $2,300. And in 2002, the fee was raised to $2,500. Later, NBPTS added a $65 administrative fee to every candidacy, bringing the current cost per candidate to $2,565.

6. Koprowicz, "What state legislators need to know," 1994.

7. It is interesting to note that the core propositions do not mention social justice, technology, schools, or a specific approach to pedagogy (e.g., constructivism or direct instruction).

8. The assessment center exercises have evolved over time. Originally, for example, the exam for AYA Science took an entire day covering postsecondary-level content material in science and pedagogical knowledge in the science classroom. Today, the exam has been reduced to a four-hour exam focused entirely on science content. For a complete description of the assessment process, see NBPTS, *Guide to National Board Certification,* 2010a.

9. The nature of this collaboration, and in particular the role of National Board teachers mentoring candidates in their schools or districts, has attracted recent attention. There are numerous ethical issues associated with this relationship and

the feedback process. For further discussion on this important issue, see Sato (2008) and Shulman and Sato (2006).

10. While the restrictions on length and evidence help to make portfolios easier to assess fairly and efficiently, they also serve to help weed out the weaker candidates. Candidates who fail to use the given amount of space or provide less evidence than the maximum allowed are less likely to score well with assessors.

11. Prior to 2003, there were thirteen standards for AYA Science. However, the current AYA Science standards have been revised and rearranged to include just twelve. Because the study discussed in this book began in 2002, the original configuration of thirteen standards is used for the purposes of discussion.

12. For a detailed description of the second edition of the standards for AYA Science, please see NBPTS (2003).

13. It should be noted that starting in 2001, the revised format for portfolio construction was phased in over a two-year period. The original portfolio required six entries. An entry called "Assessment" was incorporated into the other classroom performance entries and the "Documented Accomplishments for Professional and Community" were combined into one. Both formats were involved in this study during year one, though which candidates had which form is unknown. The teachers in years two and three had to complete the new four-entry version. Though this unexpected change in the intervention could be perceived as a threat to the study's validity, it is unlikely to be a cause of too much concern. The new version still addresses the same thirteen standards and requires candidates to provide evidence for each.

14. For a complete description of how to construct a portfolio for a specific certificate, see NBPTS, "The portfolio," 2010b.

15. All portfolio prompts shared in this discussion originated from NBPTS, *Instruction manual for adolescence and young adult (AYA) science certification,* 1997.

16. In 2003, the revised assessment extended the page limit to thirteen pages, but a 12-point font was required. Therefore, the amount of evidence presented remains about the same. This type of change makes it more comfortable for the assessors to read the evidence.

17. For a discussion of all the incentives and requirements to be an NBPTS assessor, see NBPTS, "Become an assessor," 2010c.

18. Silence may be the most difficult aspect of being an assessor. After examining entries of wide-ranging quality and witnessing both examples of amazing and scary teaching, the assessors cannot discuss what they see or read with their fellow assessors. Every lunch and break time is filled with banter that has nothing to do with accomplished teaching, which is the most pressing issue on each person's mind.

19. The four portfolio entries represent 80 percent of a candidate's evaluation. The assessment center exercises count toward the remaining 20 percent of the candidate's final score.

II

LEARNING

The Plan to Measure Candidate Learning

Chapter 4 presents a brief overview of the research design and investigative strategies used in this study of teacher learning from National Board certification. Before this research, education stakeholders expressed a lack of consensus regarding the value of National Board certification as a professional learning opportunity. Even though many candidates for certification talked openly about its benefits, a general sense of skepticism pervaded significant sectors of the education enterprise.

Assertions from critics attacking the Board as "a costly and largely misguided and ineffective effort" were met with testimonials and survey results from candidates claiming "it made me a better teacher."[1] The back-and-forth salvos between these two opposing positions contributed to the National Board's status as a controversial reform effort.

By 2001, the population of National Board–certified teachers (NBCTs) had reached 16,000 and was considered large enough to be examined through more robust investigations. The Board responded by announcing an unprecedented effort to understand the impact of certification on teachers, students, and schools. A request for proposals was issued, and more than one hundred proposals were submitted for review.

The RAND Corporation was hired to provide an independent evaluation of the proposals and identify those that were most deserving of funding. In the end, just over twenty studies were selected for funding. Some studies focused upon the effectiveness of NBCTs to improve student achievement on standardized tests while others were more qualitative in nature and examined the impact of Board-certified teachers on a school's learning environment. The study presented in part II of this book was selected for funding through this initiative.

The study distinguished itself from other proposals because it focused on certification as professional development and its effect to bring about teacher learning. The mixed-methodology approach seemed to appeal to both those who valued empirical investigations of cause and effect and those who embraced the more nuanced qualitative strategy of constructing understanding through in-depth observations.

For advocates of scientific approaches, the study utilized an efficient and elegant quasiexperimental strategy known as the *recurrent institutional cycle design (RICD)*. The RICD (sometimes referred to as a "patched-up" design) is a modified experimental approach that allows for participants to be observed before and after a specific intervention, while controlling for numerous threats to validity. The design makes it possible to look for significant gains from before ("pre-") observations to after ("post-") observations associated with the defined intervening program.

However, the pre- and post-observations are not traditional pencil-and-paper tests, as is common in many repeated-measures investigations. Rather, a more sophisticated structured interview approach was employed to develop data and evidence of change. The structured interview attempted to reproduce the construction of a portfolio on a much smaller scale. The completed interviews were then transcribed and formatted to look and read like a portfolio entry, which was then scored by an assessor.[2]

The interviews also provided a wealth of qualitative information that was used to contextualize and further understand any quantitative differences identified through pre-post comparisons. Together, the complementary strategies promised to bring detailed understanding about the role of National Board certification as a meaningful professional learning opportunity.

The validity of any new understandings that might emerge from a research project of this magnitude is contingent on the validity of several key assumptions. In this chapter, two of these assumptions are examined. The first assumption pertains to the homogeneity of candidates from one year to the next. The RICD assumes the three cohorts being compared (2001,

2002, and 2003) are homogeneous. If each cohort is derived from the same population each year, and that population does not change with regard to key demographic characteristics, then the causal-effect agent can more clearly be identified as the intervention.

For example, if 65 percent of the population pool were female in one year, it would be important that other years in the study not vary significantly from 65 percent. Any identified differences between cohorts would need to be explained and taken into consideration as possible confounding variables. Was it the difference in population that was responsible for the observed change, or was it the intervention? Conducting analyses that compare population and participant-demographic characteristics can provide information that can reduce these alternative explanations.

The second important assumption concerns the accuracy and precision of the assessment instruments developed for this research. If the protocols used to interview candidates do not accurately measure the specified construct (the standards of accomplished secondary science teaching as defined by the National Board), then the reliability of the results would be called into question. The degree to which the protocols are in alignment with the standards addresses the accuracy of the instruments to measure the identified phenomenon.

Accuracy (how close one is to the true situation) is addressed with the quality of the protocols used, but precision is an issue that depends on the conversion of interviews into measurable data. The quality of the scoring procedures is a measure of the level of precision of the findings.

The interviews may accurately address knowledge, experience, and skills within the framework of the thirteen standards of accomplished teaching, but without a precise means of scoring the data, potential differences could get lost in the noise resulting from a high degree of variance between the individuals who identify the participants' scores (assessors). Therefore, a fair measure of agreement is required between what the preponderance of evidence in a transcript indicates and what assessors report. This agreement can be expressed in terms of inter-rater reliability. The focus of chapter 4 is a discussion that assesses these two key assumptions and clarifies the implications of each on the interpretation of results.

The chapter is divided into four sections. The first section puts the current study in the context of previous research that examined what teachers may or may not be learning from National Board certification. The second section presents the research design in sufficient detail to appreciate both the strengths and weaknesses of the approach.

The third section describes the population of teachers who participated in the study. Understanding the similarity of these teachers to each other and the degree to which they represent the larger population pool from which they originated is vital to establishing the validity of observed results. Finally, the fourth section explains how the study's instruments (interview protocols and scoring rubrics) were used to convert interview data into quantifiable information.

From the following discussion of design, demographics, and instrumentation, an interesting and unique story of research emerges. What are teachers learning from National Board certification? The discussion presented here explains how an answer was achieved. It is the story of an old design used in new ways. It is the story of more than 120 secondary science teachers who agreed to participate in a study about science teaching and National Board certification. It is the story of unanticipated (but not unexpected) problems in a research project of fairly great complexity. It is a story that must be briefly told in order to appreciate and understand the findings that follow.

NATIONAL BOARD CERTIFICATION AND TEACHER LEARNING

Ever since the National Board for Professional Teaching Standards (NBPTS) issued its first certificates of accomplished teaching in 1994, the claims regarding its value as an effective professional development in stimulating teacher learning have consistently appeared throughout both the educational press and online forums.[3] What kind of research has been conducted, and what does it indicate about what teachers might be learning? In this section, a brief review of research that addresses this question is presented.

Testimonials and anecdotal reports made up the first wave of evidence regarding what teachers may be learning from Board certification. According to reports and interviews with the press, the first cohorts of candidates consistently indicated that certification had a positive impact upon their personal and professional lives.

These first-person reports indicate that Board certification might be a productive professional development. Though lacking the external validity of more rigorous pursuits, the testimonials from these teachers resonated with readers and provide the necessary evidence warranting further investigations. For example, numerous teachers have professed the benefits of National Board certification to their practice.[4] These teachers describe the effects of certification as "enlightening" (Mahaley, 1999, 5) or that it "revitalized" their practice (Areglado, 1999, 36). These accounts provide insights into the value of the National Board certification experience, but tell little about what candidates learn.

Surveys have been conducted that expand upon testimonial accounts and provide more extensive interpretations of what the population of NBCTs may be learning from the assessments. For example, NBPTS issued two reports based on survey data that provided a national profile of NBCTs and their feelings of "becoming a better teacher" from the certification process.[5] This type of information helps to validate the process as effective, but leaves open questions regarding validity of self-reports and the particulars of how the process of National Board certification could result in the professed outcomes.

Qualitative research studies that examined the outcomes of National Board certification began to clarify the possible learning outcomes from certification. These studies provided valuable knowledge that confirmed the findings in anecdotal and survey reports, and also revealed some possible explanations regarding how certification might facilitate professional growth.[6]

Other studies that were structured around support groups for teachers who were involved in the certification procedures provided compelling evidence that candidates learn from Board certification by participating in extended professional communities.[7] Studies have also attributed professional value to the NBPTS standards documents and portfolio instructions.[8] These investigations provided meaningful insights into the means and ends of Board certification, but were lacking in the generalizability of their results. They remain bound by the self-reporting nature of their evidence.

The first waves of research on National Board certification developed evidence for the following conclusions:

1. Most teachers find the experience of National Board certification to be effective professional development.
2. The discourse communities that form around the assessment experience are powerful avenues for candidate learning.

3. The NBPTS materials, such as standards documents and portfolio instructions, are a valuable resource for teachers' acquisition of knowledge.
4. Teachers learn to be "more reflective practitioners" as a result of the certification process.

It was within this context of promising qualitative investigations that the
research presented here was conceived. The study discussed in this chapter
represents one of the first quasiexperimental studies to examine the effectiveness of National Board certification as a professional development tool.
Recent literature identifies a need to complement the rich collection of qualitative studies on teacher learning with quantitative investigations that attempt
to clarify, identify, and substantiate specific outcomes.[9]

How might research move beyond the "more reflective practitioners" description of teacher learning from National Board certification? Is it possible
to identify and substantiate specific learning outcomes? The following discussion describes this investigation's plan for achieving these goals.

THE RECURRENT INSTITUTIONAL CYCLE DESIGN

Two important insights led to the design of this research. The first insight
addressed the issue of how to measure teacher learning. Many different approaches were considered, including case studies, traditional testing strategies, and surveys. However, each approach had significant disadvantages
when it came to addressing a possible causal relationship between certification and teacher learning.

It was decided that a more empirical approach that depended on sophisticated measurement tools was needed. However, identifying instruments
that might be available or might be developed to measure teacher learning
from Board certification remained a major obstacle. After much reflection
and analysis, an idea came to light. The National Board had spent millions of
dollars on the development of a valid and reliable set of instruments to assess
the quality of a teacher's work. What if these tools were slightly modified to
assess teacher understanding of specific aspects of practice?

The Board's assessment tools help to identify and quantify evidence from
candidate work to support each of the standards of accomplished teaching
associated with a specific certificate. The assessor then makes an informed

judgment based on the preponderance of all observed evidence as to whether the candidate's work is accomplished or not. However, before making this final judgment, assessors informally evaluate a candidate's evidence according to each individual standard.

The idea to formalize this important step of the assessment process and to consider the quality of a candidates' work in light of each standard represented the important innovation that made this research project possible. Rather than ask assessors to make a final judgment about the overall quality of evidence, assessors scored a candidate's work according to each of the standards for accomplished teaching. Rather than generate four scores for a portfolio of evidence, the assessors in this project produced thirteen scores (one for each standard of Adolescence and Young Adult Science [AYA Science]) according to the evidence presented in the transcribed interview.

The second insight pertained to the discovery of a research design that was new to K–12 education. The RICD has been used to evaluate treatments that recur on a cyclical schedule where one group of individuals is finishing and another group is just beginning.[10] By combining both cross-sectional and longitudinal components into the research design, the RICD allows for data to be compared within and between groups.

Numerous studies in the social and medical sciences have used some variation of the RICD to address questions pertaining to program impact on participants. In particular, Lafferty (1998) used the RICD to determine the effects of an intervention on leadership development and Conroy and colleagues (2003) used the design to evaluate assisted-living programs for individuals with developmental disabilities. However, this study marked the first time it has been used to examine teacher learning from professional development. Since National Board certification adheres to a rather regular yearly cycle (with a new cohort registering to start certification while the previous cohort is learning the outcome of the completed process), it was a good match between design and intervention.[11]

While a fully experimental design would have been optimal (e.g., a Solomon Four Group Design with random assignment to treatment), it was not practical for this investigative effort. One reason the experimental approach could not be used pertains to the self-selected nature of the population pool. Since candidates volunteer themselves for candidacy, a random assignment to treatment was not feasible.[12]

In response, the RICD's quasiexperimental approach accounts for the voluntary self-selected nature of the subjects' participation while providing effective means of addressing an array of threats to validity. The result is a design that provides an effective means of establishing some degree of causality between the treatment and the observed results.

Applying the RICD to investigate the question, "What are teachers learning from National Board certification?" provided numerous advantages with acceptable limitations appropriate for a study of this scope and size. The model is diagramed in figure 4.1 where X is the cyclical treatment (NBPTS certification), O is the collection of data (interviews), and R is random placement within Group 2.

As figure 4.1 illustrates, RICD allowed for data relevant to teacher learning to be collected across groups simultaneously and longitudinally from the same group over time. Time is measured along the x-axis and groups of participants are along the y-axis. Group 1, Group 2, and Group 3 were selected from National Board candidate cohorts 2002, 2003, and 2004 respectively.

Over a period of nearly fifteen months (September 2002 through November 2003), data was collected from three selected groups sampled from three consecutive cohorts of AYA Science candidates, as illustrated in figure 4.2. The design allows for the comparison of the pre- and post- measures between groups (cross-sectional) and within groups (longitudinal). One of the advantages of this particular design is that the effect of the treatment can be demonstrated by more than one comparison.

The establishment of causality between teacher learning and National Board certification does come with some restrictions. The limitations mani-

Group 1 $X \rightarrow O_1$

Group 2_A $R\, O_2 \rightarrow X \rightarrow O_3$
Group 2_B R $X \rightarrow O_4$

Group 3 $O_5 \rightarrow X$

X—Intervention
O—Observation by Interview

FIGURE 4.1
Design Model

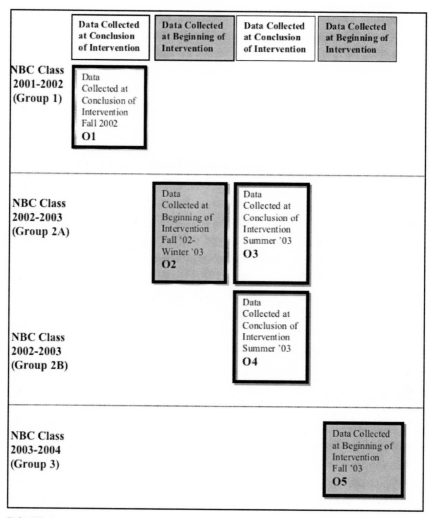

FIGURE 4.2
Overview of Data Collection According to Study Design

fest themselves with external and internal threats to validity. External threats to validity limit the generalizations of outcomes to only those individual teachers pursuing the current version of certification in AYA Science and not to all science teachers or National Board certificates.

Attacks on internal validity originate from a number of sources (e.g., history, maturation, testing, instrumentation, regression, selection, mortality, and others). Though no design is perfect, the RICD puts measures in place that address the most likely and potentially devastating vulnerabilities.

The RICD's "patched up" aspect allows for built-in control measures that strengthen internal validity. Since the One-Group Pretest-Posttest Design is so weak (i.e., only Group 2A), the addition of Groups 1 and 3 provide greater opportunity for verification. If Observations 1 and 2 are examined in isolation, the resulting design can be called a Static-Group Comparison. In this comparison design, two distinct groups are observed.

Observation 1 looks at a group that just completed the treatment and Observation 2 looks at a group that has not yet experienced the intervention. However, the timing of these observations is simultaneous. History, testing, instrumentation, and regression are each controlled as possible confounding variables in this design, but selection and mortality are not.

Thus, the Static-Group Comparison complements the One-Group Pretest-Posttest Design well. As Campbell and Stanley state, "The right combination of these two inadequate arguments might have considerable strength" (1963, 57). It is this "patched-up" approach to the methodology that provides for a reasonable measure of internal validity on all threats except maturation, which is discussed later.

To account for the possible test-retest effect, cohort two was divided into two groups. Group 2A was interviewed both before (Group 2A-Pre) and after (Group 2A-Post) intervention, whereas the second half of cohort two was only interviewed after intervention (Group 2B). This strategy allows for any effects of observation (sometimes called the *Hawthorne effect*) to be identified.

In other words, comparing Group 2A-Post and Group 2B allows for the experience of being interviewed before the intervention to be taken into consideration as a possible cause for observed changes. Was the phenomenon under study altered as a result of studying it? Group 2B is designed to address this question by providing a control to Group 2A.

Since the scheduling of the intervention is such that post- data for one group and pre- data for another group can be collected simultaneously, Group 3 is added without too much additional expense. Group 3 serves as a redundant pre- measure that can be used to understand Group 2A pre- scores. For all its "patched-up" characteristics, the final methodology for this study proved quite elegant and cost effective, with three years of data collected in only two.

FIGURE 4.3
Overview of Expected Model of Interaction

The RICD still relies on the basic hypothesis that the specified intervention will result in improved or increased response concerning the particular characteristics being measured. Put more simply, gains attributable to the treatment can be observed by comparing the pre- observations with the post-observations in this study. Figure 4.3 illustrates the basic model to be tested with this research design.

Many comparisons between different observations within the RICD framework are possible. Almost all of these comparisons contribute to the evaluation of the model rather than the assessment of candidate learning. For example, tests were conducted to compare the post- observations of Group 1 with the post- observations of Group 2. The results should have been equivalent since both represent post- observations.

Similarly, a series of nonequivalent comparisons were also made, such as the pre- observations of Group 3 with the post- observations of Group 1. The results of most of the equivalent and nonequivalent comparisons were consistent with expectations for the model.[13] With the validity of the model secure, attention could be paid to analysis that examined teacher learning.

The overall hypothesis in this study states that observations of the post-certification group should be significantly greater than the observations made of the precertification group. It is the one comparison that involves every participant. After all data was gathered, a statistical analysis of these two groups would reveal whether or not a significant improvement in scores was observed.

If scores improved significantly from pre- to post- observations, then this would serve as evidence of teacher learning from National Board certification. Based upon the RICD, table 4.1 presents the overall hypothesis being tested in this study. Figure 4.4 presents the overall hypothesis in graphic form.

"Learning" is operationally defined within the context of this investigation and refers to observed pre- to post- gains. The individual candidate's status

Table 4.1. Summary of Overall Hypothesis

Alternative Hypothesis	Predicted Relationship	Type of t-Test	Shorthand
Combined	(Groups 1 + 2B) > (Groups 2A–Pre + Group 3)	Independent one-tailed	(O1 + O4) > (O2 + O5)

with regard to the National Board certification process serves as the independent variable. The dependent variable is represented by the assessed scores of each candidate in each of the thirteen standards of accomplished secondary science teaching.

In the RICD, the timing of data collection demands closer inspection. More specifically, an observation's temporal relationship with the candidate's certification experience must be considered. Collecting data at the appropriate time is crucial to securing the most valid results.

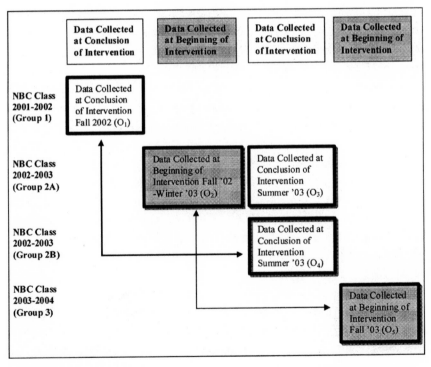

FIGURE 4.4
Diagram of Overall Hypothesis

In this investigation, the timing of interviews for both the precertification groups and the postcertification groups was a top priority. For the precertification teachers, interviews were conducted after the candidate had paid the full $300 registration fee, but before any significant or meaningful work had begun on the construction of the portfolio. For Group 3, this process worked quite well, with candidates being interviewed prior to the commencement of portfolio construction.

For Group 2, the process was more problematic, with some candidates being interviewed after 15 percent to 45 percent of their portfolio was completed. This problem is further discussed in the limitations section of chapter 6.

The postcertification teachers were interviewed after they had submitted the completed portfolio and taken the four-hour content exam, but before they learned of the outcome of their efforts. All postcertification teachers were interviewed within this period without exception. The proximity of the interview to the end of work on certification ranged from a couple of days to a few months. The fact that candidates finished the process by mid-July and did not learn the results until after Thanksgiving provided assessors a sufficient window of opportunity to contact, recruit, arrange, and conduct the interviews.

STUDY POPULATION

In an empirical study of teacher learning, several assumptions are made. For example, it is assumed that random selection will result in an accurate sample of the population. In this section, the process by which candidates became participants and the analysis of their representativeness to the greater population of candidates is discussed.

This investigation focused on the population of secondary science teachers who self-selected themselves to be candidates for National Board certification in AYA Science. To be a candidate for Board certification, teachers are required to (1) be certified in the state in which they teach, (2) currently teach at least two classes in the area of certification, and (3) have at least three years of full-time teaching experience. The population pool for this study was made up of all registered teachers for AYA Science certification for each of the three years of the study.

The final list of participants was determined on a first-to-reply basis. Recruitment of teachers ended once each of the three groups reached the needed forty teachers. Due to institutional and logistic issues beyond control of the research team, recruitment procedures from year to year were not perfectly congruent.

At the time of the study's inception, it was anticipated that the National Board would provide a list of available candidates for a particular year. The list would be randomized and a predetermined percent of the population would be contacted and invited to participate in the study.

Based on the results from the pilot study (Lustick, 2002), this process of recruitment had over a 50-percent positive response rate. Therefore, with an estimated population in any particular cohort of approximately five hundred teachers and a need for forty participants for the study, it was estimated that one hundred teachers would need to be invited to achieve the required number.

For Groups 1 and 3, this approach worked well, with an acceptance rate of nearly 50 percent. The first forty teachers to accept the study's invitation completed each group, respectively. However, Group 2 was more problematic, with an acceptance rate of 12 percent. To address the problem, the entire population pool was invited to participate. While this accommodation took a little longer, it did produce the needed number of candidates to complete Group 2. In all, 40 teachers from each of the three cohorts became the study's 120 candidates.

Does each cohort of candidates in this study accurately represent the population from which it came? Are participants from one year significantly different from other years? The answers to these questions give an indication of the samples' quality. The study's population quality can be calculated by comparing the demographic variables between each of the three groups.

To be meaningful, the study's goal of comparing pre- and post- results between different cohorts of teachers necessitates an understanding of how the three groups compared according to a few basic demographic variables such as years of experience or gender. Any differences found between groups could become a confounding variable that might rival the project's hypothesis regarding the intervention's effectiveness. Therefore, it is imperative to examine the available data to best understand how the candidates from different cohorts compared with each other and their respective parent populations.

In analyzing the similarities and differences between Groups 1, 2A, 2B, and 3, twelve different characteristics were compared. Table 4.2 provides a summary

Table 4.2. Group to Group Comparisons on Demographic Variables

Demographic Characteristic	Group 1	Group 2A	Group 2B	Group 3
Grades	ND	ND	ND	ND
Content	ND	ND	ND	ND
School	ND	ND	ND	ND
Region	ND	ND	ND	ND
Students	ND	ND	ND	ND
Gender	ND	ND	ND	ND
Years of Teaching Experience	ND	ND	ND	Different
Class Size	ND	ND	ND	ND
Length of Profiles (WORDS)	ND	ND	ND	ND
Learn of National Board	ND	Different	ND	ND
Incentive for National Board	ND	ND	Different	ND
Support for National Board	ND	ND	Different	ND

ND—Not Different.

of significant differences identified. Of those areas that showed difference (i.e., years of experience; learning of, incentive for, and support for National Board certification), the most important appears to be years of experience.

Comparisons between groups indicated that Group 3 had twelve years of experience compared with fourteen years of experience for Groups 1 and 3. Though significant ($p = 0.051$), this difference is not considered a viable explanation for observed results. The parent population of each group was revealed to be very consistent for each of the three years.[14] Aggregated to the entire study, the participating teachers had the following characteristics:

- Represented forty-two different states.
- Had content specialties including biology, chemistry, physics, and earth science.
- Averaged thirteen years of teaching experience.
- Were a female majority.
- Were evenly split between suburban schools and urban or rural settings.
- Worked primarily in public schools.
- Received some form of financial incentive to pursue National Board certification.
- Learned about National Board through a colleague.

After a detailed and thorough analysis, the teachers who participated in this study were proven to be remarkably consistent with each other and representative of their respective populations, thus satisfying the assumption that groups of candidates from one year to the next were not significantly different from each other. Because of a high degree of homogeneity both between and within groups, any findings generated by this research are more likely due to the intervention rather than population variance, and results may be generalized to the greater population of AYA Science candidates.

INSTRUMENTATION

The second important assumption in a study of this type pertains to the instruments and procedures used to generate data. Two investigative instruments (the interview protocols and the assessment rubrics) were used over the course of this study. The interview protocols were developed during the pilot investigation (Lustick, 2001) and later refined during the initial interviews of this study.[15]

The protocols were designed to mimic the entire portfolio construction process, but on a much smaller scale. Whereas the average candidate might spend hundreds of hours constructing his or her portfolio over a four- to nine-month period, this investigation sought to collect the same sorts of evidence with a seventy-minute interview. In a sense, the interview provided a sampling of a candidate's knowledge and understanding concerning secondary science teaching and learning.

The structured stimulus-response interview was employed because of its advantages for collecting richer data when compared with surveys and self-reporting instruments. Mullens and his associates (1996) conducted evaluative research and found that a structured interview can result in a more robust database.

Since the goal of this study was to assess knowledge and possible changes in knowledge as a result of certification, the use of a structured interview seemed appropriate. Because data collection by structured interview is more labor-intensive and less practical to use on a large scale, it is much less common than other forms of data collection, such as surveys or self-reports.

The structured interview developed for this study emerged in part from a technical report by Kennedy, Ball, and McDairmid that examined changes in teacher knowledge through research. In this report, the authors state that one possible way of identifying changes in what teachers know is by "presenting teachers with hypothetical teaching situations" (1993, 6).

A reliance on standardized teaching scenarios meant that the amount of irrelevant, idiosyncratic differences in responses could be reduced and the detailed, contextualized information about teachers' perceptions of practice would be increased. According to the Kennedy study, focusing the protocols on teaching situations and standardizing them for all study participants "allows for researchers to see how the various aspects of expertise—knowledge, beliefs, attitudes about learning, teaching, and subject matter were drawn on to make teaching decisions" (1993, 7).

Such an approach to assessing teacher knowledge minimizes the degree of self-reporting by teachers and maximizes their analytical focus on a third party's practice. How they interpret, analyze, and evaluate the work of another teacher provides a window into what these teachers know and understand about accomplished teaching. By scoring these analyses according to the thirteen standards of accomplished teaching for AYA Science, a good estimation of what each teacher knows about the standards becomes possible.

The structured stimulus-response interview for this study had six sections representing all parts of the portfolio construction. Each section was modeled after each theme of the four mandatory portfolio entries, and was aligned with the background and school context information that is also required. The section included a pedagogical "scenario" typical of a secondary science classroom. Table 4.3 summarizes a comparison between the structured interview protocols and the requirements (portfolio and assessment center exercises) for certification.[16]

For each interview, teachers received a packet in the mail containing instructions, artifacts, and a videotape. Candidates were asked to refrain from reviewing the materials until instructed to do so during the interview. While candidates could review the five scenarios, they were not given the questions

Table 4.3. Structured Interview and Portfolio Construction Comparison

Required Aspects	Structured Interview Protocols	NBPTS Portfolio Entry
Introductory Questions	Teacher Background School Context Student Profile	Teacher Background School Context Student Profile
Scenario 1	Teaching a Major Idea in Science Over Time	Teaching a Major Idea in Science Over Time
Scenario 2	Scientific Inquiry	Scientific Inquiry
Scenario 3	Best Practice	Assessment Center
Scenario 4	Whole-Class Discussion	Whole-Class Discussion
Scenario 5	Community, Professional Development, and Leadership	Community, Professional Development, and Leadership

they would be asked about each one. Each question asked during the interview (except for scenario 3) was modeled after the same set of prompts provided in each entry of the portfolio construction. By modeling the protocols on the portfolio construction process, data was collected in parallel with what the National Board collects in the finished portfolio. Entry 3 asked candidates to reflect on a recent example of their teaching that they thought was successful in terms of what students learned.

Just as the portfolio construction prompts can be linked to one or more of the thirteen standards of accomplished science teaching, each question in the protocol can also be traced to the same list of thirteen standards. The weight and balance of these standards as reflected in the portfolio prompts is the same in the structured interview questions. For example, 10 percent of the questions can be linked to the standard "Equity in the Classroom" in the portfolio prompts. In the interview questions, 10 percent also pertain to "Equity in the Classroom."

INTERVIEW PROTOCOLS

The structured interview utilized a series of teaching scenarios to address the respective themes of each portfolio entry. The interview experience needed to closely parallel the portfolio construction process without being cliché, trite, or obvious. It also had to limit the amount of self-reporting data and maximize the third-person analytical data. The questions and artifacts had to be recognizable as legitimate science classroom possibilities falling within the providence of a typical science lesson.

And yet all but one scenario would be new situations for each candidate. The candidates had never seen the artifacts, heard these conversations, or watched the video. Their assessment and analysis of each scenario based on the questions they were asked would provide a unique glimpse into their knowledge, values, and beliefs, which could later be measured according to the National Board's thirteen standards of accomplished teaching in AYA Science.

The basic assumption was that if teachers in the study were presented with some artifact of teaching and learning similar to their own portfolio artifacts, the analysis they would provide would be a good indication of how they would address the same question in their own portfolio construction. For example, if a question asked about equity in the scenario, and the candidate said very little about equity, then one might assume that in his or her own self-analysis for the portfolio, the teacher would also have said very little about equity.

The following is a brief discussion of each of the six parts of the protocols. The protocols as presented here remained basically unchanged over the course of the study. Even when weaknesses were later identified, they were not corrected for fear of altering or influencing the results.

Scenario 1 was modeled after the portfolio entry "Teaching a Major Idea in Science." It included an artifact that the teacher used to assess students' understanding of kinetic theory of matter before and after the unit. Kinetic theory was chosen as the topic because of its presence in most general science, chemistry, and physics classes. It is also a topic addressed to differing degrees in middle school. Being such a general idea in science, it was anticipated that most secondary science teachers would have some familiarity with it, and therefore it was not so esoteric as to be a surprise. Also, it is a challenging and abstract concept for students of all ages to learn.

The questions asked of the candidates during the interview closely resemble the portfolio prompts for the entry on "Teaching a Major Idea in Science." Scenario 1 was a difficult and demanding task of analysis for the interviewee, since it required the teacher to analyze and comment on someone else's work. Because of its perceived difficulty, teachers discussed scenario 1 immediately after the introductory questions.

Scenario 2 continued with the analysis of another teacher's work, but this time it was focused on the life sciences and the difficult concept of natural selection. This scenario was modeled after entry 2, which is titled "Active Scientific Inquiry." The theory of natural selection was chosen for this section because of its inclusion in nearly all high school textbooks and classrooms. It also allowed for teachers to voice ideas on the controversial (in some areas of the country) topic of how evolution is taught.[17]

A transcribed dialog between a group of students working cooperatively on an introductory activity commonly known as the "peppered moth investigation" was presented as a situation that allowed teachers to express their ideas about scientific inquiry, equity, engagement, and learning environment. In many respects, it was the most complex scenario of the interview, requiring participating teachers to analyze content, student understanding, scientific inquiry, equity, and science pedagogy all at the same time. Once again, the interview protocols closely followed those of the portfolio prompts.

For scenario 3, the interviewee was given the opportunity to report an instance of best practice in a guided self-reflection format. The five teachers' descriptions of lessons about the periodic table from chapter 2 were responses to this part of the interview. After two sections of intensive analysis of someone else's teaching, it was a relief for most to be able to discuss their own teaching. This scenario was not modeled after any particular entry in the portfolio, but rather was more of a summation of the reflective process present in all four entries, addressing all four areas of standards with a special emphasis on content knowledge. An evaluation of the candidate's understanding of content was possible due to the open-ended nature of the question.

Scenario 4 was modeled after entry 3 of the portfolio, "Whole-Class Discussion in Science." For this scenario, the interviewees watched a six-minute continuous clip from an actual twenty-minute video included as evidence in a portfolio for AYA Science. The whole-class discussion on the video takes place during a field trip for an Environmental Science class.

The clip showed a long table outside with the teacher at one end and a class of eighteen students sitting on either side. The class had been studying a forest ecosystem for the last six months with the goal of determining its environmental status. The exchanges around the table reveal students debating whether the observed changes over time are indicative of a forest in decline or seasonal fluctuations.

A six-minute clip was intentionally chosen from the twenty-minute video that included many interesting moments. Some moments in the video discussion were quite strong, while others were quite weak according to the National Board's standards. The clip allowed for a well–thought out and balanced analysis of the teacher's work. The candidates had ample opportunity to observe teacher actions that promoted discussion, evidence of student learning, and comments between students that reflected both content specific concepts, but also indicated views on the nature of science.[18]

Since it did not seem to be an efficient use of time or a reasonable task to ask an interviewee to watch a twenty-minute video during a seventy-minute interview, the six-minute clip provided a sufficient opportunity to observe a discussion and answer relevant questions. Teachers were asked not to watch the sealed tape until after instructed to do so during the interview. Every teacher indicated that they had abided by this request.

The interview protocols that followed viewing the video address many of the standards dealing with collegiality, assessment, understanding and goals, engagement, and knowledge of science. For most teachers who teach biology, chemistry, or life science, the concepts were familiar. A few physics teachers in the study commented that they did not know much about "ecology," but the discussion was not just about content—it was also about the process of scientific inquiry and discourse. The results from this part of the interview were quite interesting and informative.

The final section, scenario 5, once again gives teachers an opportunity to discuss their own experiences and ideas. It was modeled after entry 4 of the portfolio, "Documented Accomplishments Outside of Class." The section was divided into two equal parts: "Professional Development & Leadership Experiences" and "Community & Family Experiences." In both sections, teachers were asked which activities and accomplishments (out of a list of fifteen) they experienced directly. If they had direct experience, they were asked to rate each item on a scale of 1 to 5 with regard to the item's impact on their ability to improve student learning.

For items that teachers did not experience, the assessment was left blank. In addition, the teachers were asked if anything was missing from the list that they thought was especially helpful in improving their ability to bring about learning in their students. The list was by no means exhaustive, but did provide an indication of the candidate's depth of professional and community experiences.

At the completion of the interview, candidates were instructed to put all materials in the self-addressed, stamped envelope and return it to the research team at their earliest convenience. Upon receipt of the materials, each participant was given a twenty-five dollar online gift card as a professional courtesy for their time. During this same time, a cassette tape of the interview was transcribed by a third party. The completed transcription required one more step before it could be scored.

Before interviews could be scored by assessors, it was necessary to process them into readable documents. Each interview transcription needed to be "cleaned up" with regard to its appearance and its readability. The following is an example of one candidate's response to an interview question prior to processing:

INTERVIEWER: Suppose this teacher also said she had a goal of ensuring fairness, equity, and access for all students. What steps should the teacher take to fulfill this objective?

CANDIDATE: I think the first thing would be to ask questions of Alejandra. Uhm but personally they would be . . . they wouldn't be the most challenging on-the-spot questions. But they would be more questions to make sure that she feels comfortable with the group and comfortable speaking with the group. And I guess it really depends too, she's from Ecuador, and it depends on if she is uncomfortable speaking English. I would also probably try and take that into account. If she doesn't speak English at all or very, very little uhm . . . you know . . . taking notes would be kind of a challenge. I'm assuming that she speaks a little bit. Uhm . . . that would be definitely one of my first steps. Uhm . . . I guess it depends on the classroom environment and why she has Evan working with three gals and that kind of stuff . . . it's tough to say.

INTERVIEWER: Has Evan working what?

CANDIDATE: With three gals . . . girls.

INTERVIEWER: Oh I'm sorry . . . Is that something that would be . . . you'd want to know why . . . is that what you said?

CANDIDATE: Uhm . . . it wouldn't well I . . . I'm interested in it if . . . if one of her professional goals is working on equity in the classroom. Uhm . . .you know . . . it depends on the ratio of guys to girls in the classroom and that kind of stuff; but.

INTERVIEWER: Anything else?

CANDIDATE: Nope that's it.

The transcription is difficult to read for a number of reasons. The presence of verbal ticks (e.g., "uhm") might unfairly distract assessors from the meaning of a teacher's response. Also, the presence of the interviewer asking clarification questions are also distracting and unnecessary for the assessors to evaluate the available evidence. After processing, the passage appears as follows:

Suppose this teacher also said she had a goal of ensuring fairness, equity, and access for all students. What steps should the teacher take to fulfill this objective?

I think the first thing would be to ask questions of Alejandra . . . but they wouldn't be the most challenging on-the-spot questions. They would be more questions to make sure that she feels comfortable with the group and comfortable speaking with the group. And I guess it really depends too, she's from Ecuador and it depends on if she is uncomfortable speaking English. I would also probably try and take that into account. If she doesn't speak English at all or very, very little . . . then . . . taking notes would be kind of a challenge. I'm assuming that she speaks a little bit . . . that would be definitely one of my first steps.

I guess it depends on the classroom environment and why she has Evan working with three gals and that kind of stuff . . . it's tough to say. I'm interested if one of her professional goals is working on equity in the classroom. It depends on the ratio of guys to girls in the classroom and that kind of stuff.

While it is still quite obviously a written version of an auditory response, the passage is easier to read and score as if it were part of a real portfolio. To hand the assessors in this study a "raw" transcript would have impeded their ability to adequately and fairly evaluate the written words. National Board is a stickler for format (font, margins, spacing) and the researchers wanted the interview transcripts to visually resemble a real entry as much as possible.

Details such as the italicized (or bolded) question and the double-spaced response mimic what assessors are accustomed to seeing during a summer scoring session. The goal of transcription processing was to change the appearance and clarity of the candidates' ideas while maintaining the meaning of their responses. A fully processed transcription was about thirteen pages long and required about forty minutes to read, document, and score. The scoring process represents the second instrument for this study.

Scoring the transcript was the crucial point in the project where evidence became quantified. Therefore, only the most qualified individuals were solicited to participate. Experienced and knowledgeable National Board assessors for AYA Science were recruited to score the interview transcripts. Assessors spent the equivalent of one day's training learning how to adapt the National Board's assessment tools to the purpose of the study.

Due to the almost eight years of assessor experience represented by all three individuals, it was thought that eight hours of training and practice would be sufficient. The rubrics (based on the thirteen standards of accomplished secondary science teaching discussed in chapter 3) remained unchanged, as did the protocols for reading through a transcript one time to collect evidence.

The only real difference between scoring portfolio entries versus interview transcripts was the very last step. For portfolio entries, assessors reviewed the preponderance of evidence for all thirteen standards to determine a representative score on the four-point scale. For the transcribed interview, the assessor reviewed the evidence available for each of the thirteen standards and then determined a score for each of the thirteen standards. Instead of producing one overall score, assessors produced thirteen scores for each transcription. It is these scores that serve as the basis for the analyses described in chapter 5.

Each transcript was scored at least two times by different assessors.[19] Assessors used a form that closely resembled the rubric used to score portfolio entries. Figure 4.5 provides the training example of this form with the specific

Standard to Assess	Evidence to Support Standard	Score
I. Preparing the Way for Productive Student Learning		
a) Knowledge of Students	Does the teacher know how their students learn, actively come to know them as individuals, and determine students' understanding of science as well as their individual learning backgrounds?	
b) Content/Pedagogical Knowledge	Does the teacher have a broad/current knowledge of science and science education along with in depth knowledge of a subfield of science which they use to set important learning goals?	
c) Instructional Resources	Does the teacher select and adapt instructional resources including technology, laboratory, and community resources and create their own to support active student explorations in science?	
II. Advancing Student Learning		
d) Science Inquiry	Does the teacher develop in students the mental operations, habits of mind, and attitudes that characterize the process of scientific inquiry?	
e) Goals for Conceptual Understanding	Does the teacher set learning goals that are aligned, appropriate, and central to students and are a variety of instructional strategies used to expand students' understanding of major scientific ideas?	
f) Connections and Contexts of Science	Does the teacher create opportunities for students to examine the human contexts of science, relationships with technology, ties to math, impact upon society, and conn ections across disciplines?	
III. Establishing a Favorable Context for Student Learning		
g) Engagement	Does the teacher stimulate interest in science and technology and elicit all their students' sustained participation in learning activities?	
h) Equitable Participation	Does the teacher take steps to ensure that all students, including those from groups which have historically not been encouraged to enter the world of science, participate in the study of science?	
i) Learning Environment	Does the teacher create/promote a safe supportive learning environment that fosters high expectations for the success of all students and reflects values inherent in the practice of science?	
IV. Supporting Teaching and Student Learni ng		
j) Family and Community Outreach	Does the teacher proactively work with families and communities to facilitate ongoing mutually beneficial interactions that serve the best interests of each student's development and education?	
k) Assessment	Does the teacher access student learning through a variety of means that align with, enhance the learning of, and further learning goals?	
l) Reflection	Does the teacher accurately and insightfully analyze, evaluate, modify, and/or strengthen teaching by suggesting next steps or alternative approaches that may improve students' learning?	
m) Collegiality and Leadership	Does the teacher contribute to the quality of their colleagues' practice, the instructional program, and the work of the professional community throug h collaboration or leadership?	

FIGURE 4.5
Scoring Form with Guiding Questions

questions assessors were to ask about each standard while reading through the interview. In the version used by assessors, the area with questions was left blank to record evidence.

While an instrument analysis indicates a high degree of agreement between the interview prompts and the portfolio prompts, the measure of inter-rater reliability was not as successful. The assessors in this study demonstrated an overall reliability of 0.458, which is considered low to moderate. With such a complex and difficult assessment task, a reliability of 0.458 represents an important weakness of this investigation. All findings derived from this study should be conditional upon a less-than-ideal inter-rater reliability.

The methodological assumption regarding the adequacy of the assessment instruments' accuracy and precision is satisfactory to a limited degree, but limits the generalizability of this study's findings. The effect of the moderate reliability is to inflate the variability of the scores, making the tests of the hypotheses statistically more conservative—that is, making it more difficult to reject the null hypotheses. The results of these tests are presented in the next chapter.

SUMMARY

This chapter dealt with the issues and approaches associated with the research methodology. This study intended to fill a noticeable void in research that examined National Board certification as a professional learning opportunity. The RICD was chosen to investigate a series of hypotheses that would identify observed effects of treatment upon secondary science teachers in this study.

Through both cross-sectional and longitudinal data set comparisons, most threats to internal and external validity were controlled for with this methodology. The model of interaction and the hypothesis for this investigation were presented. The demographic information regarding cohort participants indicated a high degree of similarity between and within groups.

In the next two chapters, the results of this research effort are presented. Chapter 5 examines the quantitative differences observed as a result of National Board certification and chapter 6 discusses the qualitative evidence to ascertain the degree to which the two forms of evidence agree.

NOTES

1. Bellevue School District (N.D.); Boyd and Reese, 2006, 51; and National Board for Professional Teaching Standards, 2001b, 4.

2. For the complete set of interview protocols, see appendix A.

3. For detailed documentation of candidate comments about the certification process see Tracz et al., "Improvement in teaching skills," 1995; and Kowalski et al., "Professional development," 1997. For more recent research on NBPTS and teacher learning, see Standerfer, "Learning from the National Board," 2008; and Tracz et al., "The impact of NBPTS," 2005.

4. See Bailey and Helms, "The National Board certified teacher," 2000; Benz, "Measuring up," 1997; Gardiner, "I leave with more ideas," 2000; Haynes, "One teacher's experience," 1995; Jenkins, "Earning board certification," 2000; Marriot, "Increased insight," 2001; Roden, "Winners and winners," 1999; and Wiebke, "My journey," 2000 for examples of anecdotal evidence for Board certification as a productive professional learning opportunity.

5. National Board for Professional Teaching Standards, "The impact of National Board," 2001a and National Board for Professional Teaching Standards, "I am a better teacher," 2001b represent the first research efforts conducted by the National Board to document the effects of certification on candidates and their teaching.

6. See Athanases, "Teachers' reports," 1994; and Chittenden and Jones, "An observational study," 1997 for examples of research that examines possible mechanisms of professional learning from Board certification.

7. For research on the sociocultural aspect of candidate learning see Burroughs, Schwartz, and Hendricks-Lee, "Communities of practice," 2000; Manouchehehri, "Collegial interaction," 2001; and Rotberg, "National Board certification," 1998. See Anagnostopoulos et al., "Dollars, distinction, or duty?" 2010 for an institutional perspective on NBPTS and teaching.

8. For a thorough analysis of the NBPTS materials as learning resources, see Kowalski et al., "Professional development," 1997.

9. For in-depth discussions about multiple approaches to research about teacher learning, see Crawford and Impara, "Critical issues," 2001; Floden, "Research on effects," 2001; and Porter, Youngs, and Odden, "Advances in teacher assessments," 2001.

10. For examples of how this design has been used in prior research efforts see Campbell and McCormick, "Military experience," 1957; Jimenez, "Psychosocial intervention," 1999; and Shavelson, Webb, and Hotta, "The concept of exchangeability," 1987.

11. It is important to note that the NBPTS has altered the process to make it less contingent on all candidates following an identical schedule of events (i.e.,

registration in the fall, portfolio construction in the spring, testing in the summer, and results provided in the fall). While a majority of candidates still abide by this calendar, a growing number of candidates do not, as indicated by the option to stretch the experience over a three-year period through the "Take One" program.

12. For a further discussion about the threats to internal and external validity for different quasiexperimental designs, see Campbell and Stanley, *Experimental and quasi-experimental*, 1963; Cook and Campbell, *Quasi-experimentation*, 1979; Merriam and Simpson, *A guide to research*, 1995.

13. The comparisons that involved observation number two (O2) was shown to be problematic. This issue is addressed in chapter 5.

14. For a complete analysis of the populations, see appendix B.

15. For group 1, forty-six teachers were recruited and interviewed. The first six interviews served as an opportunity to revise the instruments and train the assessors. The data from these initial observations were not included in the final analysis.

16. For a detailed comparison of the interview protocols with the portfolio prompts, see appendix C.

17. It is interesting to note that not one teacher in this study made a negative remark about this content area. In fact, there were numerous comments regarding the importance of teaching natural selection to students.

18. The original twenty-minute clip was used by the National Board in their assessor training as their benchmark example of accomplished whole-class discussion in science. In other words, the tape was used to demonstrate to assessors what a "4" or highly accomplished video of a whole-class discussion looked like.

19. As one of the three assessors, I scored every transcript while the other two assessors each scored half. On occasion, when there was significant disagreement between assessors, the third assessor was asked to score the transcript. To address possible bias, I took several important steps. First, a period of three to five months passed between the time of the interview and my opportunity to assess. Second, the only identifier on the transcript was the candidate's project number. Third, while I did recognize some of the transcripts and could recall the specific interview, I made a conscious effort to focus on the evidence presented. Did I influence the results, or was my work consistent with that of the other assessors? To answer this question, all analyses were repeated using only the two other assessors' scores and none of mine. The results were identical, indicating that my work did not sway the results one way or the other.

5

Quantitative Evidence for Candidate Learning

Anyone who has visited a carnival or county fair knows how the bright colors, flashing lights, and constant motion of the rides can overpower the senses. It is an environment that manipulates an individual into feeling a sense of excitement, anticipation, and sometimes a little anxiety. However, the carnival's illusory glitz and glamour can hide the less attractive reality. Peel back the pretty sign or look under the public façade and the more problematic aspects of the carnival might be revealed.

Carnivals would not stay in business long if visitors had complete access to the carnies' hidden world. Pieces of wood used to level the Whirly Bird. Repairs to the Ferris Wheel that do not quite meet code. Food prepared in less than ideal conditions. Rides that function but need key parts replaced. Visitors to the carnival are not well informed of these problems. On the rare occasion, a ride might be closed, sending the message that safety is a concern.

However, it is in the carnival's short-term financial interest to take the risk and encourage everyone to go on the rides. People do not always make the same assumptions and choices because of the same criteria—a carnie must weigh the cost of closing a ride for needed repair against the potential income it would generate. Sometimes the ride is shut down and sometimes it isn't. There is a degree of risk for anyone who climbs aboard for a momentary thrill.

In some ways, educational research is not so very different from the carnival. While the standards may be more rigorous and the researchers more

educated, carnies and principal investigators both could be considered ped-
dlers of illusion. How could educational research possibly be compared with
a traveling carnival? Both enterprises depend on the imperfect efforts and
judgments of people.

Like the carnival, educational research tends to have two faces: the public
and private. The public face of educational research is the final written version
that appears in print, such as can be found in professional journals and websites. Any publicity or news reports generated by a peer-reviewed publication
may also contribute to the public face of research.

The public face is neat and tidy. It is clean and official looking. It is highly
processed and sanitized by the editing, revising, and formatting efforts. The
public sees beautifully set text, impressive tables and charts, and authorita-
tive-sounding conclusions. These elements help to generate a view of research
that is "scientific," meaningful, and error-free.

Even when a study addresses its limitations, this often occupies a small
percentage of the total narrative, and may or may not provide meaningful
information. Most principal investigators take the limitations sections seriously, as evidenced by their carefully worded, strategically placed, and cau-
tiously presented information. While authors are ultimately responsible for
what they write, the journal's rules for manuscripts also influence what ends
up in print.

A journal publication's limitations on length ensure that a report of research is communicated as efficiently as possible. Authors must make choices
about what to include and what to edit out. Even if everything seems relevant
to the project, authors are forced to prioritize and to make difficult choices.
The items that are perceived to be most problematic and the least central to
the overall argument are the first things cut. Unfortunately, the end result
further promotes the public face of research and helps to cover up its less attractive underbelly.

Research is a messy business. No matter how sterile a report appears, no
matter how much antiseptic has been applied, educational research has an
ugly (but real) private face. The private face of educational research is usually
only known to the principal investigator and a few select individuals, such as
the co-principal investigators, or a few trusted colleagues.

It is a face that deals with all the headaches and frustrations, stupid mistakes, and careless errors that might seem minor at the time, but have the

cumulative effect of decreasing the overall quality of the investigation. These aspects of research are not the exception; they are, most probably, the rule. The more open and honest researchers can be regarding the problems they faced, the solutions devised, and the potential impact on findings, the closer the public and private faces become. Unfortunately, sometimes honesty gets usurped by cleverness.

Educational researchers, as a group, tend to be very talented at disguising the impact of their limitations upon the end result. It is for this reason that so much time and energy is dedicated to helping the next generation of educational researchers develop strong critical analysis skills. When an article is assigned for a course in education, the reader learns to be a more scrutinizing consumer of information. Informed and skilled readers will appreciate both faces of research, and learn to piece together how each relates to the other by noting what an author says and does not say. Such game playing is the business of educational research and peer-reviewed publications.

Unlike a journal article, a book allows for a more in-depth and detailed discussion that can shine a bright light equally upon the public and private faces of education. Chapter 5 is divided into three sections. The first section describes the procedures and strategies for collecting data. The collection of data in a study like this is very different than a study that might utilize laboratory apparatus to investigate a natural property of life or matter. The interview, exchange of information through the mail, and the tools of technology all contribute to the complexity of the data collection process and the opportunity for error.

The second section presents the analytical strategies used to arrive at the results. The strategies are then followed by the identification of specific standards most closely associated with the observed learning outcomes. Last, the chapter concludes with a significant discussion of the project's private face—otherwise known as procedural issues that fell short of the ideal. These shortcomings help to understand the limitations of the study's conclusions.

While the presentation of a robust limitations section could be interpreted as indicative of a weak study, it is hoped that just the opposite will be achieved. By being blatantly honest about problems encountered during this human enterprise, the findings' significance will be better understood and appreciated.[1]

In a world where written documents are an attempt to manipulate the reader, the idea that something is "objective" or without a purposeful agenda is ridiculous. Therefore, the goal of this chapter is to provide the most thorough presentation of results, while embracing the problems encountered during the implementation of the project.

The description of the research process provided in chapter 4 can be summarized according to the following steps:

Step 1: Recruit 120 National Board candidates to participate in a study.

Step 2: Conduct 140 structured interviews lasting seventy minutes each.

Step 3: Transcribe and process each interview into a readable document.

Step 4: Arrange for at least two National Board assessors to score each document according to the thirteen standards of accomplished teaching.

Step 5: Compare scores from the teachers in the precertification group to those in the postcertification group to identify and quantify gains.

While short on details, these five steps represent an efficient description of the major actions needed to find an answer to the research question: What are teachers learning from the certification process? Chapter 5 provides an answer in four sections. Each section corresponds to a specific goal. After reading this chapter, the reader will:

1. Understand how the data collection procedures deviated from the expected, and how this might impact the validity of the project.
2. Appreciate the result of hypothesis testing that reveals the strengths and weaknesses of the project design and theoretical model.
3. Learn about specific areas of candidate learning by examining the overall hypothesis.
4. Explore possible threats to validity through an analysis of candidate "status."

COLLECTING DATA

After recruiting each participant as described in chapter 4, data collection began with a completed consent form, and then continued with the telephone interview of the teacher-candidate. After the audiotaped interview was transcribed, a "processed" version of the transcript was then scored by at least two assessors using the rubrics and standards of the National Board certification process.

The assessors then provided one score for each of the thirteen standards of accomplished teaching in Adolescence and Young Adult Science (AYA Science) described in chapter 3. Next, the thirteen assessed scores for each candidate were aggregated to the group level so that means representing different observations could be compared for significant differences at the overall, set, and individual standard level of analysis. The pathway for collecting and analyzing data is illustrated in figure 5.1.

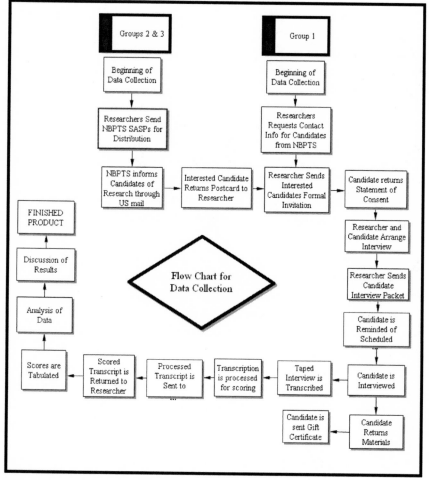

FIGURE 5.1
The Pathway to Data Collection

The lower right-hand corner of figure 5.1 represents the point in the process where the candidate was interviewed. Each of the 140 interviews conducted for this study was the culmination of arduous preparation, endless patience, and dedicated persistence. Prior to the interview, Group 1 required six important steps, while Groups 2 and 3 each required eight steps to reach completion. Before a candidate could be interviewed, each step needed to be accomplished successfully. The amount of logistical planning, high-level organization, and compassion for the teachers willing to participate cannot be overestimated.

Each interview was unique and routine simultaneously. For example, while all interviews consisted of exactly the same set of questions based on the same artifacts and evidence, each one took place at a different time and place. One day a candidate from Georgia might be interviewed at noon and the next day a candidate from Hawaii might be interviewed at three in the morning. Some interviews were conducted in winter and others in summer.

It is assumed that most of these differences do not impact the quality of results, but there is no way to completely rule out the possibility. On one occasion, technology was the cause of a problem. A teacher from the East Coast was being interviewed. The interview went well, with the candidate sharing detailed and insightful responses for each of the six scenarios. After forty-five minutes, when the cassette was to be flipped over to continue recording, it was discovered that the tape had stopped working only twenty minutes into the interview.

The interview was completed, but the data could not be used in the study. How might the results of this study have been impacted had the tape not gotten tangled? It is difficult to say, and probably not worth the effort to figure out, but it is an example of how an obstacle can force researchers to make accommodations.

The top priority for every interview was that it be conducted within the time constraints imposed by the research design. Precertification data were to be collected after candidates self-selected themselves for Board certification by paying the nonrefundable $300 registration fee, but before meaningful work on portfolio construction had begun. Postcertification data were to be collected in the period after a candidate submitted the completed portfolio and finished the assessment center exercises (around June), and before they were notified by the Board of whether or not they passed (late

November). However, abiding by this timing rule proved a difficult challenge, as this chapter addresses later.

The analysis of data represented the second half of the research process, and was much less impacted by time constraints. However, the analysis of data faced some of its own special and unforeseen issues. How much training was sufficient to prepare assessors for the scoring of interviews? What training practices were most efficient and effective? Within the financial limitations of the study, how could the highest quality of work be ensured?

While the procedures and protocols for research were meticulously attended to during the proposal stage, unexpected problems had a way of changing things. As John Steinbeck said when he paraphrased Robert Burns, "The best laid plans of mice and men often go awry." This project did deviate from the expected on a number of occasions, but considering the complexity of the process, these issues did not seriously impact the quality of the overall investigation.

QUANTITATIVE RESULTS FOR THE VALIDITY OF THE MODEL

Before identifying what the results say about potential candidate learning, it is important to ask, "To what degree do actual observations compare to their predicted relative value?" As described in chapter 4, the recurrent institutional cycle design (RICD) allows for a series of hypotheses to predict expected relationships between the five observations. These equivalent and nonequivalent hypotheses test the overall validity of the model investigated.

Namely, if candidates for National Board certification learn about practice from the process, then post- observations should be significantly greater than pre- observations. Likewise, the model gains strength if no differences between post- observations or between pre- observations are observed.

The results from testing the validity of the model indicate a fairly good level of confidence in the predicted impact of the intervention. In other words, those observations that should be the same did not differ significantly from each other and those that are predicted to change do indeed demonstrate significant gain with one important exception. Tests that involved the pre-observation for Group 2 (O_2) were problematic, providing good evidence that O_2 was qualitatively different than the four other data sets.[2]

The problem with the pre- observation for Group 2 suggests that either the model is incorrect or the procedures used during O_2 were flawed or at least

```
┌─────────────────────────────────────────────────────────────┐
│                                                               │
│   Group 1      X → O₁                                         │
│   ---------------------------------------------------------   │
│   Group 2_A    R O₂ → X → O₃                                  │
│   Group 2_B    R       X → O₄                                 │
│   ---------------------------------------------------------   │
│   Group 3                              O₅ → X                 │
│                                                               │
│   X—Intervention                                              │
│   O—Observation by Interview                                  │
│                                                               │
└─────────────────────────────────────────────────────────────┘
```

FIGURE 5.2
Design Model

different from the rest. Why might O_2 be flawed compared with the other pre- observation (O_5)? This issue is explored later in the limitations section. With O_2 identified as the weakest part of the model, the results of the overall hypothesis are now presented.

For the reader's convenience, the design model is provided in figure 5.2.

QUANTITATIVE RESULTS FOR TEACHER LEARNING

All the hard work dedicated to ensuring the timely collection of data according to the research design was an investment in the research process. Researchers invested significant time and resources into the data collection process to obtain the highest quality evidence for analysis. In this section, the strategy used and the outcomes produced are presented.

The flowchart for analyzing the results of the overall hypothesis is presented in figure 5.3, which provides a branching schematic for the decision-making process associated with this hypothesis. In this approach, testing continues only when significant differences are identified at the overall, sets, and then the standards levels of analysis. The analysis can be reduced to addressing the following three questions:

1. Are the precertification scores significantly different from the postcertification scores?
2. If a significant difference exists, which set(s) of standards is/are most responsible for the observed difference?
3. Of the set(s) identified as responsible for change, which individual standards demonstrate the most change?

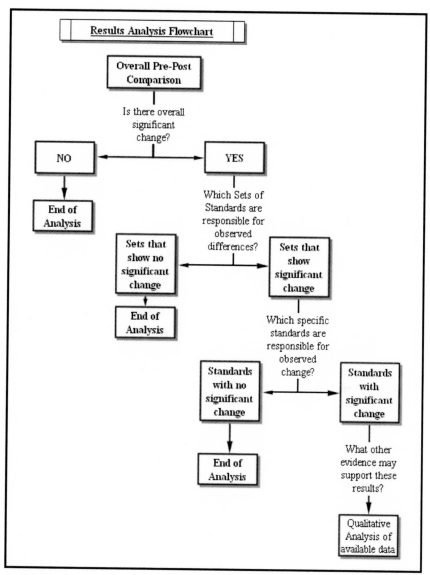

FIGURE 5.3
Analysis Flowchart

Table 5.1. Descriptive Statistics for All Groups in the Overall Hypothesis

Group	Obs.	N	Mean	Std. Deviation	Std. Error	95% Confidence Interval for Mean		Min.	Max.
						Lower Bound	Upper Bound		
Group 1	1 (post)	40	2.811	0.453	0.072	2.666	2.956	1.654	3.692
Group 2 A	2 (pre)	18	2.641	0.559	0.132	2.363	2.919	1.702	3.615
Group 2 B	4 (post)	20	2.792	0.425	0.095	2.593	2.991	2.038	3.644
Group 3	5 (pre)	40	2.540	0.391	0.062	2.415	2.665	1.538	3.192
Summative		118	2.690	0.457	0.042	2.607	2.773	1.538	3.692

The RICD for this study yielded a total of five observations. Table 5.1 presents the descriptive statistics for the overall hypothesis, which uses four out of the five observations, pooling data from all 118 participants.[3] All data sets except for Group 2A's post- observation (O_3) are included in this comparison.

Throughout this phase of analysis, one-tailed contrast t-tests were used to determine significance. T-tests were used to compare two post- groups with two pre- groups. Analysis of variance between groups comparing the four groups without consideration of pairings produces similar—if not less significant—results. Since the comparison is between pairs of groups, and not four groups independent from each other, the contrasting paired t-test is most appropriate.

According to the study's model of interaction, the National Board certification promotes learning as evidenced by observed gains from pre- to post-observations. Table 5.2 provides the results. There are 114 degrees of freedom, indicating every participating teacher in the study was taken into account for this comparison. The value of the contrast has a p value of 0.009, which is significant at an alpha level of 0.05. The corresponding effect size of this observed difference is 0.473 or 47 percent of a standard deviation, which is a relatively strong indication that the answer to question one is yes, meaningful differences between pre- and post- group scores exist.

Table 5.2. Test of Significance for the Overall Hypothesis

Hypothesis	Contrast Value	Standard Error	t	df	Sig. (1-tailed)	Effect Size
Overall	0.423	0.176	2.400	114	0.009*	0.473

*Significant at p = 0.05 level

Because a significant change from pre- to post- was identified in the overall comparison, the second question can be addressed through closer analysis. Four sets of standards for AYA Science require four separate t-tests for analysis with the same data sets. To reduce the chances of committing a type-1 error (finding significant change when no real change exists), a Bonferroni adjustment procedure was employed.

According to Yip (2002), this conservative adjustment reduced the risk of a family-wise error, while still allowing for the identification of observed differences. Because the study wished to maintain a 0.05 alpha level for each of the four tests, significance was determined at an alpha level of 0.0125.

At this level, as table 5.3 reveals, the contrasts for Set II (Advancing Student Learning) and Set IV (Supporting Teaching and Student Learning) were both found to be significant at $p = 0.008$ and $p = 0.005$, respectively. Set III (Establishing a Favorable Context for Student Learning) was found to be marginally significant at $p = 0.013$. Set II and Set IV had effect sizes of 0.482 and 0.524, respectively, indicating the main areas of observed learning. Because significant differences were identified in three of the four sets, it becomes possible to examine each set in more detail to identify the specific standards that may be responsible for the observed learning.

Sets II, III, and IV have a total of ten standards requiring ten t-tests. Once again, a Bonferroni adjustment procedure was used to reduce the chances of a type-I error due to repeated use of the test. To maintain an overall alpha level of 0.05, the significance for each test was set at $p = 0.005$. At this level, two standards are significant and two are marginal, as shown in table 5.7. Scientific Inquiry from Set II and Assessment from Set IV are significant at 0.001 and 0.002, with effect sizes of 0.606 and 0.596, respectively.

Table 5.3. Test of Significance for Sets of Standards

Set	Value of Contrast	Std. Error	t	df	Sig. (1-tailed)	Effect Size
I. Preparing the Way for Productive Student Learning	0.304	0.176	1.727	114	0.043	0.341
II. Advancing Student Learning	0.494	0.202	2.442	114	**0.008***	0.482
III. Establishing Favorable Context for Student Learning	0.461	0.204	2.253	114	0.013**	0.444
IV. Supporting Teaching and Student Learning	0.459	0.173	2.656	114	**0.005***	0.524

* Significant at $p = 0.0125$ level
**Significant at $p = 0.05$ level

Table 5.4. Test of Significance for Individual Standards

Set	Standard	Value of Contrast	Std. Error	t	df	Sig. (1-tailed)	Effect Size
II. Advancing Student Learning	**Science Inquiry**	0.667	0.217	3.073	114	**0.001***	**0.606**
	Goals & Conceptual Understanding	0.494	0.206	2.392	114	0.009**	0.472
	Contexts of Science	0.321	0.279	1.151	114	0.126	
III. Establishing Favorable Context for Student Learning	Engagement	0.477	0.208	2.294	114	0.012	0.452
	Equitable Participation	0.448	0.242	1.851	114	0.033	0.365
	Learning Environment	0.457	0.223	2.049	114	0.021	0.404
	Family & Community Outreach	0.174	0.217	0.803	114	0.212	
IV. Supporting Teaching and Student Learning	**Assessment**	0.647	0.214	3.022	114	**0.002***	**0.596**
	Reflection	0.607	0.241	2.515	114	0.007**	0.496
	Collegiality & Leadership	0.409	0.180	2.276	114	0.012	0.449

*Significant at p = 0.005 level
**Significant at p = 0.01 level

The two standards that were marginally significant included Goals and Conceptual Understanding from Set II and Reflection from Set IV at $p = 0.009$ and 0.007, respectively. Though marginally significant at the level of the Set, Set III did not have any significant standards at the 0.005 level. After all of the interviews and the assessors' work to score each transcript, two standards (Scientific Inquiry and Assessment) proved most responsible for the observed gains from pre- to post- observation.

While evidence exists that candidates probably learned about Goals and Conceptual Understanding and Reflection, it remains unclear whether candidate learning is occurring around these standards. In chapter 6, a review of the qualitative evidence provides additional perspective on the validity of these observations.

At this point in the analysis, evidence suggests two possible explanations for the observed gains. The first explanation focuses on the likelihood that the model is accurate and the improved scores are the result of the certification experience. The second explanation considers the identified weaknesses in the observations (e.g., O_2—Group 2A's pre- observation) sufficient cause to undermine the validity of the model. The following discussion about participant "status" considers the problem of Group 2's pre- observation in detail. If the issues associated with O_2 can be better understood, perhaps its threat to the model can be minimized. The following section discusses this possibility more fully.

THE STATUS OF GROUP 2

As per the design, postcertification observations of Group 1 were to take place at the same time as the precertification observations of Group 2. However, the recruitment and selection procedures for Group 2 ended up being quite different than planned. As mentioned in chapter 4, a list from the Board of registered candidates for cohort two was to be obtained, randomized, and then a portion invited to participate. Those candidates agreeing to participate would then be randomly assigned to either Group 2A or Group 2B, until each subgroup had twenty teachers.

Group 2A was to be observed both before and after intervention, whereas Group 2B was to be observed only after intervention. However, the recruitment procedures varied from this plan. The procedural adjustments for identification and recruitment of Group 2 had their basis in three different areas of circumstance: (1) legalities, (2) institutional constraints, and (3) a policy change at the National Board.

Legalities

Unlike Group 1, which was composed of candidates who had completed their portfolio and assessment center exam at least three months previous, Group 2 consisted of candidates who had only just registered for certification and had paid the non-refundable $300 registration fee. Observations were to be made during the period between the payment of the registration fee and the beginning of meaningful and earnest work on the portfolio. However, the National Board was not allowed to provide a list of new registrants to be randomized and invited to participate. The National Board highlighted the need to maintain confidentiality with these newly identified candidates.

The Board's rationale was sound and understandable: If the National Board shared the contact information of these new registrants with a third party, those candidates who were not successful at achieving certification later on might point to the "harassment" of the third party precipitated by the National Board as reason for their unsuccessful attempt to be certified. For Group 1, it made no difference, because all their work had already been submitted. However, for the pre- groups, no direct contact would be possible for fear of contaminating their chances of success. A new procedure was needed that was satisfactory to the Board and to the investigation.

After a couple weeks of discussion and e-mail exchanges, a new procedure was devised. In the revised approach, a letter would go out from the Board to the newly identified registrants. The letter explained the purpose of the communication and provided a brief description of the study, contact information, and a self-addressed postcard that could be returned to learn more about participating in the research.

Upon receiving this letter, the candidate could choose to "learn more about the study" or ignore it completely with no consequences. Those wishing to learn more returned the postcard with their contact information directly to the investigative team. These steps are illustrated in figure 5.1. Upon receipt of the postcard, communication with the potential participant was identical to communication with Group 1. A formal letter of invitation and a consent form were mailed to the candidates. If they chose to participate, the candidates completed, signed, and returned the consent form in the self-addressed stamped envelope.

As a result of the additional steps required to recruit precertification candidates for the study, the rate of return dropped from 65 percent for Group 1 to 10 percent for Group 2A-Pre. Not only did the rate of return drop dramatically, but the added steps delayed the successful recruitment of candidates.

The time between an individual's first appearance in the National Board's database and the individual's interview averaged from six to eight weeks. This is compared with a roughly three-week turnaround time for Group 1. While the added communication steps proved an important challenge for Group 2 recruitment, the institutional shortcomings may have been even more detrimental to the research.

Institutional Shortcomings

The second problem associated with data collection for Group 2 involved institutional shortcomings at both Michigan State University and the National Board for Professional Teaching Standards. At the Board, significant time delays for the exchange of information between the various departments involved in supporting research initiatives was a problem. The executive department was responsible for all correspondence with the investigators, including answers to specific questions and access to data needed for the study.

After an investigator submitted a request in writing, the contact person then forwarded the inquiry to the appropriate individual for a response. The Board's response was then returned to the official contact person, and then sent to the investigator. All of this communication was done through electronic mail. Getting an answer from the Board could be as quick as a few minutes or as long as a few weeks.

To compound the communication issue, the Board's contact person for the research project also became responsible for contacting each registered candidate who qualified for Group 2. Depending on the workload of the contact person, this process could take anywhere from a day or two to a few weeks. Many days would pass with no word regarding the status of the mailings to candidates.

It is difficult to determine if the contact person at the Board truly appreciated the time-sensitive nature of the task. The actions (or lack thereof) of the contact person could be explained by a number of different possibilities, all of which are not relevant to this study.[4] What is true and relevant is that the convoluted procedures resulted in significant time delays between identification of possible participants and the actual collection of data.

On one side, bureaucratic constraints by the National Board were making the timely recruitment of candidates difficult. On the other side, Michigan State University presented an entirely different—but no less important—obstacle, pertaining to how the U.S. Mail was sorted and delivered to faculty.

During the recruitment phase of the investigation, the postcards returned by candidates were as precious as gold to the investigative team. Every day the lead researcher visited the mailbox with great anticipation. How many postcards would be returned that day? Where would they be from? How soon could a candidate be interviewed? A lot was riding on those little postcards waiting to be picked up from the mailbox. With Group 1, it was not uncommon to receive a dozen cards each day for a week.

However, when it came time to recruit Group 2 candidates, the number of postcards returned dropped to a trickle. One or two postcards would be returned, when ten to fifteen were expected. All too often, no cards were found. At the time, such a disappointing rate was hard to explain. Was Group 2 so different then Group 1? Was the initial contact from the National Board somehow poisoning the pool? Why were far fewer candidates than expected returning their postcards?

One explanation for the poor return rate became apparent several months later, after Group 2 was identified. An undergraduate student helper for the department secretary was assigned to distribute the mail into individual faculty mail boxes. For some reason, this undergraduate could not find the individual mailbox for the postcards' addressee.

The mailbox with the matching name was located on the top shelf at eye-level in the far left-hand corner. Rather than ask the secretary for assistance, the undergraduate student placed the postcards in an unmarked mailbox located at the bottom lower right corner. The postcards were discovered while checking other mailboxes to see if some project mail had been misplaced.

Approximately fourteen cards were in the unmarked mailbox. According to their postmarks, these cards were some of the first returned, and raised the rate of return to more than 10 percent. From that moment on, mail was checked at the building's point of entry every day, before being sent to the department for sorting.

Two immediate consequences resulted from this unfortunate human error. First, randomly dividing Group 2 into 2A and 2B was not possible. The priority became to collect preintervention data from Group 2A as soon as possible, before candidates were too far along in the intervention. Therefore, each new Group 2 participant identified was immediately placed into Group 2A.

Only after Group 2A was complete were additional candidates placed into Group 2B. Because Group 2B was a postintervention observation, a race against the clock was not necessary. It took over five months to solicit the participation of the more than forty teachers necessary to complete Group 2. Whereas data collection for Group 1 was completed in six weeks, Group 2A took several months to finish.

No degree of foresight or planning could have prevented this particular problem. In any research endeavor, a certain level of trust exists between those doing research and those providing supportive services. The garbage gets picked up, the electricity stays on, the water flows from the faucet, and the mail gets delivered. While often taken for granted, the most inconspicuous aspects of life can have unforeseen consequences upon the quality of research when something goes wrong.

The best a researcher can do is to expect the unexpected. While the mishandled mail is unfortunate, compromises to procedure could be made to compensate. However, no amount of planning for a project or altering research procedures can sufficiently deal with unforeseen circumstantial events. The policy changes at the Board present an excellent example of such a problem.

Policy Changes at the National Board

The last reason for the difficulties in identifying and recruiting participants for Group 2 rests with policy changes at the Board. The changes pertained to when and how teachers could register for National Board certification. Prior to the class of 2002–2003, applicants would register over the summer and during the fall, and begin the process of certification just before or after Christmas vacation. This meant that most of the construction of the portfolio would take place during the spring semester. However, with the 2003 cohort, changes were implemented that made it possible for candidates to register and begin work on their portfolios with much more flexibility throughout the calendar year.

While a majority of candidates still used the traditional calendar to complete the requirements of National Board certification, a significant number opted for the more flexible schedule. The impact of this change on the study resulted in a smaller pool of candidates than anticipated for the September through December registration period. If the timing of registration was problematic to the study, the revised registration options for candidates were devastating to the concept of "preintervention observation."

The study was conducted under the assumption that data would be collected in clearly identifiable pre- and postintervention conditions. Post- observations were made after a candidate completed and submitted a portfolio and had taken his or her assessment center exams, and before he or she had received word from the National Board as to the final outcome. In all post-observation cases, this timing was achieved successfully, producing "true" postcertification data. However, for the pre- observations, circumstances became problematic due to the Board's embracing of technology. As the Board moved away from paper registration, the concept of a "true" pre-observation faded.

During the Board's first ten years of operation, teachers registered through the mail. The time between submitting a check for $300 and receiving "the box" of instructions and materials could be one to three months.[5] This period was considered ideal for collecting precertification data. With the development of online registration, this window instantly disappeared. Candidates could pay the fee online with a credit card and immediately have access to the information in the "box" as downloadable digital files. This one change effectively eliminated the one- to three-month period of relative inactivity for some candidates.

As a result of these developments, additional information was collected from each candidate in a precertification group. At the start of the interview, candidates were asked to describe how much work they had already put into the construction of their portfolio. After further analysis of this data, it became quite evident that the pre- observation as originally intended no longer existed.

In the end, every candidate observed as part of the pre- groups had already experienced part of the intervention to some extent. Candidate experience included reading the instructions, working on entries, collecting data on students, videotaping, attending workshops, and engaging in conversations with local support groups and virtual communities.

Any and all of these activities would effectively prevent a candidate from being labeled a true pre- subject in the original sense. A candidate's experience in Group 2 ranged from a low of 2 percent of the portfolio process completed to a high of nearly 50 percent, with an average of around 20 percent of the portfolio process completed.[6]

Status Issue for Pre- Observations

Was the nonexistence of a "true" precertification observation responsible for the weaknesses identified in the model?.If so, how might this problem best be addressed to understand how it impacted observed outcomes? The analysis presented here explores the status of Group 2's observation as a possible explanation for its problematic characteristics. If the research model is accurate, then the more exposure a candidate has to the certification process, the higher his or her assessed scores should be.

One way to test this theory is to more closely examine the relationship between the precertification scores assessed to each member, and his or her reported status with regard to the Board's assessment process. The more exposure to the certification process, the higher the final assessed scores should be.

A meticulous review of candidate information allowed for an estimate of a candidate's status with regard to the certification process. The calculation of status was based on a listing of all the steps common to the completion of a portfolio. From receiving materials to analyzing a video, each step of the process was listed, and a percentage of the total assigned.

Completing a portfolio involves four basic steps: plan, organize, collect, and analyze. Each of these steps was worth 5 percent of the total, making all four entries worth 80 percent of the total work. The remaining 20 percent was divided into smaller actions and steps that lead up to the actual portfolio construction. Items such as reading instructions, reviewing standards, collecting permission slips, or talking with colleagues are examples of actions that were each assigned a 2-percent value of the total.

Candidates were asked at the start of the interview to describe what, if anything, they had done toward certification. Candidate responses were then coded to determine an estimate of how much work they had completed at the time of the interview. While a visual inspection of a candidate's work to date would have been optimal, the candidate's self-report of progress was the best that could be achieved.

The status of each candidate could then be graphed according to the total score of all thirteen standards assessed from the interview transcript, and a correlation determined. A line of best fit provides a visual indication of the correlation. The higher the correlation is between status and total score, the stronger the relationship. The correlation for Group 2 is presented in figure 5.4.

The result was a moderate and positive correlation between a candidate's experience with the intervention and the observed scores for that candidate. Considering that both the assessed scores and the estimate of status were

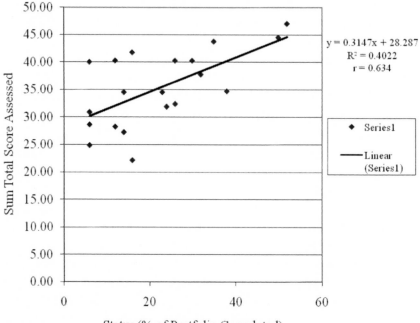

FIGURE 5.4
Total Assessed Scores versus Status of Group 2

constructs, a Pearson correlation (r) of 0.634 (square root of R squared) is indicative of a relatively strong relationship.

If this analysis demonstrates that the pre- observation is correlated with status, then it should also be visible with Group 3's pre- observation. To test this idea, an identical analysis was performed on Group 3 to see if the status issue shared any common characteristics with Group 2. Figure 5.5 illustrates the findings of this analysis.

The result is a positive correlation with a Pearson coefficient (r) of 0.4961, indicating a fair relationship between status and score,[7] but not as strong as with Group 2. This lower correlation might be explained by the size of Group 3 (n = 40) compared with Group 2 (n = 18). Or it could be the result of improved efforts to contact and recruit candidates earlier in the certification process. Group 2's average status was 22 percent, while Group 3's average status was 20 percent.

It is also interesting to note that the status analyses with Groups 2 and 3 produce a line of best fit with nearly identical y-intercepts of just over twenty-eight, suggesting that the pre- groups began the process with similar levels of understanding about the standards of accomplished teaching. With evidence that a candidate's status may correlate to the final sum of assessed scores, a

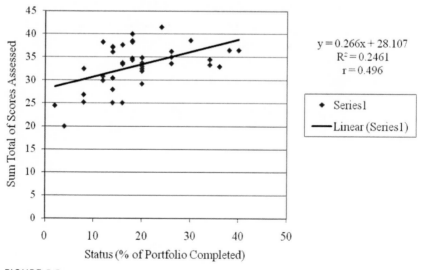

$$y = 0.266x + 28.107$$
$$R^2 = 0.2461$$
$$r = 0.496$$

FIGURE 5.5
Total Assessed Scores versus Status of Group 3

regression analysis was conducted to find out the possible impact of the problem on the observed results.

What might the data for Group 2 have looked like if candidates were interviewed closer to the time of their registration? In other words, if a candidate's status were reduced by a certain percentage, how would the testing of the project hypotheses change? At what percentage of "status reduction" does a particular hypothesis become significant at the .10 and .05 level? Answers to such questions would provide a way of comparing the relative strength of each hypothesis to the overall model, and substantiate the claim that Group 2 was plagued by important data collection issues rather than a flaw in the theoretical model.

In table 5.5, an analysis of percent reduction in status and the consequential change in significance is present for both the equivalent hypotheses (1–4) and the nonequivalent hypotheses (5–10). This regression analysis begins with the actual outcomes of all tested hypotheses. Hypotheses 6 and 9 show a significant change. Then the status is reduced according to the identified correlation by 15 percent, 30 percent, and 55 percent.

At 15-percent reduction, hypotheses 5 and 8 become significant at the $p = 0.05$ level. At 30-percent status reduction, hypothesis 10 becomes significant at the same level, while hypothesis 7 becomes significant at the $p = 0.10$ level. It is not until status is reduced by 55 percent that hypothesis 7 ($O_3 > O_2$) shows a significant difference at $p = 0.05$. This exercise illustrates the relative weakness of the pre- observation for Group 2 compared with the other observations. This extension of data is intended to explore the problematic nature of Group 2's pre- observation (O_2) and its possible impact identifying meaningful gains.

Table 5.5. Percent Reduction in Status and Projected Change in Significance

Hypo.	Comparison	Type of t-test	df	No. of Tails	Sign. w/no status	Sign. 15% status	Sign. 30% status	Sign. 55% status
1	O3 = O4	Indep.	36	2	0.615	0.578	0.622	0.622
2	O2 = O5	Indep.	56	2	0.430	0.657	0.242	0.066
3	O3 = O1	Indep.	56	2	0.485	0.445	0.490	0.490
4	O4 = O1	Indep.	58	2	0.878	0.875	0.875	0.875
5	O1 > O2	Indep.	56	1	0.112	**0.045**	**0.015**	**0.001**
6	O1 > O5	Indep.	78	1	**0.003**	**0.001**	**0.000**	**0.000**
7	O3 > O2	Depend	17	1	0.199	0.205	0.091	**0.019**
8	O3 > O5	Indep.	56	1	0.056	**0.043**	**0.003**	**0.000**
9	O4 > O5	Indep.	58	1	**0.013**	**0.009**	**0.000**	**0.000**
10	O4 > O2	Indep.	36	1	0.176	0.096	**0.033**	**0.003**

Is the inconsistency of observed gains due to (1) an ineffective intervention or (2) an unforeseen problem with data collection? The "status" issue holds promise for explaining the observed results. The unexpected methodological problems encountered during the collection of data from the pre- groups should not cloud the possible meaning of the results. Just as it would be unwise to conclude that the intervention had no observable effect because of a methodological issue, it would also be foolish to ignore the problems and irresponsible not to try to compensate for them.

These projected outcomes shine a light on the relative strengths and weaknesses of the nonequivalent hypotheses. With only a 15-percent reduction in status, five out of six nonequivalent hypotheses become significant at the $p = 0.10$ level, supporting the expected model of interaction. Furthermore, this hypothetical analysis demonstrates and confirms the fact that hypothesis 7 is the weakest of all, becoming significant at the .10 level with a 30-percent relative reduction in status and not significant at the .05 level until a full 55-percent reduction in status is achieved.

The impact of this regression analysis on the nonequivalent hypotheses is interesting. Equivalent hypotheses 1, 3, and 4 show no change as status is increased, indicating that these comparisons are very similar. However, equivalent hypothesis 2 moves closer to being significant, with a p value changing from 0.43 at 0-percent reduction to 0.066 at 55-percent reduction in status. It is the one equivalent hypothesis to include the Group 2 pre- observation, suggesting it might be different from the other precertification observation (O_5).

These hypothetical results clarify the situation with Group 2. One interpretation is that the collection of data was nominal, and no change was observed pre- to post- in Group 2. If this were true, then other indicators would emerge to support the idea that Group 2 was somehow different on measured scales than the Groups 1 or 3. However, the demographic analysis suggests that Group 2 was not unique on any of the recorded characteristics. Therefore, the idea that it would behave dramatically differently than the other groups is not supported by available evidence.

The second interpretation promotes the idea that unanticipated errors in the data collection process made a true pre- observation for Group 2 impractical. A weakened pre- observation due to status issues would reduce the likelihood of identifying significant gains in candidate understanding. As described in this section, evidence exists to support this interpretation.

Recruitment issues due to legal, bureaucratic, and policy changes made the Group 2 pre- observation problematic. In addition, the fact that Group 2A was the smallest of the five observations (n = 18) does not help the situation. Since each of the hypotheses without Observation 2 tested according to expectations, the most likely interpretation points to a procedural error with Group 2, rather than a lack of an effective treatment.

This foray into hypothetical situations and analysis is presented here only to better understand the issues associated with Group 2's pre- observation (O_2). It was not used to identify candidates' learning outcomes from the certification experience. While the analysis of status remains far from definitive, the results do provide additional evidence to support that the problem with Group 2's pre- observation had more to do with investigative procedures than any group characteristic or weakness in the model.

This problem might have been avoided or minimized had the size of Group 2 been increased. Group 2A played a more vital role in this analysis than any of the other four groups, yet it was the smallest. This situation can explain many of the methodological issues associated with this analysis. Instead of forty teachers in each of Groups 1, 2, and 3, thirty teachers in Group 1, Group 2A, Group 2B, and Group 3 may have allowed for less variance in results.

Dividing 120 teachers by four groups rather than three may have consequently facilitated the identification of significant differences associated with Group 2A pre- to post- observation. While the obstacles discussed in this section would still exist, Groups 2A and 2B would be larger to correspond with their greater role in the investigation.

The lack of a true "precertification" impacts the limitations of this work. Most notably, the lack of consistency in recruitment protocols for each of the three groups diminishes the quality of the empirical results. Inconsistent use of random selection and random assignment limits the generalization of the study's findings. Only Groups 1 and 2B were randomly selected for data collection. Because of the pressure of time, the pre- groups were interviewed on a first-come, first-served basis, making random assignment to one of the two parts of Group 2 impossible.

Improved recruitment procedures would have allowed for more consistent use of random selection for all three groups, and random assignment within Group 2 to either 2A or 2B. Because of this inconsistent use of random selection and the quasiexperimental nature of this research, the conclusions drawn from this study are generalizable to secondary science teachers who self-select themselves for National Board certification in AYA Science. Thus, external validity is limited to this population of teachers.

A critic of this study could point to the lack of significant differences found in four out of the six nonequivalent hypotheses, and could conclude that the intervention is ineffective in promoting teacher learning. To draw such a conclusion would be to deny other valid explanations and supporting evidence that suggests that the intervention does affect teacher learning.

To ignore the status issue would be irresponsible. To fully understand and explain the observed results, all possible explanations need to be explored. "Status" as an unforeseen procedural problem remains an important issue, but one that should not impede the process of substantiating possible learning outcomes that teachers demonstrate from National Board certification.

CANDIDATE LEARNING AND CERTIFICATION

The last result that needs to be discussed pertains to the relationship between observed learning gains and the candidates' final outcome of the candidates' attempt to become National Board–certified. Is there a relationship between candidate learning and success at achieving Board certification? An analysis of the data indicates some interesting possibilities.

Regardless of whether one is successful or not at achieving National Board certification, the amount of learning that takes place is almost the same. Table 5.6 provides a synopsis of the relevant findings, and shows that 61 percent of all candidates in this study for AYA Science were unsuccessful in their initial attempt to achieve certification. A 40-percent pass rate for this certificate as indicated in this study is consistent with the historical passing rate for this certificate. This is further evidence that the study's sample of candidates is a good representation of the parent population of candidates.

A deeper inspection of gain scores associated with those who passed and those who did not pass reveals an interesting pattern. Those who passed were assessed higher both in the pre- condition and the post- condition compared with their unsuccessful peers. However, both categories of candidates demonstrated almost identical score gains from pre- to post- observation with a 0.06 gain and a 0.08 gain for those who did not achieve and those who achieved, respectively.

Table 5.6. Group-to-Group Comparisons on Continuous Demographic Variables

| | Group 1 | Group 2A | Group 2B | Group 3 | | | | Comparisons of the Sample Groups | | | |
					Source	df	Sum of Squares	Mean Square	F Value	Pr > F
N	40	18	20	40						
Years Experience										
Mean	16.4	15.3	14.7	11.0	Model	3	635.1	211.7	3.24	0.0248
Std Dev	7.6	10.2	9.0	7.0	Error	114	7452.0	65.4		
Class Size										
Mean	25.5	24.7	25.8	25.1	Model	3	14.2	4.7	0.16	0.9244
Std Dev	5.4	4.9	5.3	5.8	Error	114	3425.2	30.0		

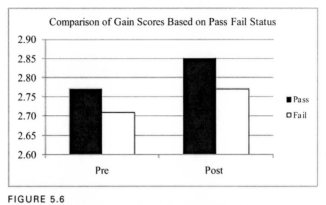

FIGURE 5.6
Comparison of Gain Scores Based on Pass Fail Status

This evidence strongly suggests that regardless of the final outcome, both candidates who achieve and those who do not achieve certification were observed to learn about the standards of accomplished teaching. Interestingly, those who were unsuccessful started off with less understanding than their peers who passed, but by the end had improved their understanding to the point where their peers had begun the process. Figure 5.6 illustrates the observed gains for these two groups.

SUMMARY

For all the efforts to make sociological research scientific, it remains a very human enterprise, and one prone to all the failings of individuals and institutions. While the results of candidate learning presented in this chapter appear valid and strong on the surface, problems with procedures and bureaucratic support reveal real threats to internal validity. These issues translate into a more cautious embrace of the results and limitations on the generalization of findings to the larger population of secondary science teachers.

The strategy employed to test for significant gains from pre- to post- observations at the overall, set, and individual standards levels identified candidate learning in the areas of scientific inquiry and student assessment. While reflection and conceptual understanding were marginally significant, a final assessment of whether or not they are substantiated learning outcomes will wait for the qualitative analysis of data. Just as significant is the finding that regardless of whether a candidate achieves Board certification or not on the initial try, evidence suggests that all candidates are learning about the standards of accomplished teaching.

The chapter also described the complex procedures used to recruit candidates and collect data through structured interviews. More than 140 interviews were conducted with 120 teachers from forty-two different states for this project. Analysis of population demographics indicates a high level of homogeneity between and within groups, lending greater strength to the overall model of interaction between the intervention and the candidates. While some weaknesses in the model were identified through the testing of equivalent and nonequivalent hypotheses, the integrity of the design remains in tact. However, the problems associated with Group 2's pre- observation encourage a conditional acceptance of the results.

To further substantiate what candidates appear to learn about inquiry and student assessment, chapter 6 examines the qualitative evidence. The comments and ideas expressed by candidates will be analyzed to ascertain the degree to which identified learning outcomes are supported. The use of additional data helps to triangulate observed outcomes and bring greater overall confidence in the validity of the proposed model that National Board certification is a productive learning opportunity.

NOTES

1. This open approach to research was inspired by Annette Lareau's (1989) classic book, *Home Advantage.* In this work, Lareau makes a conscious and deliberate effort to share the tiniest detail with the reader in an appendix that is nearly as long as the chapters that precede it. Her brutal honesty about the trials and tribulations of ethnographic research into the lives of learners has the interesting effect of making her conclusions all the more plausible in a counterintuitive manner.

2. See appendix D for a more thorough discussion of the equivalent and nonequivalent hypothesis testing.

3. In Group 2A, one more subject than anticipated dropped out of the certification process (I anticipated six dropping out of the certification process and the study, but the actual number was seven) and technical problems with the tape recorder during one interview allowed for only eighteen usable pre-post comparisons.

4. It is important to note that this was not the only study being conducted at the time. Approximately twenty other principal investigators were working with this one contact person at the Board. It is understandable how delays might happen.

5. "The box" is a reference to the ten-pound box of materials and instructions necessary to construct a portfolio. Numerous candidates referred to this rather large and heavy package that arrived by mail as "the box." Among candidates from this era, "the box" represents an insider's joke about the magnitude of the certification task.

6. See appendix E for a complete discussion of how status was calculated.

7. This correlation does not include one outlier who had a very high status, but one of the lowest scores. If this outlier is included, Pearson correlation drops to 0.3461.

6

Qualitative Evidence for Observed Learning Outcomes

The carnival metaphor for education research in chapter 5 referred to a visual inspection of the rides. A lot can be learned about the quality and safety of a ride just by making repeated observations. In this metaphor, the results indicate that the ride is strong, though some concerns are noted. To make a more accurate assessment, additional information is needed.

In chapter 6, the researcher returns to the carnival, but this time to talk with the folks who spent a great deal of time going on the rides and experiencing what the carnival had to offer. Getting their perspective should complement what has been learned through observation alone. National Board certification is similar to a carnival ride in that it offers candidates an intense experience filled with highs, lows, and a fair amount of tedium. However, unlike an amusement park, the work of the Board is serious, with implications for schools, teachers, and students.

Chapter 5 identified and quantified the observed learning outcomes for candidates. The purpose of chapter 6 is to substantiate candidate learning associated with the scientific inquiry, assessment, and reflection standards of accomplished teaching. The chapter addresses two specific questions:

1. What evidence do candidates provide in their comments for identified learning outcomes?
2. How can these examples of learning be understood in the context of National Board certification?

The goal of this study was to investigate teacher learning by quantitatively comparing preintervention and postintervention scores on thirteen standards of accomplished teaching as defined by the National Board for Professional Teaching Standards (NBPTS). The assumption for this approach was that changes in observed pre- to post- scores for a particular standard could then be interpreted to represent the candidate's "learning" or change in understanding associated with the specified domain.

The three standards that demonstrated the most improvement as determined by the assessment process (Scientific Inquiry, Assessment, and Reflection) are discussed. Though only marginally significant, Reflection is included in this analysis for two reasons. First, reflection is pervasive and central to the National Board certification process. Second, teachers in this study commented on "reflection" more than any other standard. If the status issue of candidates in the pre- observation group had been improved only slightly, "reflection" would have been identified as an area of candidate learning.

While caution characterizes this decision, it would be irresponsible to ignore the possibility entirely. Do these learning outcomes make sense in the context of the National Board certification process? How can these examples of learning best be described and explained? To answer these questions, qualitative data collected during the interviews with each candidate will be used to contextualize and enrich the discussion. It is therefore important to understand the genesis of this qualitative data.

QUALITATIVE DATA

Many candidates who graciously accepted an invitation to participate in this study incorrectly assumed that the "conversation" with the interviewer would serve as a sounding board to voice their opinions and ideas about the certification process. The official letters of contact with the candidates never indicated or implied that National Board certification would be the focus of the interview. Rather, the letter stated that the conversation would be based on their "ideas and experiences related to teaching and learning."

Still, many teachers indicated that they wanted to discuss their specific experiences with the process, especially those teachers in the post- groups. To prevent speculative and hearsay-type responses from teachers in the preintervention groups included in this analysis, only evidence from postintervention interviews (n = 78) were considered for this aspect of the analysis.

How could candidates be asked about their specific certification experiences without interfering with their responses to other parts of the structured interview? When would be the optimal opportunity to query candidates about their experiences? What questions should be asked? Since the requirements for National Board never ask for candidates' opinions on the process, the questions needed to be separate from the other protocols so that results could be easily isolated and removed during transcript processing.

Candidate opinions about the process could not be part of the transcript scored by assessors. The questions also needed to be toward the end of the interview, so that nearly all data could be collected without the interviewer or assessor knowing what the candidate might think about the actual process. Therefore, imbedded deep in the first list of professional development experiences of scenario 5, "National Board certification" is listed as the second to last item.

In this part of the interview, teachers were presented with a list of fifteen professional development experiences.[1] Figure 6.1 shows the form candidates completed during this part of the interview. They were asked to indicate those items with which they had direct experience. Then they were to rate each item they checked on a scale of one to five, regarding how well the experience helped them "improve their ability to bring about learning in their students." Since they had all completed the certification process, "National Board certification" was checked and rated by every teacher.

At the time of response, no questions were asked about specific items in this list, or reasons for rating. However, after each table was completed, candidates were asked, "Is there anything in particular missing from this list that you found especially helpful in improving your ability to bring about learning in your students?" When both tables (the professional development history and family and community outreach) and follow-up questions were complete, candidates were asked, "From these two tables, which one item do you think was most helpful in improving your ability to bring about learning in your students?"

In response to this question, teachers contemplated both lists, and then responded with their choice and the reasoning behind it. The candidate's answer remained part of the transcript. If they answered "National Board certification," then no further inquiries were required by the interviewer. However, if they chose an item other than National Board certification, they were asked about their certification experience at the conclusion of their response.

FIGURE 6.1

List of Professional Activities and Accomplishments

Professional Activity/Accomplishment	Yes	No	Rating
Attending educational conferences/workshops			
Professional development activities at school			
Reading educational literature			
Reading scientific literature			
Writing educational articles (professional)			
Writing scientific articles			
Serving on an advisory committee at the school or district level			
Serving as a Union representative			
Developing science curriculum for your class, school, or district			
Mentoring a new/student teacher			
Leading a professional development workshop for your colleagues			
Taking a science course at a local university			
Collaborating with colleagues on an interdisciplinary project			
Pursuing National Board certification			
Taking an educational course at a local university			

More specifically, they were asked, "By the way, could you talk a little bit about why you rated National Board certification a _____?" The blank was filled in with whatever ranking on the one to five scale they specified. The candidates responded with an explanation that provided detailed evidence regarding their overall experiences, whether positive, problematic, or both. While candidate comments from this special question in the interview were not available to assessors, they were used for the qualitative analysis.

From figures 6.2 and 6.3, it is clear that the number of candidates' comments regarding specific standards correspond with the actual observed results. The standards that demonstrate the most gain (Standard 4: *Scientific Inquiry*, Standard 11: *Assessment*, and Standard 12: *Reflection*) also resulted in the most qualitative responses for those same areas.

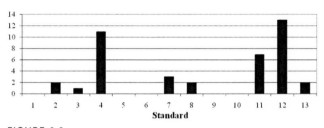

FIGURE 6.2
Number of Comments Corresponding with Standards

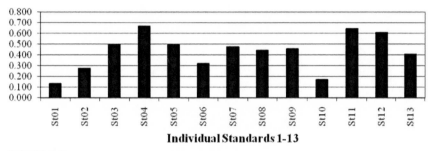

FIGURE 6.3
Observed Gains for Individual Standards on a 4-Point Scale

This agreement between the quantitative and qualitative data streams provides further support for the validity of observed learning outcomes. The topics teachers chose to share regarding Board certification map nicely onto the areas of observed gains. In the discussion that follows, each of these three observations will be explored, explained, and understood in the context of learning resources available through the certification process.

STANDARDS WITH SIGNIFICANT OBSERVED GAINS

Standard 4 (Scientific Inquiry), demonstrated the greatest gain from pre- to post- with an effect size of 0.606, or nearly 61 percent of a standard deviation. Of all thirteen standards measured, this represented the greatest amount of improvement from pre- to post- observations. The second most significant gain was found in Standard 11 (Assessment), with an effect size of 0.596, or nearly 60 percent of a standard deviation. Finally, the third largest observed gain was in Standard 12 (Reflection), with an effect size of 0.496, or nearly 50 percent of a standard deviation. The following discussion examines each of these outcomes and how they make sense in the context of National Board certification.

Scientific Inquiry: Evidence for Learning

Shortly after the Soviet Union launched Sputnik in 1957, the United States began focusing time and resources on improving science education. As part of that science literacy movement, the term *scientific inquiry* gained popularity as the new way to teach science. Its meaning as a pedagogical strategy has continually changed and continues to evolve. One of the first promoters of this new approach was Joseph Schwab. Schwab (1962) described scientific inquiry as a mode of science education that would more accurately reflect the scientific process. In this view, the teacher, when presenting material in lectures or reading content from textbooks would model the habits of mind involved with scientific inquiry such as questioning, analyzing, and evidence gathering.

Rather than just disseminate scientific facts and concepts to receptive students, this view of science education stressed that students learn how to ask questions, challenge assumptions, and seek validity to perceived truths. In the forty years since its introduction, scientific inquiry has developed an array of labels and catch phrases such as *discovery learning, hands-on activities, exploration, teaching by problem solving,* and *inductive methodologies.* Most important, it has expanded not only to refer to how a teacher should teach science, but how a student should learn science.

The National Board's definition of scientific inquiry can trace its roots to Schwab's earlier conception of teaching science as analysis. For National Board, scientific inquiry serves both as the means and the ends of a teaching-learning process. In the extended discussion of the standard, the Board states, "It is not a basic goal of science instruction to fill students with as much information as possible; rather, it is to help students acquire the mental operations, habits of mind, and attitudes that characterize the process of scientific inquiry—that is, to teach them how scientists question, think, and reason."[2]

According to the standard, the best way for teachers to reach this goal successfully is to have students take on an "active role" in their learning by arranging frequent opportunities for "hands-on" science activities and "open-ended investigations," complete with time after the activity for reflection and analysis of results. Teachers' understanding of scientific inquiry as a pedagogical strategy is reflected in the types of choices and decisions made during their planning, lesson management, and assessment techniques.

Teachers choose age- and skill level–appropriate classroom activities that are as much "minds-on" as they are "hands-on." Other indications that a teacher effectively employs scientific inquiry in the classroom pertain to questioning style, wait time after asking a question, discussion management, and an acceptance of the "unpredictable consequences of an activity and student-centered pedagogy."[3]

Though the definition of scientific inquiry may be broad, and may have different meanings to different teachers, the National Board defines it with specific characteristics and observable qualities. A literal laundry list of skills, dispositions, habits of mind, and pedagogical approaches characterize a teacher who knows this approach and is able to use it effectively in the science classroom. Therefore, if assessment in this study finds improved scores from precertification to postcertification, it could be assumed that teachers are learning to more closely align their practice with this conception of scientific inquiry and teaching. Does the evidence support this assumption?

For those teachers who commented on the scientific inquiry aspect of certification as a significant area of learning, it is apparent that the National Board's version of "scientific inquiry" was a new approach to teaching science. For example, when Sharon, a teacher from Wyoming, was asked what she learned from the certification process, her response expressed a recurring theme among many candidates.[4] She said:

> I would point to the increased use of inquiry within my classroom. I think that it has had some strong benefits in terms of helping students to think about what science is. Science is a process and not just a memorization of facts and spew them back out at the teacher. And I do think that doing the National Boards has helped me to incorporate that more into the classroom.

Sharon articulated precisely the National Board's conception of scientific inquiry. She described a learning environment where the teacher is not the sole authority on content knowledge and student-centered active learning results in the learners constructing their own understanding of natural phenomenon. Seeing value in this approach, Sharon pointed to an "increased use" of this approach presumably because of "strong benefits" to student learning. Finally, this teacher described how a scientific inquiry approach helps students understand not only the content of science, but also the process of science as a valid and important goal.

For other teachers, the certification experience motivated them to incorporate more scientific inquiry into their classroom instruction. For example, Mike, another teacher from Wyoming, stated, "National Board is making me look at how much scientific inquiry I'm doing and where the students are actually doing the inquiry versus me just regurgitating."

By doing more inquiry-based lessons, Mike came to an understanding regarding a clear distinction between teacher-centered, lecture-based instruction and student-centered, activity-oriented learning. Rather than simply "regurgitating" information, scientific inquiry allows students to have more of a participatory role in the learning process.

For both of these teachers, National Board certification allowed them to revisit, rethink, and retry a process with which they were already familiar. However, for some teachers, scientific inquiry represented a whole new way to teach. In attempting to fulfill the requirements of the portfolio, they were "forced" to try to teach according to a scientific inquiry method. For example, Susan, a teacher from Arkansas, commented:

> I had a real tough time coming up with and dealing with the inquiry base process. And I found out that other science teachers that had gone through the National Board certification—some who got it and some who didn't—had a tough time with that. It's very difficult to not want to jump in and help the kids. And to see them sort of struggling and kind of thinking "what they needed to do" type thing; I had to be very careful with my questions so that they would think of what they had to do next without me giving them an idea as to what to do.

Susan described her experience trying to teach in a new way. The efforts were difficult, and went against her existing tendencies and habits of mind. Certification encouraged her to be much more self-conscious regarding how she asked students questions, and how her responses to students were formulated. For an experienced teacher with well-rehearsed scripts for interacting with students, scientific inquiry proved to be a difficult challenge, but likely a powerful learning experience.

One reason why scientific inquiry proved to be an arduous task for some teachers may pertain to the perceived change in the teacher's role as classroom authority—the present adult who needs to control what happens and when. This idea manifests itself by how teachers described their handling of unexpected consequences or events that happened during a lesson. For example, Condoleezza from California said:

> I noticed that there was almost as much learning going on from students making mistakes as students doing the right thing. Whereas before I had done that—kind of stepped away and allowed students to pursue inquiry truly at their level—their own experiments—their own ideas of what would happen—their own analysis—and peer discussion of what was happening in their experiment. I tried to control the situation and make sure that the students would get the right outcome.

For Condoleezza, the requirements of National Board certification forced her to relinquish control over the learning process and encourage students to take on more responsibility in developing their own investigations, predictions, and group explanations for observations. "Making mistakes" becomes an aspect of the "right thing" in teaching science, rather than a dreaded deviation from the anticipated path of the classroom lesson.

Prior to certification, this teacher was strongly focused on students getting the "right outcome." As a result of certification, she now has an appreciation for the means by which students look for answers. Rather than being completely motivated by the students' acquisition of content, this teacher now expresses a value for the student's role in defining what content is learned and by what means. Condoleezza continued by saying, "Instead of being so controlled in making sure that the students gained all the content, it [National Board certification] forced me to step back and have a more student-centered environment."

Some might argue that "making sure the students gained all the content" is a good thing, and that the steps this teacher has taken have weakened her effectiveness, rather than strengthened it. However, adapting scientific inquiry as required by the National Board may not replace the goal of content learning, but rather support and enrich the endeavor for students and the teacher. The National Board standards of accomplished teaching for Adolescence and

Young Adult Science (AYA Science) may emphasize scientific inquiry, but it would be incorrect to assume that inquiry replaces direct instruction or the acquisition of accurate understanding of concepts.

Nowhere in the standards does the National Board dictate the amount of scientific inquiry a teacher should use. Rather, accomplished teachers need to demonstrate that they can use the strategy when most appropriate for specific learning goals. One possible reason that scientific inquiry provides a strong learning experience for the teachers pertains to the consequences of giving up control over the information flow during class. For those teachers new to the pedagogical approach, moving to a more "student-centered environment" is synonymous with relinquishing control to particular aspects of classroom management.

However, once those teachers overcome their apprehension, they often experience unexpected results that become productive "teachable moments." For example, Mike from Wyoming described a situation where he was working with a group of students who appeared to be stumped by the results of a procedure. The group's troubles caused him to pause before engaging them with questions. Although his immediate inclination was to explain and resolve their impasse, Michael suggested, "Let's take another look at this." He then described what might happen as a result of this comment: "Hopefully something would be sparked in somebody's brain that would propel the group in the right direction."

Michael has made a conscious effort to place more control over the learning process in the hands (and minds) of the students in the group. He said, "I'm gearing more of my labs toward open-ended investigations if the approach lends itself to the content. So that way the students take more of a self-discovery approach rather than a cookbook type lab. I'm avoiding the cookbook type labs." The results from this decision are known with less certainty than if the students were just told the answer. But even with increased uncertainty, Michael saw enough benefit to continue with this process.

Scientific inquiry was observed in this study to be the standard of greatest improvement from pre- to post-observation. For those teachers who commented on this aspect of the certification process as significant to their learning, several reasons emerge:

1. Scientific inquiry for some was a new experience that, once tried, resulted in some positive effects in the classroom.
2. Scientific inquiry was difficult for some teachers because it required a change in the position of the teacher as the single authority in the classroom.
3. By giving more responsibility to students for their own learning, teachers experienced unexpected situations, which gave rise to productive teaching and learning opportunities.

How those teachers determined whether a moment was productive or not pertains directly to how a teacher assesses student understanding. It is toward the assessment of student understanding that the discussion turns next.

Assessment: Evidence for Learning

Assessment in educational circles has a wide range of meanings: from standardized tests that provide a particular view of what students may or may not understand to more immediate classroom-based practices. It is this later categorization that is most applicable to this study. Assessment in this sense (commonly referred to as *embedded, formative, continuous,* or *classroom-based assessment*) is defined as the process of gathering information and then evaluating students' ideas and reasoning about the particular subject matter being taught.

The results from this process are then used to inform instructional decisions.[5] Effective assessment relies heavily on a teacher's strong understanding of content. The National Board agrees with this definition of "assessment." In their detailed discussion of Standard 11: *Assessment,* the National Board defines it as "the process of using formal and informal methods of data-gathering to determine students' growing scientific literacy, understanding, and appreciation" (National Board for Professional Teaching Standards [NBPTS], 1997, 45).

Evidence in support of learning related to assessment in this study is substantial. The National Board's incessant requirement of focused, detailed, and extensive review of artifacts to support assertions of student learning places a priority on identifying and using evidence of effectiveness. For many teachers, this represents a new approach to practice. Many are accustomed to a traditional "teach and test" mentality that results in assessment practices that focus primarily on factual recall ability. Through the efforts to construct a meaningful portfolio, issues of student assessment were explored in richer detail. The process "made" Kate, a teacher from California, think about her lessons "in more detail and think about assessment." Another teacher, Karen, who is from Kentucky, expanded upon this theme by saying:

> Well, like I used to just grade a test. Based on how the grades were on the test that would kind of be my indication of if the kids learned or not. And now, I just see that there's all types of assessments and that how a student does on your test is going to have an influence on your teaching and how you instruct. You know I never looked at that as a tool for changing my instruction.

Karen expressed a deeper understanding and appreciation for assessment than she possessed prior to the certification process—proving that the practice of teaching is enriched by assessment, not plagued by it. Assessment becomes a tool for improving student learning instead of only a requirement for the report card.

Another effect of the detailed assessment requirements of National Board was Karen's changed view of her students as each being unique. She continued by saying, "I realized that you really need to look at a student's individual needs and style. For a long time I taught just college-bound kids and you kind of think that they are just all the same. And they are not . . . it just made me individualize more."

Karen described a 180-degree readjustment regarding her approach to teaching and learning—from a teacher-centered, passive learning environment to a student-centered, individualized learning community. Assessment facilitated this change by allowing the teacher the opportunity to more closely examine what individual students may or may not be learning, and the teacher's causal relationship to the assessed outcome.

Another teacher echoed this idea of discovering more value for assessment than just a grade at the end of a unit, and for using assessment practices to see one's self as more directly responsible for eliciting (or not eliciting) learning from students. During part of the portfolio construction that required close assessment of student learning, Madeline, a teacher from Rhode Island, stated:

> I actually noticed things that the kids didn't understand. Under other circumstances I probably would have just gone right by it and not put it all together. But in the larger context—when I was looking at an extended unit and the various pieces—I noticed that there were several things the kids just didn't get. If I hadn't spent the time to analyze it, I probably would have just gone right by it. And just said, "Oh, they just didn't get it." But I really saw that there was definitely a problem somewhere with the way I structured the lesson or the way that I delivered the lesson or something that I did that said they didn't get it. And it caused me to step back and change the way that I'll teach that again. Normally, I probably wouldn't have done that.

Madeline articulated an appreciation for assessment practices that did not exist prior to certification. Not only was a problematic concept identified from an assessment, but also reasons for the lack of learning were formulated. In this case, the teacher expressed a belief that the students "didn't get it" because of a problem with the teacher's pedagogical decisions or her delivery of the lesson in class. The teacher cited that National Board certification provided a set of "circumstances" that were different than "normal."

These different circumstances can be interpreted to mean the additional requirements demanded of the teacher while constructing the portfolio. Without the particular needs of the portfolio construction, Madeline would probably have never taken the time to explore assessment to the extent demonstrated here.

The qualitative data indicates that the learning that takes place in assessment is more profound in character than that observed in scientific inquiry. For example, once the power of detailed and intensified assessment of student learning is experienced, it actually may change the way a teacher thinks about practice. For example, Rita, a teacher from Kentucky, reinforced this notion by stating:

> And it truly—and it has already carried over to this year—you know when kids don't write very well—you almost dread reading their writing. But I find myself really wanting to read their lab reports and stuff. And I feel like what I say to

them on their papers—I definitely give them more feedback. But my feedback is more direct. So I feel like I analyze their work better than I did before.

In this example, Rita "looks forward" to a task that previously was "dreaded." Assessment has not only improved her understanding of student ideas and reasoning, but has also led to an improved appreciation for effective engagement through appropriate and more thorough feedback. Finally, the teacher learning exemplified here appears to represent immediate change to the teacher's practice that has carried over into the semester following completion of National Board certification requirements.

The immediacy of change associated directly with assessment procedures is found in the following quote from Marsha, a teacher from Florida. Marsha stated:

> I know I've changed the way I correct papers after having to go through that process. There is that one section in your portfolio where you had to put in student work and your comments. I pulled some student work and I started looking at it and it was just full of misconceptions. This was a physics worksheet and I said, "My God, these would have just gone right by me if I hadn't taken the time to sit down and read every word that they wrote." So, I have now changed the way that I correct papers. The kids—there is more red on the paper when they get it back than their original writing. So I correct papers with just a real eagle eye now. I read everything that they write. To me that was the biggest eye opener I've had in a long time.

The development of an "eagle eye" with regard to what students are thinking as reflected in their writing echoes many of the other ideas already explored in this section on assessment. Marsha has changed her practice as a result of experiences with assessment that were brought about because of the requirements of the portfolio construction. This enriched assessment practice has also resulted in improved feedback or engagement with the students, as indicated by Marsha's description of "more red on the paper . . . than their original writing."

These types of self-reports suggest that for at least some of the teachers sampled, a rather profound shift has taken place. Perhaps these changes point to the kind of self-sustaining, generative learning now recognized as a relatively rare event in the literature.[6] How long such effects may last cannot be answered in the context of this study. But in the annals of teacher learning, the reports are remarkable against the backdrop of so many teachers' dismal accounts of professional development experiences. The process of Board certification appears to have been a transformative experience for at least some teachers on selected dimensions of practice.

Reflection: Evidence for Learning

The literature on reflection is as deep as it is wide. There is a consensus in the educational community that some form of reflection links effective practice with inquiry and continuous professional growth. John Dewey first used the term *reflection* and defined it as "an active, persistent, and careful consideration of any belief or supposed form of knowledge."[7] In the 1980s, the idea was revisited in Schön's (1983) *The Reflective Practitioner.* Schön believed that experience alone was not enough to move a novice teacher to the realm of an expert. He maintained that "reflection in action" and "reflecting on action" were intertwined means of developing expertise in teaching. These ideas of reflection have strongly influenced the way the National Board defines and uses the term.

According to the National Board, *reflection* is the act of regularly contemplating "the effects one's actions and initiatives are having on fostering student learning."[8] From this view, reflection becomes a means of self-education and being a "life-long learner." As figure 6.1 indicates, Standard 12 (Reflection) garnered the majority of comments, further bolstering its significance as an area of candidate learning. Though Standard 12 was the third-highest observed gain out of the thirteen standards, it had the most comments.

This situation might be explained by the fact that reflection directly or indirectly supports the other twelve standards. Teachers may reflect on equity, resources, assessment, scientific inquiry, engagement, or learning environment, but only focus on the act of reflection as significant. In the discussion that follows, examples are shared that illustrate the value of active reflection and focus on a specific issue or problem related to practice.

A common theme that runs through many of these comments pertains to the value of reflection that is "forced" upon the teacher by the certification process. As Judy, from California, said, "It really makes you stop and take a look at every little nit-picky thing you do. And you see things that you didn't see before because you don't have time to see them. So it forces you to take the time to really reflect on what you are doing." Kim, from Maryland, added a similar voice when she stated, "I think it's very good to take time out and look at what you are doing and why you are doing it."

Judy and Kim suggested that making time for reflective work adds to the perception of certification as a beneficial learning experience. Annabelle from Alabama echoed this view when she said that National Board certification was "the most beneficial thing that I've ever done in terms of real personal, professional development. Because it made you take a good hard look at yourself and your teaching practice—which otherwise a teacher never would do. Because no one ever asked you to do that." These teachers' comments suggest that being "forced" or "made" to engage in critical reflection through the certification process was a new and powerful experience.

However, it's not just the act of reflecting that is important; it is also the quality of what teachers mean by *reflecting on practice*. In terms of quality, reflection for many teachers in this study referred to self-examination that peered beneath the obvious. For example, Melinda, from Virginia (who also echoed the "required" nature of the reflection process), commented on the character of the reflection when she stated:

> [National Board certification] has really required me to do more analysis of my daily teaching then I might have conducted otherwise. And it brought things to my attention that I probably wouldn't have noticed on my own. Like sitting down with students' work for the one entry and the written work and really reading it in-depth and reading in between the lines and picking out what it is trying to show me; and all of that kind of stuff. It sort of helped me see how my students were doing in a different atmosphere than I would have considered them originally.

Melinda indicated that reflection was effective because it forced her to "really" read students' work "in-depth," and to "read between the lines" in order to find out hidden or less apparent meaning. From this kind of description, one could infer that under nonreflecting circumstances, the teacher only considers student work in black-and-white or right-and-wrong contexts. Certification promotes something richer where candidates are asked to "really read" student ideas beyond the simple answers. The product of this detailed analysis results in an assessment of student understanding "in a different atmosphere," or knowing them in a way that the teacher had not considered prior to certification.

Another way to think about this reflection as in-depth analysis is represented by the comments of Kelly, from Oklahoma. Kelly expressed the "revealing" nature of the reflection process as very productive. She stated, "It made me realize that some of the things that I was already doing—how profound an impact it had. And how I could do more of it. And it also showed me things that I didn't even think made a difference that do make a difference." In this example, the reflection process caused the teacher to rethink some prior assumptions about instruction and make connections perceived to be "profound" in nature.

Another way to think of the "profound" nature of this experience is that it increased the teacher's awareness of the complexity of a task previously assumed to be quite simple and straightforward. For example, Carol, from North Carolina, stated:

> I didn't realize until I did National Boards how—how much actual thought goes into a lesson. You know—after a few years you just kind of do it by instinct. But when you have to really think about managing all these kids; for example does that girl who doesn't speak Spanish very well, get what I'm saying? It just brings it all back up to the forefront and makes you think about it.

Carol not only repeated the idea that reflection causes a teacher to "really think" as opposed to just "think," but also indicated a new appreciation for the complexity that teaching entails. Carol also pointed out the role reflection plays in solving problems. She questioned whether or not an English language learner (ELL) comprehended the intended objectives. Finally, Carol mentioned the idea that National Board certification "makes" a teacher reflect in a purposeful and meaningful manner.

In addition to focusing on the act and quality of reflection, many teachers make a connection between reflective activities and their improved ability to bring about learning in students. Whether a teacher mentions it specifically or not, the sense is that *it's all about the students*. For example, Natalie, from Georgia, said:

> I could really see my teaching. What did I do? What did I *not* do in my classroom right now to meet those standards? It also helps you assess how you teach and what you teach. Meaning, are you really teaching the concepts that you are supposed to be teaching or are you kind of skirting around your science

concepts? Are you teaching in a way that is useful for your students or not? So most of what I liked about National Boards was that it really made me reflect and assess what I'm doing in the classroom. And do I do it in such a way that my students can figure out what I want them to get out of each day's lesson.

Natalie connected reflection to teaching content. The types of questions Natalie posed form a template for future circumstances with students in other classes. These questions guide instruction and allow teachers to make alterations to best meet the needs of learners. Natalie's emphasis on reflection as a daily activity indicated the potential value of certification to foster change in practice.

For candidates like Natalie, reflection is not something they only did for certification. Rather, it is something they learned from certification and have incorporated into their postcertification practice. If the experience of reflection from National Board certification results in new habits of mind around questions like these, then who is the likely beneficiary? One could conclude that students would ultimately benefit from a teacher so intent on meeting the needs of both the mandated curriculum (e.g., science concepts) and students' learning.

Reflection may lead to better teaching and learning. Markus, from Washington, made this point when he stated, "I think whenever you start analyzing why you are doing what you are doing—the impact on students and student learning is definitely going to be positive; because you seek a deeper meaning for each of the things that you are doing."

Jillian, also from Washington, provided further insight into the connection between effective reflection and better instruction:

As you try to explain to somebody else why you think something is good for student learning—you may go through the process of going, "Wow, maybe that's not so good. Maybe I always thought it was good—but where is the evidence that it was good?" And so it really made you think about why you choose to do something and what evidence you have now to suggest that it is good for students. And sometimes I think teachers—we as teachers don't do that. We think it's good because we think it's good. And we like it. But it may not always be good for student learning.

For Markus and Jillian, reflection caused them to rethink, reconsider, or reassess particular assumptions, ideas, or beliefs about teaching and learning science. It would appear that teacher learning associated with reflection attempts to get beneath the surface of the apparent to question or consider the less apparent or hidden meaning.

In particular, Jillian's questioning about assumptions she might have made about what is taught, how it is taught, and how it is learned by the student is very interesting. Jillian's shift from an instinct approach to teaching (i.e., "It's good because we think it's good") to a more evidence-based form of instruction (i.e., "Where's the evidence that it was good?") is a powerful example of the quality of learning the certification process seems to promote in some candidates.

This last teacher comment is special. It is special not for what was said, but more for how it was said. It is as if the teacher was caught in the act of reflection, and it provides a glimpse into how the teacher's mind may work through the reflection process effectively. It is also an example of how the video requirements of the certification serve as a valuable resource for reflective learning.

Vivian, from North Carolina, described an enzyme laboratory with a class of biology students. In her comments, Vivian described what happened when she completely mishandled the students' test tubes over lunch by setting the incubator on a temperature that was too high. Here's how Vivian told the story:

> When they came back to lunch I told them "Gee guys, I've ruined the experiment—I've boiled these." We talked about what could affect enzymes and I tried to get them to think, "OK, what could go wrong?" And they came up with the different aspects. And then I said "Oh yeah—temperature, I know I boiled your yeast to infinity." And so it was a cool lesson at the time; but when I went back and watched it, I was thinking next year if that ever happens—it would be better to have them come back from lunch, get their tubes, take down the data and realize "Oh geez, it didn't do what we thought it was going to do." And then have them try and figure out what in the world went wrong without me telling them first. So I sort of—I tipped them off without realizing it; so I realized then that I need to be careful. What I need is to let the kids discover things on their own and try to keep my mouth shut more often. So I can see that's helped me a lot. You really don't see yourself teach unless you do have a tape set up and you can go back and see what has happened in the lesson. So that part I know will help me next year.

With the use of the video, Vivian presented a description of what meaningful reflection looks like. In this passage, the teacher identified a key mistake that could have been avoided. She realized that rather than telling the students about the mistake, it may have been a more productive and effective learning experience for the students had they figured out the problem on their own.

Vivian's insight from the teacher's point of view goes to the heart of the standards for accomplished teaching. With this description, the teacher moves from being the giver of knowledge to the facilitator of learning. It represents a move from teacher-centered pedagogy to student-centered pedagogy. The comment also has relevance to the previous discussions on science inquiry and assessment involving both of those areas as more than peripheral to the reflection.

The preceding samples of qualitative evidence illustrate some of the ways reflection could be recognized as learning. The fact that reflection is involved in every aspect of the portfolio and, to a certain extent, in all the other standards makes the observation of learning in the area of reflection that much more significant. What do teachers mean when they say that certification made them "more reflective practitioners"?

The answer appears to be related to the extent and magnitude of their willingness to be self-critical. The more a teacher is willing to indicate weakness, point out mistakes in his or her planning or teaching, or more thoroughly understand what a student may or may not be learning, the clearer the indication as to how well the teacher has learned to incorporate a reflective component into practice.

Therefore, when teachers say, "I'm more reflective now" with regard to National Board certification, what they may mean is, "I am more willing to question my own judgments, assumptions, and actions to determine what is in the students' best interest. If evidence suggests that I should do something better, then I will take appropriate action to correct the situation."

What specific aspects of the certification experience are most likely to foster such a dramatic change? In the next section, the resources for learning from Board certification are considered.

RESOURCES FOR LEARNING

National Board certification is a structured process. The structures are designed to ensure that every candidate is provided every opportunity to present evidence in a specific and orderly fashion. From the Board's perspective, strict guidelines and protocols help to ensure equitable and accurate assessment. For the candidate, the process of certification serves as a curriculum that can solicit a range of outcomes.

In this section, resources of learning represent the different aspects of the certification curriculum. These resources include the directions and prompts for portfolio construction, the thirteen documented standards of accomplished teaching in secondary science, the videos, and support community. If the observed learning outcomes are accurate, then the resources should support explicit and implicit candidate learning. The following analysis discusses each of these resources as a facet of the curriculum presented by National Board certification.

The evidence provided by candidate comments about certification requires an important reminder. National Board certification presents intellectual, pedagogical, organizational, and logistical challenges to the candidate. If National Board is to promote teacher learning that translates into improved practice, then the tasks designed to assess the quality of instruction must be intellectually challenging and relevant to instruction.

As has already been touched upon, ample evidence suggests that certification is a demanding endeavor. Robert, from Montana, put it this way, "I thought the National Board Portfolio was the most difficult thing that I'd ever done in my entire career. I consider getting National Board certification far greater than getting my masters' degree or anything else. I thought it was just an enormous project and very worthwhile."

Amy, from Virginia (who was first introduced in chapter 3), gets the prize for most convincing description: "I think if I had the choice to go back and get a Ph.D. or even have triplets, I would do either of those before I'd go through National Board again. It was almost like I was opened up, I was humbled, I saw myself, I mean the real me as a teacher."

Both Robert and Amy provide evidence for the rigorous nature of the certification process. In addition, Amy's comment about seeing the "real me as a teacher" indicates that the act of critical self-reflection (when done properly) provides the teacher with a challenging and potentially rewarding experience. Amy said that it was like she was "opened up," meaning that the process had brought her to the point where she was not only confronting her teaching, stripped of any pretense, but that it was done in a public manner.

For Amy, the experience was "humbling." Amy may have come to a stark realization that her original definition of what an accomplished teacher should know and be able to do was entirely inadequate when held up to the Board's definition of excellence. It is this discrepancy between the real and the ideal that may fuel the feeling of rigor in the assessment process. For most candidates, the discrepancy is too much to overcome, and in the end, their evidence is insufficient for them to be deemed "accomplished."

Nearly 50 percent of all Board candidates do not achieve National Board certification, and those pursuing an AYA Science certificate face an even higher (60 percent) failing rate. One candidate from Massachusetts, Perry, actually found this to be beneficial for the process. In describing the value of the experience separate from the ultimate outcome of certification, Perry stated, "And actually even at the end of this month if they tell me that I didn't pass and that I have to re-do something I'm not going to—it won't bother me and I won't feel like I wasted any time. And actually, I kind of like the idea that most people don't pass."

Perry's confession is significant to one of the main findings in this study: Regardless of whether candidates are successful at achieving National Board certification, they demonstrate professional learning from the experience. The ultimate outcome for Perry has been supplanted by the fact he did not "waste" his time in the endeavor. The valuable contributions of portfolio instructions, prompts, standards, videos, and colleagues to the certification experience are vital to understanding how the process fosters the observed learning in inquiry, assessment, and reflection.

Finally, Perry's admission that he "kind of likes the idea that most people don't pass" is a real gem of a comment. It points to a future vision of teaching that not only acknowledges the value of identifying exceptional teachers, but provides a model for how the entire teacher community might begin to embrace a nonegalitarian view of the profession. It is a view of teaching that is based on respect for a colleague's ability to not only foster learning, but also to communicate clearly about the complexity of the endeavor in a rigorous and meaningful manner.

Portfolio Materials

If certification serves as the curriculum, then the portfolio prompts, instructions, and standards function like a textbook. However, this "textbook" differs from the traditional notions of what a textbook should be. Kelly, from Oklahoma, described the difference nicely when she stated, "It wasn't like they [portfolio materials] were giving me instruction on how to be a better teacher—they were just telling me how to collect data for them—so they could see if I was a good teacher."

In other words, the materials do not inform the candidate as to what lessons to teach or how to teach them, but rather provide a framework that informs the teacher how his or her practice can best be represented by evidence for assessment. This quality of the portfolio directions is quite important. It requires the teacher to continually make decisions pertaining to practice that address the needs of students, standards of accomplished teaching, and the requirements for certification.

Serving three masters could result in teachers commenting on how the certification process "forced" or "made" them reflect to a greater degree than they normally would do. This decision-making process was demonstrated by Mary, from Nebraska, when she commented, "trying to figure out what lessons I do that matched the criteria they were looking for; and if they didn't currently match, how would I fix them? So it was really preparing the portfolio [that was most helpful]."

Mary focused on the needs of the portfolio. When she said "fix them," it could be interpreted that she needed to make adjustments to her lesson so that it was more "Board acceptable." Such a decision may or may not be good for her students. The point is that she focused on pleasing the Board, and not necessarily addressing the specific needs of her students. This type of evidence has implications, as is mentioned later in the discussion regarding teacher quality.

Another teacher, however, found the materials provided by the National Board to be a good source of inspiration and ideas. Elli, from California, stated, "[W]ith National Board certification you are evaluating your own teaching and you're getting new ideas as you are reading through the materials." The "materials" serve as a source of information that the candidate must read (and in many cases, re-read) and ultimately come to understand.

Wendy, from Louisiana, described this process by saying, "Because when you look at [those materials] and go through the guidelines and you go through the objectives and you answer those questions—have you done this?—do you do that?—if you didn't, it makes you more cognizant of the fact that you probably should."

Wendy described this process of learning as if it were a conversation between the text and the teacher. The result of this interaction was a teacher who became "more cognizant" or aware of a different approach to practice. However, Wendy's comment also reflects the authority of the portfolio prompts. Wendy was focused on procedural completeness, rather than student learning.

Standards Documents

The materials provided by the National Board include a detailed description of the thirteen standards of accomplished teaching in AYA Science. This document presents a vital source of learning for the candidate. Some teachers like Naomi, from Georgia, indicated that they felt "forced" or "made" to "read those national science standards." However, others expressed a view that described the document as a rich resource for learning. John, from New York, stated:

> I bet I read that standards book after I highlighted it thirty times—maybe not all the way through—but I'd read this page and that page. I really thought a lot of the stuff in the standards book really made me reflect and *not just* the lessons that I did for part of my National Board; but you know some of the other lessons that I was doing. I actually think that that standards book should be required reading for all teachers. I thought that was excellent.

One gets an image of a very well used and loved physical text that is worn and marked up from being referred to over and over again. Such documents become cherished by the learners as representative of the learning that takes place. The comment also hints at the notion that the learning is "not just" in the context of National Board certification, but also for the "other lessons" that were not part of the portfolio construction. In other words, John's comment is evidence that the resources for learning carry over into noncertification experiences.

The standards serve multiple purposes. Not only do they function as a text from which a teacher may acquire relevant teaching knowledge, but they also serve as a benchmark against which current practice can be compared. As Kerri, from Kentucky, stated:

> It was just a challenge for me to meet the standards that are outlined in the National Standards for Professional Teaching. Just to put yourself up against

those standards was awesome, humbling, and motivating all at the same time. They describe what the qualities of accomplished teaching look like.

Kerri describes a mixture of emotions when she says "awesome, humbling, and motivating." Such words reveal the power of this document to instill meaning and relevance to a teacher's practice. The standards articulate a system of teaching that some candidates identify as relevant to their efforts in the classroom.

Video Recordings

Another valuable source of learning for candidates can be found in the videos they produce and submit. As part of the portfolio construction, candidates are required to submit two twenty-minute videos. One video is focused on active scientific inquiry and the other looks at whole-class discussion in science.

Powerful and abundant evidence is available that the video portion of the assessment process was a fertile area for learning. For example, Molly, from Maine, states, "Videotaping yourself in action allows you to sort of step back and look at the way you design your stuff. Looking at it through different filters really allows you to ask whether or not you think you are the teacher that you sometimes feel that you are."

As anyone who has had to confront himself or herself on video may know, the experience can be difficult, painful, and powerful. What is observed on the screen is at times far removed from the perception of one's self as a teacher. Molly expressed this phenomenon when she stated that the experience helps one assess "whether or not you think you are the teacher that you sometimes feel that you are." Such an experience could easily motivate a teacher to adjust, make another video, and reassess the performance. The examination of one's practice compared with the standards of accomplished teaching (or as Molly called them, "filters") promotes a kind of self-examination that can facilitate dramatic learning.

The video was not just a source of learning about the teacher; it was also a source of information about the students and their engagement with the teacher. For example, Daphne, from New York, stated:

I'd never worked with videotaping before and so I wanted them [the students] to be comfortable. And I videotaped like—probably about fifty hours worth of class time. And initially it was very funny because they all behaved a certain way in front of the camera. Then later on, it became much more revealing because I could see what was happening. The tapes provided me with ways to question my honor students for my bio class. Last year, they wouldn't answer any questions in class.

Daphne used the video to address a problem regarding engagement with students. She also indicated that the video analysis became "much more revealing" about a particular issue regarding student behavior. Video analysis could facilitate learning in areas of engagement, assessment, learning environment, knowledge of students, and scientific inquiry.

Daphne also shared an important insight about reconciling the requirements of certification and the needs of her students. She described the effect of the intrusive nature of the video camera on her students by the fact that she wanted them to be "comfortable." To make the documentation of her practice more authentic, Daphne repeatedly used the camera until students got accustomed to its presence in the classroom.

Once students were acclimated to being on camera (i.e., "fifty hours worth of class time"), their behavior became "more revealing" because she could "see what was happening." This type of analysis suggests that Daphne approached the process of making a video not so much as a requirement of certification, but as an integrated part of her classroom teaching.

The resources described thus far represent learning opportunities for teachers that are best explained by Sfard's (1998) acquisition metaphor of learning. The candidates' comments all involve interacting with an artifact of the certification process. Whether that artifact is a standards document, portfolio-related material, or video, the text for learning remains fixed and unchanging, even though different teachers may interpret, learn, or experience each piece quite differently. For example, Constance, from South Carolina, describes her experience with the documented resources as follows:

When you see things that are part of the standards, because you have to know those standards so well, when you see things that you should be doing but aren't doing—when you are going through the process—you make sure that you do those things, because you know that you are supposed to be doing them. And if you haven't done them before, you start. And that's good because they are all very positive things we should all be doing.

Constance attempted to fulfill the requirements and meet the standards to the best of her ability. From this teacher's description, one gets the sense that these documents are fixed and unchanging, and that it is the teacher who is trying to change to fit the standards. In the last resource to be considered (colleagues), a participation metaphor for learning such as Lave and Wenger's (1991) situated learning model is more important in explaining the observed outcomes.

Colleagues as Resources for Learning

One way to appreciate the value of a support network in relationship to the certification process is to see what someone with no support had to say. Bonnie, from Ohio, stated:

> I found National Boards to be a solitary process. . . . For me, National Boards did not have that collaborative element. And I think that collaborative element with other educators is a huge piece. I think that analyzing the student work is an incredibly valuable experience. I mean the pieces that went into it were powerful. I think that to analyze student work with a group would be more powerful. Or to analyze that videotape in some detail with a group of peers would be more valuable.

As the evidence that follows indicates, Bonnie may be correct in her assessment of the situation. A collaborative strand to the certification process does provide for an opportunity to learn in a different manner.

Take for example, Shannon, from Arkansas. Shannon's comment about her experience placed the emphasis on colleagues as a vital source for her learning. She stated:

> Pursuing National Board certification has impacted me more than anything I've done since I've started teaching. I've learned from going through the projects more about what it is to help my students. And I've learned more about myself than anything else has taught me. And I have met the most high-caliber teachers I've ever known through the application process. Other teachers, who were applying last year, went with me to support groups and we became friends. And we are still e-mailing each other and going to conferences together. And there were some National Board–certified teachers in Little Rock who met with us to encourage us and were readers for us. I never would have interacted with those teachers. And they are fantastic teachers. And I've been influenced by

them and helped by them. And that would never have happened if I had not been going through National Boards. Just the encouragement, just the energy level and the expectation level that those teachers have has stimulated me I guess to want to do better and to try harder and it's just been great. Whether I make it or not—it has definitely impacted me.

Shannon presented the idyllic example of National Board certification promoting teacher learning through an evolving sense of participating in a community. Shannon described the relationships that arose from the experience and how those relationships shaped her experience and sense of mission in becoming a better teacher. The community was inspiring and supportive, guiding and collaborative, respectful, yet critical. The certification process for Shannon facilitated professional communications and expectations of excellence because of her exposure to "accomplished teachers."[9]

In this view, National Board becomes not only a vehicle for developing dialogue between teachers, but also an elite kind of fraternity where "membership has its privileges." Among the advantages that Shannon identified is the sense of communing with teachers who appear to have greater abilities, enthusiasm, energy, and knowledge about teaching. Such a positive group of peers may inspire or motivate a new "member" toward higher achievement and effectiveness in the classroom.

It should be noted that Shannon's desire to "try harder" can be interpreted in several ways. Does it mean she is trying to be a better teacher, Board candidate, or both? Her mention of the role these "fantastic" teachers play as "readers" hints that this support group could be focused on improving Shannon's chances of achieving certification, and not necessarily improving instructional practices.

Shannon's comment also points to a common weakness of the local school community. If Shannon is finding the individuals from other districts who she can model, emulate, and connect with, then she is most likely not finding this type of professional satisfaction within her school. While conferences and university course work may also bring teachers together, the experience of National Board certification seems to bring driven individuals together to form productive professional relationships around fundamental issues about improving practice.

In a more specific example of how collaboration can facilitate learning, Clare, from Kentucky, described her experience wrestling with the term *significant,* which was used frequently by members of her support group. Clare stated, "See this whole word *significant* was something that baffled me throughout the entire National Board group. They used that word so much. I'm just saying it was so funny because my mentor and I we were just pondering on *significant, significant, significant.*"

This is an interesting example of National Board certification bringing professionals together through a support group that might not normally interact, to discuss concepts that may not originate from everyday practice. Clare described a connection between herself and her mentor that the support group nurtured. She does not say what they determined *significant* to mean, or that they ever resolved the issue. Rather, her story represents a form of professional bond between the mentor and the candidate. Because Clare repeated *significant* three times, one gets the sense that this was a form of "inside joke" that only the two of them shared.

In essence, these candidates may have been constructing their own understanding of "significant" quite independent of any definition from the National Board or the support group. This kind of learning indicates the potential for the National Board to promote sociocultural learning through communities of practice. Further research into the collaborative nature of candidates working together seems warranted. However, in the context of this study, it is fairly safe to conclude that collegiality and collaboration had an implicit impact on shaping what candidates learned. There is just not enough specific evidence from the qualitative review to make a more defined connection.

Another form of community that has become available and vital to the process of certification takes on a virtual form. With the rise of Internet- and web-based communications, candidates are likely to find answers to questions, moral and emotional support, and guidance about portfolio and assessment issues online. For example, Yahoo Groups has an online community just for AYA Science candidates. Teacher-candidates can access archived messages or post one of their own. Such efforts often result in meaningful and long-distance relationships centered on classroom practice and the certification process. For example, Vicki, from North Carolina, stated:

> I had gone to a couple of community workshops or district workshops. I attended everything I could and had some good support. I even found a lady that read my entries over the Internet. She lived a couple of hundred miles

away from me. I helped some other teachers that were doing the advanced work (these are teachers that didn't pass part of it [certification] the first time). I helped them even though I'm not sure that I knew what I was doing. But, I felt like I had gained a lot and helped them to work on their video skits and to analyze it and help them put the right words in their questions and that kind of thing. And see I like doing that, too. I like working with other teachers and that's the collaborative thing.

Vicki had participated in traditional support group settings within her district, but she also found support over the Internet. The give-and-take Vicki described in this passage reveals a quality of learning that is missing from descriptions of other sources for learning discussed previously. Vicki found an intrinsic reward in helping others, even when together the teachers were unsure what the correct solution may be.

One gets the sense that the experience of certification facilitates common experiences that translate into professional (and possibly personal) relationships. Like strangers in a lifeboat adrift on the ocean, candidates struggling to make sense out of the demanding tasks of certification reach out and try to help one another succeed. Granted, part of this comment is disturbing, such as the reference to the video being a "skit," but this is explored later in chapter 7.

The next example provides evidence that National Board certification plays a crucial role in school communities as a rallying point for educators. Mike, from Wyoming, described this activity by saying, "I talked seven of our department members into trying the National Boards this year—so we could all sit there and work together and help and collaborate on ideas and try and understand what in the heck they are asking us and stuff."

Mike was able to convince fellow department members to pursue National Board certification together, so that they could try to understand "what in the heck" was needed to complete the portfolio successfully. According to Mike, the tasks and challenges that National Board certification presents to the candidate are best addressed from multiple perspectives and ideas as represented by a group of colleagues.[10]

So far, the resources for learning associated with a participatory metaphor have examined school support groups, online virtual communities, and district workshops. Another interesting milieu of collaboration can be found at the university setting. In many places, colleges of education are establishing support networks between academia and local teachers pursuing National Board certification.

Such networks have the potential to open lines of discourse between professional researchers, academics, and classroom teachers in new and interesting ways. For example, Bob, from Washington, states, "I was the only teacher in the school [pursing certification], but there was a college that was sponsoring Saturday workshops, once a month, so we'd get together for three hours then with people all over the state and discuss it [National Board certification]."

Bob described his efforts at overcoming isolation by participating in a statewide support group centered at a college. This comment provides no indication about the relative value of the experience or the nature of the learning, but it remains important because it demonstrates how different components of the educational system can come together for a common purpose and create a distinct community that would not have existed had it not been for National Board certification.

SUMMARY

In chapter 6, the qualitative evidence for learning from National Board certification was presented. Both the quantity and quality of the candidate comments about their National Board certification experience support the observed gains for Science Inquiry, Assessment, and Reflection reported in chapter 5.

In addition, teacher learning in these areas was linked with available resources associated specifically with Board certification. The resources described here support both an acquisition and participation explanation of teacher learning from the certification experience.

Part III of this book considers what candidate learning might mean to classroom practice, and the implications of this work to various diverse educational stakeholders. In particular, suggestions for improving the certification process and ensuring the future of the National Board for Professional Teaching Standards will be considered.

NOTES

1. See appendix A for details.

2. National Board for Professional Teaching Standards (NBPTS), *Instruction manual*, 1997, 31

3. Ibid., 32.

4. To protect the identity of participants in this study, all of the teachers' names in this discussion are pseudonyms.

5. See Gallagher, *Teaching for understanding,* 2000, for a thorough discussion of how assessment informs practice in science.

6. See Franke et al., "Understanding teachers' self-sustaining, generative change," 1998, for further discussion on the concept of self-generative learning.

7. Dewey, *How we think,* 1910, 9.

8. NBPTS, *Instruction manual,* 1997, 53

9. Darling-Hammond and McLaughlin, "Policies that support professional development," 1996, describes meaningful teacher communication about real issues of teaching and learning as vital to a successful professional development experience. Traditional teacher in-service training workshops often fail to achieve this kind of relevancy.

10. It is interesting to speculate how this support group might influence the school community or its fate upon hearing about who passed and who did not. What would happen? How would personal and professional disappointment play out against others who felt triumphant and "accomplished"? How would personal feelings influence professional conduct? Further research on this aspect of the candidates' experiences would be most revealing and relevant.

III

NATIONAL BOARD CERTIFICATION

7

Implications for Teacher Quality

What good is "teacher learning" if it does not improve work in the classroom? One can learn to be a better cook, but unless the knowledge and skills acquired are used in the kitchen, the same old meals are going to be served. In teaching, a similar situation exists. Just because teachers *learn* about practice does not necessarily mean they will *change* their practice. In this chapter, the relationship between what teachers learn and how that learning introduces possible changes to instruction is explored.

Determining the effects of professional development on classroom practice is notoriously difficult. While candidates for Board certification learn about inquiry, assessment, and reflection, it is a very different goal to link these outcomes with changes to practice. For example, teachers might acquire new knowledge or skills, yet choose not to deploy them in their practice. Or they might make changes initially, but gradually revert back to old ways. Another possibility is that the changes they make might not enhance their practice. Compounding the problem of linking professional development to student learning is the teacher's crafty predilection for tweaking reforms to meet their needs.

Prior scholarship reveals teachers importing only certain aspects of reforms into their teaching, with uncertain overall and long-term effects. Describing such problems, investigators have resorted to such metaphors as "hybrids" to indicate the distinctive mix of grafting the new onto the old.[1] Furthermore, "change" does not automatically mean "improvement." The latter term requires a value judgment, as well as an empirical result. The discussion that follows offers a qualified interpretation of impacts based on both available evidence and a dose of insightful speculation.

While direct observation of candidate teaching was beyond the scope of the investigation described in this book, subtle and meaningful evidence exists from the teacher interviews that shed light on possible patterns of impact. To understand how learning might influence the work of teachers, interviews were revisited and recoded to look for comments that focus on teacher perceptions of the relationship between certification and possible changes to teacher quality.

This chapter shows that candidates from this study fall into three distinct categories of learning: dynamic, technical, and deferred. *Dynamic learning* translates into immediate improvements in teacher quality. *Technical learning* refers to the situation where candidates demonstrate improved understanding, but make no attempt to change the quality of their instructional practices. Last, *deferred learning* describes those candidates who are unsure how their learning will affect their teaching. Like the technical learner, the deferred learner's quality of instruction remains unchanged, but a possibility of improvement in the future exists.

In the following discussion about dynamic, technical, and deferred learning, teacher quality is defined as the capacity to generate and sustain effective student engagement.[2] According to the Eisenhower Grant Program for Professional Development in Math and Science, teaching quality impinges directly on the efficacy of student work through professional competence in two areas[3]:

1. Teachers' content expertise expressed as knowledge of a specific discipline and knowledge of how to teach that discipline.
2. Teachers' pedagogical expertise (expressed as the ability to develop academic tasks with appropriate content and challenge) uses a variety of instructional strategies to assess students' knowledge and skill and manage a classroom environment for optimal working conditions.

The first area is very similar to Lee Shulman's (1986) concept of pedagogical content knowledge while the second area is reminiscent of the types of content and skill emphasis found in teacher preparation programs.[4]

This study reveals that National Board candidates learn about assessment, reflection, and scientific inquiry. What do the observed "learning" outcomes mean in terms of change in teacher quality, teacher effectiveness, teacher knowledge, or teacher beliefs? It would be wrong, for example, to conclude that because there was a significant increase in the mean scores for scientific inquiry, teachers are necessarily better at teaching with a scientific inquiry method or that they now know more about teaching with scientific inquiry.

Kowalski and his associates (1997) also observed professional growth from the certification process, but went on to conclude that the assessment process appears only to change the classroom behaviors of the candidates secondarily. Their observations indicate that teacher quality may or may not be improved as a result of National Board certification. However, the wealth of data collected from the participants in this study provides evidence unavailable at the time of Kowalski's work.

The evidence indicates that roughly half of candidates improve their teaching immediately as result of certification (dynamic learners) while the other half do not (technical learners). Technical learning about assessment, reflection, and inquiry served to improve a candidate's chances of achieving certification, rather than improve instruction. However, before getting to the details of these possible impacts on teacher quality, it is prudent to first discuss some of the assumptions on which these ideas are based.

Three important assumptions are relevant to this discussion. For purposes of analysis, all three assumptions have been considered "true" in order to focus on possible relationships with the intervention. The three assumptions identified here concern amount of work, rate of learning, and learning style.

The amount of effort or work a teacher puts into the process is a difficult construct to measure. Some teachers may be 100 percent committed to success, while others might be only mildly interested in achieving a goal. Different teachers place differing priorities within the responsibilities in their lives. For many, National Board certification may be their number one priority during the year of certification, but for others it may rank third or fifth, and does not receive the same focused attention and effort.

As a result, it becomes problematic to compare Teacher A's learning experience with Teacher B, because their learning outcomes may have nothing to do with the intervention and everything to do with the level of commitment toward the task. In practical terms, Teacher A, who has set a high priority for Board certification, may not be hindered by the technical requirements of the certification process, whereas Teacher B, who has other more pressing responsibilities, finds the technical requirements a tedious burden. Therefore, it is assumed when looking at teacher learning that all teachers are trying their best to succeed at any given task.

The second assumption pertains to the rate of learning. It is assumed in this study that all teachers learn at the same rate. For example, if two teachers begin the process in September and complete it in June, then the assumption might be made that they obtain the same amount of knowledge in the same amount of time. Again, this assumption is problematic. Teacher A may demonstrate all the learning outcomes in January that Teacher B will not understand until the following October. Both teachers acquired the same knowledge and skills, just in differing amounts of time.

The third assumption pertains to a teacher's capacity for learning (or learning style). For purposes of this study, it is assumed that all teachers have an equal capacity for comprehending and acquiring knowledge and skills relevant to practice. However, not all teachers have identical capacities to learn the same knowledge and skills in the same manner. Whereas Teacher A may be very able to learn concepts and skills associated with scientific inquiry, he or she may have a more difficult time when it comes to understanding or appreciating the value of reflection in practice. Whereas Teacher B finds the knowledge and skills associated with reflection to be quite easy to acquire, he or she may struggle with the concept of inquiry.

In addition, the environment in which teachers learn varies greatly. Some teachers may be more effective learners in a community environment, whereas others prefer learning on their own. Each teacher's unique learning style, coupled with the unequal access to different resources, makes an assumption about learning styles problematic. With the understanding that these assumptions present serious challenges to any discussion about learning, teacher quality, and professional development, the following exploration of learning and teacher quality is presented.

DYNAMIC LEARNING

In dynamic learning, identified preintervention to postintervention gains translate into immediate, effective, and meaningful changes in a teacher's beliefs, understandings, and actions in the classroom. For example, teachers who learn about inquiry in a dynamic manner change their practice to match their new understanding. In this interpretation, teacher quality is characterized as "improved" or "increased." The following comments and analysis try to illustrate precisely what is meant by this categorization of learning.

Dynamic learning results in immediate qualitative change to practice that is often described as an improvement in ability to foster learning in students. Penny, from Hawaii, provided the first piece of evidence when she stated, "The analytical part of learning doesn't just end with sending in your paperwork to National Certification. It's something that you can't help but continue to do. The questions that I had to answer in written form pop into my head now all the time." Carina, from Florida, presented another example of this idea when she stated that the experience of serious reflection from the certification experience is "carried over and you are just different. You think about it [teaching, learning] differently."

Both Penny and Carina internalized the National Board framework of reflection and action. The skills they acquired pertaining to reflection on practice and student learning persisted months after the certification process was over. Carina said she "can't help" but continue with the same approach that was repeatedly employed during the portfolio construction. Penny described the effects of learning as "carrying over" into the current semester. These teachers could be described as "more effective" or of "higher quality" because of the reflective learning brought about by National Board certification.

For some teachers, the changes are more specific to particular aspects or standards of practice. For example, Ron, from New York, described his incorporation of rubrics as a means of communicating expectations more clearly with students. He said:

> This year is going fantastic—even compared to last year—which was a very good year for me. This has been my best year in the physics classroom. One of the biggest reasons why was realizing that I wasn't getting the quality of student work because I didn't have standards. When I realized that I needed to give the kids the standard by which they would be judged—and I sat down and deliberately thought about everything that I thought was important as far as scientific inquiry—I came up with my investigation rubric inspired by my portfolio construction. These efforts totally changed the quality of work that I get from my kids. From garbled incomplete chunks of incomprehensible garbage—really for a lot of them—to a more focused, a more complete, a more in-depth understanding.

Ron described tangible and observable differences in the way he thought about, planned for, and implemented a scientific inquiry lesson. He demonstrated learning associated with the standards of assessment, engagement, scientific inquiry, and reflection. The teacher "realized" that the problems associated with the low quality of student work might be corrected by his decisions and actions. Ron "deliberately thought" about how to solve, or at least address, the problem. This teacher acted upon a newly acquired understanding involving the use of rubrics and standards that are used extensively through the construction of the portfolio entries.

Not surprisingly, and in agreement with observed pre- to postcertification gains in the standards, many comments from teachers indicated that their teaching had changed the most with regard to scientific inquiry. For example, Sarah, from New York, remained involved with portfolio-like activities. She stated, "I'm still doing more inquiry-based labs, more projects. My classroom has become much more student-centered and having students be more analytical and critical thinkers."

Sarah learned an appreciation for a more "student-centered" approach, as well as learning to encourage more "analytical and critical" thinking in her students. Another example is presented by Charity, from California. Charity described how becoming more self-confident provided the necessary strength to do more inquiry with her class. She said, "From the skills that I gained last year in focusing on good teaching and the things that they make you focus on in your portfolio, I gained a lot of confidence in those skills and they became more natural and easy for me. Whereas I might not have taken that risk had I not gone through the process."

The interesting distinction between Charity and Sarah is that Charity hinted that prior to certification, the skills in question were present, but remained weak or underdeveloped. In particular, the skills associated with conducting a more student-centered class where the teacher does not dispense knowledge but rather helps students create their own understandings were revitalized. Charity said that these skills became "more easy," which implies that they existed before the intervention, and that certification provided an opportunity for them to develop. Charity made a direct connection between the experience of National Board certification in the previous semester and new lessons implemented in the current term.

Dynamic learning might best be described with another teacher's description of learning from National Board certification. With regard to his experiences as a candidate, Perry, from Massachusetts, stated, "If you can get a kid to think about a subject that you are teaching—if you can get a kid to internalize it—then he'll have it forever. It's the same thing I think with adults." Perry implied that candidates who internalize their learning from certification are more likely to be changed by that learning "forever." From this perspective, learning is not pragmatic for the purposes of achieving certification, but rather it's something that teachers carry with them for their entire careers.

While dynamic learning may be "internalized," as Perry suggests, it is the immediacy of change catalyzed by learning new knowledge, skills, or understandings that make this type of learning so important to improving teacher quality. How long will this improved teaching continue? How effective will the "improvements" regarding student-learning outcomes be? What is the longevity of this type of learning? Is it forever, as Perry suggests? Or is it cast aside after a few months, while the old (often easier) ways creep back into practice? These are interesting questions, and worthy of future research.

What kinds of candidates are likely to be dynamic learners? It might be that teachers who are intrinsically motivated to pursue National Board certification are more likely to demonstrate dynamic learning. For example, Daphne, from New York, described her reasoning for pursuing National Board in this way: "I need to do something to get out of this rut. I had looked at National Boards since I think it was like 1998 I had considered it. But then with all the state assistance and everything, it was more financially okay to do—so I went ahead and did it."

Veteran teachers with more than ten years of experience often describe National Board certification as an opportunity to "get out of a rut" or overcome teacher "burnout." They have heard good things about the process and its ability to help with professional fatigue. While extrinsic financial incentives may make the process possible, it is the important intrinsic reasons that might make it valuable. For the technical learner, extrinsic concerns overpower all others.

TECHNICAL LEARNING

Until this section, the comments about National Board certification have taken on a very positive and productive tone. The evidence used to describe technical learning has a distinctively different flavor. The negative connotations of these comments are not meant to imply that technical learning is bad, but rather that it is different from dynamic learning. For example, Gabriella, from North Carolina, described the National Board experience in the following terms: "I found the whole experience kind of humiliating. I mean the whole thing was so incredibly frustrating and humiliating."

To clarify, most of Gabriella's issues arose because of communication problems with the National Board and the district protocols for covering the costs of certification. However, the situation never improved from this unfortunate beginning. Not all candidates find the experience to be such a wonderful, life-changing professional development experience. However, just because an individual does not enjoy the certification process does not necessarily mean that he or she did not learn from certification efforts.

Technical learning describes changes in thinking that are procedural in nature. They are linked closely with the goal of succeeding with the certification process. Teachers are learning about scientific inquiry, but only in the context of how they can most impress the assessors. In other words, teachers are learning how to be better candidates for National Board certification, but not necessarily learning how to be better teachers.

In this interpretation, teacher quality remains unaffected. Becoming skilled at Board certification does not necessarily make a teacher more effective in the classroom. The following comments illustrate and serve as evidence for technical learning.

Constance, from South Carolina, observed phoniness in other candidates that could indicate technical learning. She stated, "While I think that for some teachers it's going to make them better teachers, some teachers are going to do what they have to do for certification and not change what they are really doing. They are putting on a show and they just do that well. And whether you maintain [that kind of teaching] afterwards is what I question." The idea expressed that some teachers "put on a show" for certification is echoed by Mark, from Virginia, who said, "But I haven't put on a dog and pony show this year where I'm inventing all of these terrific lessons that I didn't have before."

Mark would probably agree with Constance. They both perceive some of their colleagues as not being honest with the spirit of self-reflection, self-realization, and professional development that are part of the National Board certification process. These "dog and pony" teachers put their efforts not into improving practice, but into impressing the assessors who evaluate the videos and portfolio artifacts. They are playing to a specific audience that does not necessarily include students—and rather than be true to the standards, they attempt to manipulate them for purposes of financial gain.

One teacher in the study confessed to being one of those "dog and pony" teachers. Kim, from Maryland, described the certification experience as follows: "I felt like it was more of an exercise in trying to find out what they were looking for. And so I spent more of my energy doing that than in actually reflecting on my own practice and writing about it."

Kim did not appear to be intentionally phony for the assessments, but somewhere along the line, she got some advice that ended up interfering with the quality of her experience. Kim's focus was on what she thought "they" wanted—"they" being the National Board portfolio assessors. Kim committed valuable time and energy toward chasing down a goal of pleasing the assessors, rather than addressing the students or her own needs.

Where might a candidate receive this kind of advice or direction? According to Ellie, from California, the support groups (which many teachers claimed enriched the certification experience through professional discourse and community) represent one such source of advice. Ellie said:

> I had a group that I met with once a month to discuss what we were doing. Those discussions were "Are we meeting the requirements of National Board?" They weren't really discussions about our instruction and assessment. Instead, we were expected to evaluate each other's papers and decide whether or not we thought they were good papers.

Ellie expected the support group to be focused on conversations around "instruction and assessment." Instead, she found the support groups focused on technical issues—issues associated with writing, answering questions efficiently, and the particular requirements of the different entries in the portfolio. These types of conversations may result in a teacher learning more technical knowledge and skills on how to succeed in certification. This learning, however, may not translate well into changes in classroom practice.

Perry, from Massachusetts, voiced a similar observation about his support group, but went on to make a very insightful remark. He said:

> I did sit in on three of their meetings and at least at the workshop that I attended it was all about how do we get through and how do we pass and how do we write what the readers want you to write. They were saying that they were going to give us deadlines that we had to have our video done by and they were going to do this and that—it was just too contrived. I think it missed the mark of what the heart of National Boards started out to be, which I see as very good. I think much of the focus of support groups is kind of sad. I heard the president of the National Board mention that somewhere in Virginia they have a whole bank of readers that help read the candidate's paper before they are submitted to the National Board. I think it's kind of sad that the people are trying to manipulate the system to try to find ways to use all the correct buzz words but learn nothing.

Perry not only recognized the inauthentic nature of this type of support, but also felt sorry for teachers that feel the need to "manipulate the system" in order to succeed. Teachers with this mindset learn what others think are good strategies for passing the process, techniques for writing the way the "readers want you to write," and other non-standards–based skills and knowledge.

These teachers learn, but their learning is technical, and not related to classroom practice. Technical knowledge regarding the certification process has a perceived importance, as indicated by so many teachers willing to commit valuable resources to the goal of certification. The observation raises the question, "What is the value of technical learning?"

One possible answer may be found in a comment from Staci, from Florida. Staci viewed the process of certification with a cynical perspective that is in alignment with the previous comments, but added a valuable twist. She said:

> I think a lot of it is what hoops can you jump through? How well? How good are you at writing? At saying what you need to say to prove yourself based on the rubric? Are you good at being able to work through that? If you are, that's great. But someone might be a very good teacher, but based on what they submit, it might not be evidence of what they are doing.

Staci makes a very important point. Accomplished teachers may not be good at proving they are accomplished. National Board certification may be too restrictive in formatting requirements and questioning style to fit some teachers' strengths of communication.

Staci's comment also underlines the importance of the technical knowledge needed to succeed at communicating one's practice effectively through the portfolio. The choices for artifacts, decisions regarding lessons, actions taken during the video capture of a class, and the details of how to analyze student work all contribute to technical learning.

The problem would seem to be when the technical learning overwhelms and overshadows the intended focus on self-reflection and student learning. For one teacher, this problem had no resolution. Like a good science educator, Paul, from Louisiana, compared the experience of certification to the Heisenberg uncertainty principle. Paul stated: "Frankly I found that it was so difficult. It's sort of like Heisenberg's principle. You can either know where the electron is and not know what its doing or know what its doing and not know where it is. I could either teach as an effective teacher or I could go through this procedure to prove I'm an effective teacher."

The implied conclusion is that "I can't do both." Paul could not dedicate the time and energy required to communicate the quality of his practice effectively through the construction of the portfolio while also teaching with the same resource intensity that he was accustomed to without the demands of the certification process.

So, for some teachers, the certification process seemed to be a diversion from their teaching—a kind of "jumping through hoops"—rather than a stimulus for reflecting on or learning about their teaching. Technical learning from certification has value that is narrowly instrumental at best. To what percentage of teachers who fail certification would this apply? How could the process be improved to include teachers like Paul? Or does being an accomplished teacher mean that the technical knowledge is not a challenge? Does the technical knowledge somehow facilitate the dynamic learning previously discussed? These are questions all raised by this analysis; the answers must wait for future studies.

The technical learner may be motivated primarily by extrinsic rewards, but this investigation does not allow for any conclusive evidence-based conclusions. The high-stakes nature of certification created by many states' significant financial incentives may override the potential impact certification can have on improving teacher quality. It is a potential irony that the policies to encourage more National Board participation may actually diminish the quality of the experience. Some teachers faced with the possibility of significant financial gains may become myopic in their efforts to be successful with the task rather than fulfill the intent of certification.

DEFERRED LEARNING

In deferred learning, significant changes from pre- to postcertification do not translate into immediate changes in teacher practice. However, change may become apparent or take effect a few months or years after certification. In conceptual change theory, Strike and Posner hint at a "deferred" type of learning when they say that conceptual change learning was not intended to provide "a detailed account of learning that could be immediately applied to the classroom" (1992, 150). In other words, a delay between learning and action that is based on that learning is probable.

Teachers may require a certain distance from the certification experience to make sense out of what they learned and apply it to practice. For example, specific ideas pertaining to scientific inquiry may require a significant gestation period before their importance or underlying concepts are well enough understood so as to result in changes to teaching. With deferred learning, teacher quality may improve in the future, but not immediately after the experience.

Another way to think about deferred learning is to include the concept of uncertainty. To the extent that a teacher is uncertain how or if learning took place as a result of National Board certification, the possibility exists that a learning outcome might be realized sometime in the near or distant future.

When Mark, from Virginia, described whether or not National Board certification affected his practice, he made the following comment: "I'm not sure that it's changed at this point how I taught." By qualifying the statement with "at this point," Mark left open the possibility that lessons learned from the experience could become realized at a future time. Such is the character of deferred learning.

What is it about the process that might result in uncertainty regarding the learning outcomes for a candidate? One possibility relates back to the concept of the previous discussion on technical learning. For example, Melissa, from Kentucky, described her thinking on the topic as follows: "Now that I've completed everything—it's all turned in—the stressful parts of it are gone; and I have the opportunity to sort of look back and observe and see how some of the things have been incorporated into my teaching. I think that it was particularly useful."

Melissa described the stress associated with technical learning interfering with the advent of dynamic learning. What is really interesting about this remark is the phrase "I have the opportunity to sort of look back and observe and see how some of the things have been incorporated into my teaching." This act is a form of metacognition where the teacher examined her practice to identify changes and thus learning outcomes.

Melissa did not claim that she was more reflective, more student-centered, or more focused on assessment. No specific outcome is identified—yet. The teacher saw this process of learning as removed from the "self." At the time of her comment, Melissa was unaware of how her practice may have changed. It may not have changed—and then again, it may have. Melissa needed distance from the intense experience of certification, and time to look at her work and try to recognize differences in values, decision making, and beliefs that may have been instilled from the certification experience.

Malcolm, from Georgia, made a similar—if more detailed—point about uncertainty and learning. Malcolm, like Melissa, was overwhelmed by the technical learning requirements of the National Board certification process. In his comment (made approximately four months after completing his portfolio and assessment center exams), Malcolm described his learning experience as follows:

> I'm just really quickly removed from it and I haven't even found out if I've gotten it yet. I had to put a lot of time and effort into the National Board certification itself. I felt like sometimes it took away from the time I could have put into the overall classroom to help the students. By having to do some of the stuff that I was doing for National Board—such as videotaping, which is not a common practice, I was very busy. And the kids don't act the same on videotape that they would act in normal circumstances. Getting all the kids to sign the release forms—the details of the National Board—I think lead me to maybe not—think that it would benefit the students as much. Now ask me in five years after I've gotten the certification and I don't have to work on the specifics and don't have to videotape and don't have to jump through some of those hoops anymore.

The first point of interest is Malcolm's use of the phrase "quickly removed" from the certification process. Four months after finishing the requirements of certification (including a summer vacation), and this teacher was still racked with uncertainty about what, if anything, was gained from the experience.

The second important point pertains to the comment, "and I haven't even found out if I've gotten it yet." For Malcolm, a relationship between the learning experience and the status of a successful candidacy exists. If a teacher passes, he or she may look back on the experience in a more positive light, and identify learning. If unsuccessful, the opposite might occur. This comment points to the importance of collecting data from the postintervention candidates prior to the announcement of results, as was done in this study.

The third point of interest is the phrase, "I had to put a lot of time and effort into the National Board Certification itself." The use of the word "itself" is a direct indication of the technical dimension of learning associated with the certification process. The teacher did not identify specific issues of pedagogy associated with a particular entry or artifact; instead, the teacher identified the process of certification as the central issue. Malcolm went on to describe how the "certification itself" interfered with the quality of instruction for those students in class at the time of the portfolio construction.

Though Malcolm's comment provides evidence that he may be an example of deferred learning, his comment also points to the technical learning. His comments about videos, release forms, and "the details of National Board" all suggest that he learned quite a bit about the certification process.

The issue is whether the technical learning Malcolm clearly experienced interfered with or contributed to the possibility of deferred learning. In other words, if the technical aspects of certification were not such a distraction for Malcolm, would his learning be more accurately characterized as dynamic? In Malcolm's case, he might have a more definitive answer five years after the certification process.

Another way to illustrate the impact of certification on teacher quality is to consider the chemistry teachers from chapter 1, Dan and Rich. Dan and Richard provide two very different examples of how to teach chemistry. Students of both teachers performed equally well on standardized tests about the periodic table, but Dan's students were more engaged, interested, and likely to study chemistry. If Dan and Richard both went through the certification process, it is possible to guess what might happen. This hypothetical analysis further illustrates the concepts of dynamic and technical learning.

Dan's style of teaching is in much closer alignment with the Board's standards than Richard's approach to teaching. For Dan, certification confirms much of the work he currently does with students. He uses a lot of inquiry-based pedagogy to teach science. He encourages whole-class discussion on a regular basis. However, he realizes from certification that his ability to assess student learning and work with parents does not measure up well against the standards.

Dan studies about assessment and develops a series of informal instruments that allow him to focus on students' developing understanding of specific concepts that pertain to the periodic table. He also realizes that he could develop a more effective relationship with parents of some of his most difficult and rewarding students. As he tracks his communication log with parents, he begins to appreciate the value of this brief but poignant communication to the overall learning experience of his students.[5]

Dan completes his certification requirements and feels the experience confirmed his understanding of pedagogy and enriched his skills at assessment and inquiry. According to this study, Dan would be considered a dynamic learner if he immediately improves his teaching as a result of the certification process and carries those changes long after the certification requirements are completed.

Richard has a very different experience. For him, the easiest portfolio entries to complete are teaching a major idea over time and community collaborations. Richard can easily map his teaching onto the requirements and standards addressed in these entries. However, the whole-class discussion and scientific inquiry entries are very difficult. Because his conceptions of these ideas are very different from that of the Board, Richard struggles to emulate the expectations for each entry.

The video segment requirements compound the problem by raising the bar even higher. If left alone, Richard may very well finish, but feel resentment at the contrived nature of the videos and the repetitive nature of the analysis. Richard would probably be best characterized as a technical learner because he has no intention of changing his practice after completing the requirements of certification.

However, Richard's learning could be quite different if he and Dan collaborate on many of the technical issues they each face. For example, they might help each other record lessons and then talk about the videos in terms of what segments would be best to use and why.

While these discussions examine what evidence might be best to present, they are also lines of communication about teaching and learning that might not have existed if not for the video requirements. Dan can answer Richard's questions about how to go about teaching students to participate in whole-class discussion. Richard helps Dan understand his way of teaching a major idea over time. Together, they deal with the demands of the portfolio and learn from each other in the process.

If they do not collaborate, Dan passes and Richard does not. Richard learns about inquiry, engagement, and reflection, but he has no intention of continuing these approaches in the future. If the colleagues do collaborate, they might both be certified as accomplished. Richard might still be characterized as a technical learner overall, but the chance exists that he might be willing to try to promote whole-class discussion more frequently because that part of the portfolio was a positive and interesting experience. Therefore, Richard's learning might best be characterized by both some technical and dynamic learning.

It is important to note that regardless of whether Dan and Richard achieve National Board certification, the demanding certification experience acts as vehicle for both teachers to learn about their respective approaches to teaching science. According to the findings of this study, they learn about inquiry, reflection, and assessment. The precise impact this learning might have on their work with students remains a hypothetical extension of data, rather than a certainty based on evidence.

The example of Dan and Richard also reveals something quite interesting about National Board certification. While the "Dans" of the world find the process quite valuable, the quality of their instruction might not change very much, since their teaching prior to certification is already in strong alignment with the standards.

It is teachers like Richard who might be most affected by certification, since their practice is least aligned with the standards. If the "Richards" of the world are going to learn from certification in a dynamic manner, it is probable that they will need a collaborative relationship with colleagues who are understanding and dedicated.

The more mutually beneficial the collaboration, the more likely both teachers will be dynamic learners. The scenarios described here represent only two of many possible ways the experience could unfold. The following section presents not only a discussion of the likely frequency of learning types, but also some key assumptions that pertain not only to National Board certification, but to any professional learning opportunity.

FREQUENCY OF LEARNING TYPES

How often does each of these learning categories occur? What are the relative frequencies among candidates? To answer this question for the participants in this study, the portion of the interview that allowed candidates to comment openly about National Board certification was again recoded. This time, all postcertification interviews were analyzed for evidence of each of the three learning types. Comments that reflected an immediate change in practice were coded as "dynamic." Comments that focused on the process of certification, rather than on teaching, were coded as "technical." Those candidates who were unsure about the impact of the process were coded as "deferred."

Using these coding rules, a review of all responses (N = 78 teachers) reveals that approximately 40 percent of candidates fall under the dynamic learning category. Interestingly, another 40 percent of candidates could be categorized as technical learners. Roughly 20 percent of the teachers could be categorized as deferred.

While not meant to be definitive, the results suggest a possible division between science teachers and the quality of their experience with National Board that will be explored later in the chapter. If it is assumed that half of the deferred learners eventually described their experience in dynamic language, and the other half in technical terms, then it could be concluded that National Board certification improves teacher quality for approximately half of the Adolescence and Young Adult Science candidates.

EMOTIONAL CONSIDERATIONS

Dynamic, technical, and deferred learning categorized the observed outcomes in relation to their potential impact on teacher quality. However, this is but one of many possible interpretations of the results. For example, the teacher's self-reports of learning from National Board could also be interpreted from an emotional perspective. A review of the comments classified as "dynamic" could be interpreted as coming from teachers who felt "good" about the experience. For them, National Board certification was a positive endeavor. Regardless of whether they ultimately passed or failed, these teachers connected with and appreciated the process on an intellectual, philosophical, and emotional level.

Likewise, a review of comments from teachers classified as "technical" could be interpreted as originating from a more negative emotion, such as frustration, despair, annoyance, or futility. For these teachers, certification was a trial by fire that did not live up to expectations, or proved distasteful on an intellectual, philosophical, or emotional level.

The rules and requirements used by the Board to ensure a fair, equitable, and valid assessment process were incompatible with many candidates' expectations regarding what is reasonable and what is not. For those who perceived the process as too cumbersome, the learning observed is tainted by the focus on technical requirements.

The deferred learners may simply be confused emotionally one way or the other. They remain uncertain if they liked it or not and only time might someday help them resolve their situation. Perhaps whether or not they achieve National Board certification will impact their final assessment of the process. Or perhaps the process was so overwhelming and tumultuous that their lives need to recover an element of normalcy before they will understand what they may or may not have learned.

An emotional interpretation raises the question, "Why would some candidates react to the certification process in an emotionally positive, negative, or unsure fashion?" A possible answer is discussed in the final section.

As teachers reflect on the process after the fact, many may be considering how to make use of things they learned, exploring discrepancies between their preferred methods and what they perceive to be preferred by the National Board. Such reflection can move in two directions—to reaffirm a teacher's commitment to his or her existing preferences, or to provoke some change.

This study does not have data that could identify a teacher's preferred beliefs or values about his or her practice and how that practice compared with the National Board's vision of accomplished teaching prior to, during, or after the intervention. This investigation was focused on identifying what teachers learned from certification—not in actual changes to practice. However, it is reasonable to conclude that to the extent that certification unsettled some teachers' thinking, the experience holds the possibility of ushering change—but only the possibility.

MOTIVATION AND SCIENCE EDUCATORS

The identification of dynamic and technical learning outcomes divided equally among candidates in this study provides insights into the confusing world of the science educator. What might explain such a clear division among science teachers concerning the quality of their learning experience with the National Board? Possible answers include the role motivation plays in the teachers who opt to pursue certification, and the beliefs and values teachers hold regarding their personal definition of accomplished teaching.

Motivation plays a powerful role in the learning process. Teachers who are intrinsically motivated (e.g., a desire to improve) might tend to experience dynamic learning, while those motivated by extrinsic forces (e.g., money) may tend to fall into the technical category. Since 90 percent of the participants in this study had some form of financial incentive, it is unfeasible to explore possible relationships between motivation and quality of outcome on any empirical grounds. However, some interesting speculations are appropriate.

If two different groups of candidates exist—(1) those who do pursue certification because they truly want to be considered Board certified, and (2) those who do it strictly for monetary gain—then some generalizations might make sense. For example, it could be inferred that the former group would work hard, have an open mind, and probably be thought of as dynamic learners. The latter group would be those pursuing certification to get the bonus attached to success. For teachers in this group, it might be inferred that they would like to succeed with a minimum amount of work and sweat. It would be quite reasonable to think of these extrinsically motivated individuals as those who fall into the technical category.

However, such a distinction is flawed. Most likely, a range and mix of motivations is responsible for individuals pursuing National Board. Just as some extrinsically motivated teachers might embrace the standards of accomplished teaching and become dynamic learners, there could be intrinsically motivated learners who never get beyond the technical aspects of certification. With this probability in mind, what can be said about the teachers in this study? Who were they? What motivated them?

The answer may lie in the fact that these teachers self-selected themselves to participate in this study. The response rate for this study ranged from 10 to 65 percent. If these teachers belonged to the extreme end of the extrinsically motivated, then it does not make much sense that they would volunteer to participate in a time-consuming educational study.

On the other hand, if teachers had a high degree of intrinsic motivation (even if financial incentive was part of their decision to pursue Board certification), then it is imaginable that they would be more likely to agree to an invitation to participate in a study. Therefore, it can be argued that the teachers in this study could most likely be thought of as intrinsically motivated teachers. The 50 to 90 percent who never bothered to learn more about participating in this study were probably more extrinsically motivated candidates whose aim was to achieve certification with as little time and effort as possible.

Why is this speculative assertion important? Because understanding the teachers in this study helps to appreciate what it is they have had to say. More specifically, the identification of dynamic and technical learning outcomes divided equally among candidates in this study provides insights into the confusing world of the science educator. According to Adelson (2004), secondary science teachers today are caught in a bind between differing perceptions of what advanced teaching means.

On one side are those who promote and identify excellent teachers by focusing on the outcomes of practice (i.e., student achievement) and the teacher's content knowledge. The American Board for Certified Teaching Excellence represents this position. An outcome-based definition of successful science teachers does not care how teachers teach as long as they understand the content and can prove effectiveness through test scores.

Teachers who fulfill this definition tend to rely heavily (if not exclusively) on direct and undifferentiated instruction. The role of inquiry is most likely absent and assessment is only narrowly defined. How these teachers interact with colleagues, work with family and community, develop relationships with students, and contribute to the success of the school is absent from the picture.

Also missing are the knowledge and skill sets associated with how to prepare the way for productive student learning, how to advance student understanding, and how to establish a favorable context for student learning. Each of these areas of knowledge and skill are considered (or assumed) superfluous to the ultimate goal of higher student achievement.

At the opposite end of the spectrum, teachers are presented with a definition of accomplished teaching that focuses on process (the means and parameters of practice). In this view, represented by the National Board for Professional Teaching Standards, outcomes are valued, but more broadly defined. Outcomes can be test scores, but they can also be written work by students, artifacts that represent cognitive growth, or actions and achievements outside of class that contribute to the overall quality of teaching and learning.

This complex perspective of advanced teaching defines *accomplished* by not only considering teachers' content knowledge, but also by including the other dimensions associated with preparing, advancing, and facilitating student learning. For secondary science teachers, the messages received by representatives from both sides of the debate can be confusing and disorienting.

Teachers are in the impossible position of trying to find a way to serve two masters. On the one side, teachers feel tremendous pressure from school, district, and state agencies to improve student test scores by literally any means possible. For some teachers, this means teaching for the test, which often results in dull and repetitive classroom experiences. And, on the other side, teachers must wrestle with the complex nature of practice revealed to them in teacher preparation programs, colleges of education, and advanced degree programs.

If these two opposing views were not difficult enough, teachers also face desperate parents who expect their children to not only do well on tests, but also develop a healthy self-esteem, a positive self-image as a learner, and the skills and knowledge to be successful after graduation.

Teachers today find themselves in a grave and perilous position of being damned if they do and damned if they don't. This dichotomy is based on the assumption that a more complex approach to teaching and learning may not result in adequate test scores—or at least not as good as those achieved through "drill and kill" direct instruction. Even the National Board admits that a more complex approach to practice may "temporarily jeopardize students' performance on standardized tests" (National Board for Professional Teaching Standards, 1991, 25). However, one should consider the entire range of learning outcomes, and not just test scores.

In terms of possible impact on teacher quality, an analysis of candidate responses seems to suggest a mix of dynamic, technical, and deferred learning. Some teachers might regard Board certification as a genuine learning opportunity, others might undertake it for the extrinsic rewards, and still others might learn from the process in a gradually evolving manner.

Mixed motives and outcomes are more nearly the norm in human affairs than singular or pristine results. In fact, the different categories of learning described in this study support the conclusion that Board certification provides the opportunity for teachers to learn about specific aspects of their work. How that learning impacts practice, however, remains unclear.

SUMMARY

The National Board standards represent a broad consensus within the science education community that, in Joseph Schwab's evocative terms, science is a "narrative of inquiry" (1978, 271), not simply a "rhetoric of conclusions" (134). Instruction that aspires to teach students the methods of science is a critically important issue for the twenty-first century. Consequently, the underlying values represented by the National Board standards constitute a professional consensus; what these standards "teach" about instruction are eminently defensible.

However, in a field of faith and trust like education, where scientific principles answer few questions and intuition is overused, it is understandable why education leaders want a system of teacher performance evaluation that is based on concrete and assessable data. National Board certification exposes teachers to a vision of their profession that moves beyond knowledge and skill acquisition to embrace the beauty, complexity, and uncertainty that is this vision of teaching and learning. If improved practice begins with learning, then National Board certification is a good place to start.

Teachers in this study demonstrated significant learning in the areas of scientific inquiry, assessment, and reflection, regardless of whether they were successful at achieving Board certification. Therefore, it appears that the benefits of Board certification go beyond the immediate financial rewards some successful candidates receive to take the form of improved knowledge and practice in science instruction for both those who achieve and those who do not achieve certification.

If teacher learning is considered an important component to improving teacher quality and ultimately student learning, then these results point to the possibility that the process of Board certification may positively impact the quality of instruction (as defined by the National Board) and students' learning experiences. Further research on this relationship is needed to pinpoint the degree to which science teaching improves, the duration of those changes, and the impact of changes in practice on a range of student learning outcomes. On balance, National Board certification is a worthwhile form of professional development. The caveats, as always, are important, but so is the preponderance of the evidence.

NOTES

1. See Cohen, "Teaching practice," 1988; Cohen, "The case of Ms. Oublier," 1990; and Tyack and Cuban, *Tinkering towards utopia,* 1996, for examples of how teachers adapt reforms for classroom practice.

2. Mullens et al., *Student learning,* 1996.

3. Ibid., 9.

4. Holmes Group, *Tomorrow's schools of education,* 1995.

5. The communication log is part of the fourth entry of the portfolio, "Documented Accomplishments." Candidates maintain a log of all correspondence with parents and community leaders. They are then asked to reflect on the significance and role of this communication to fostering student learning in the classroom.

8

Improving National Board Certification

While this study substantiates the value of National Board certification as a professional learning opportunity, it also reveals weaknesses in the process. The discussion that follows considers a series of recommendations regarding how the Board might improve the quality of its services and adapt to a changing educational environment.

These are two very important perspectives. The first perspective teases meaning from the findings in this study and applies them directly to the task of improving professional learning opportunities offered by the certification process. While evidence from the dynamic learners makes it clear that Board certification offers teachers a unique opportunity to improve the quality of their work with learners, it is also clear from the evidence represented by technical learners that the process could be improved.

The second perspective is less grounded in evidence and based more on intense and sustained reflection. Over the course of this particular study, much thought has been paid to a wide array of questions. However, most of these queries can be summed up by asking: How can the Board better position itself in a volatile education policy environment?

The relationship between these two perspectives is complex, in a chicken-or-the-egg kind of way. Does reform begin with improved certification, which would lead to a more relevant organization? Or do institutional improvements result in a better evaluative service? While not mutually exclusive, each choice has implications to how the Board plans out its future efforts. Optimally, both strategies should be complementary and addressed at the same time. This is important to remember when considering the suggestions and ideas that follow.

IMPROVE THE ORGANIZATION'S BUSINESS MODEL

When the Board began its work in 1987, it received a grant from the Carnegie Corporation of New York. The grant was used to set up the organization and develop standards and assessments. When certification of teachers began in 1993, the Board was ready to request federal funding to support its initial work.

At the time, the Clinton administration was very supportive of the Board's efforts because they addressed a dire need to differentiate between adequate and exceptional teachers. Because of President Clinton's leadership, significant federal dollars were invested in the reform, with the goal of certifying one hundred thousand teachers. A strong federal push for the National Board was welcomed by many states, especially those in the south and west.

For the southern states, the National Board offered a viable and economical solution to a big problem. The southern states tended to pay their teachers the least compared with the rest of the country. Rather than raise everyone's salaries, National Board offered these states a valid and reliable means of identifying certain teachers who would be paid more. Certification allowed the teachers in these states to get paid more through yearly bonuses and stipends that brought their compensation up to something comparable to their colleagues in other high-paying states.

For a time, it was a very successful strategy for addressing a difficult and expensive process. Board certification gave teachers in the system hope of earning more pay. The possibility of better salaries through Board certification improved the retention of teachers and promoted a vision of teaching that schools and districts could endorse.

However, with the incoming Bush administration in 2001 and the passage of No Child Left Behind, the criteria for defining an accomplished teacher began to change. It changed from the Board's vision of teaching as an intellectual, complex, and reflective endeavor to one that focused solely on a teacher's ability to raise student achievement as demonstrated by ever-improving test scores. According to this rubric, the "superiority" of Board-certified teachers over their noncertified counterparts came under fire.

As the public discourse moved away from issues of teacher quality and toward improving test scores as a way of assessing school quality, federal support for the National Board diminished. States picked up the slack in many cases, but as state budgets have come under pressure during recessionary times, funding for Board certification has been one of the first places states look to cut spending.

Now, the Board finds itself with its hat in its hands, desperately trying to figure out how to find the funds to support the current financial model. Developing strategies that piggy back on federal legislation (e.g., Race to the Top funds) is a stop-gap measure, and not a strategy that ensures the long-term sustainability of the organization.

Compounding the problem is the politicization of the National Board. Because President Clinton provided initial support for Board certification, the next administration was less inclined to provide federal funds in part because the National Board for Professional Teaching Standards (NBPTS) was associated so strongly with a Democratic party reform. So complete was Bush's disdain of anything Clintonesque when it came to education that the reauthorization of the Elementary and Secondary Education Act (No Child Left Behind) had the word "Goal" stripped out because it was reminiscent of Clinton's education initiative known as "Goals 2000."

After struggling financially for eight years, the Board is now feeling a sense of relief with President Barak Obama's Democratic administration. However, their relief may be short-lived. While the Race to the Top funds may provide additional measures to support certification for states that win the awards, there is diminishing public support for the National Board as a reform worthy of perpetual federal funding.

Accomplished teaching is not a political issue. It should not be dependent on what party is in power or who holds the purse strings. Quality teaching is a national issue, and one that should be blind to politics, poverty, and personal convictions. To become a truly nonpartisan, nongovernmental entity, the National Board needs to wean itself off the federal government teat and establish a more sustainable and independent means of funding its work.

If NBPTS can become less dependent on, if not completely free of, government support, much of the controversy over whether it represents a worthwhile investment will also disappear. To accomplish this goal, the Board faces two considerable challenges:

1. Convince the entire teaching community to share in the cost of running the NBPTS through a $20 annual contribution. If all three million teachers in the United States each paid $20, the Board would have sufficient funds to work with twenty thousand candidates per year.
2. Work with states, districts, and unions to ensure that the National Board is integrated into salary contracts, just as graduate credit and years of experience are currently addressed.

By addressing both of these goals simultaneously, the Board can free itself from federal tax payer dollars and avoid having to legitimize itself according to whatever educative fad might come and go. After standardized tests, something else will gain the favor of the easily impressed. If the Board is to stand for a vision of teaching and learning that can withstand the inevitable waves of reform, then it must become an expression of the teaching community. National Board cannot afford to be an opportunity for a few, but rather needs to be an accepted ideal for all.

Unlike the medical profession, where the costs of certification represent a much smaller percentage of the individual's income, teachers must consider different mechanisms to support and ensure the high and rigorous standards among their ranks. One way to address the problem is to dissipate the high costs of complex assessments among greater numbers of individuals. If everyone in teaching contributed a little, then the costs of advanced certification could be brought down for those who decide to achieve such a goal.

Currently, the 3.2 million members of the National Educators Association pay on average about $100 per year in dues. The dues are divided among local, state, and national offices of the union. If 10 to 20 percent of dues could be dedicated to National Board certification, a big step in becoming a truly professional organization would be taken. In return for their support, teachers would become *de facto* owners of the program. As owners, they would want to have input into the operations, assessments, and agenda that the Board sets for itself.

Instead of having an open-ended invitation to all teachers to become candidates each year, the Board would offer a limited number of slots allocated according to population density. Each region could send up a specific number of candidates for National Board certification. Those who wish to be candidates might be preassessed by current Board-certified teachers, and those deemed most worthy of the opportunity would be encouraged to apply. The rest would receive recommendations about how to improve their chances during the next round of certification. In this approach, the rigor and integrity of the process would remain intact (if not become strengthened) and the prestige of the certificate would be improved.

While distributing costs among all teachers would go a long way to making the Board more sustainable, it would not cover all the costs associated with certification. Other sources for funding include candidates, districts, and foundations. For example, every candidate should probably pay for a small portion of the certification process. Whether it is $50 or $200, the candidate should shoulder some of the burden. After all, he or she will be the immediate benefactor of the process, and therefore should provide some support for the costs. This is especially true if the outcome of certification is integrated into a teacher's compensation schedule.

Districts can also share in the costs of this process, but not necessarily as funders. Rather, NBPTS should be included in the local district contracts and handled in the same manner as professional development opportunities such as conferences, summer institutes, graduate credits, and professional development hours.

If approached from this perspective, the incentive to pursue National Board is integrated into the fabric of the contract, and would not represent any additional cost to the district in terms of bonuses or yearly stipends. At the same time, teachers would have the opportunity to pursue National Board certification at the appropriate time in their careers, without worrying about whether state-level funding will be available.

If the Board can succeed in convincing the community of teachers that they share a common vision of exceptional teaching, then market pressures will go a long way to fostering change. Those districts or states that do not offer support and rewards to teachers for participating in the National Board certification process will be less attractive to prospective teachers than areas that do.

While the addition of National Board as an institutionally accepted means of improving teacher quality would cost no more than current practices with formal graduate education, it would offer teachers an additional option for professional growth. It would also provide the much needed consistency regarding what accomplished practice looks like from one year to the next. By institutionalizing National Board certification within the framework of union contracts, the Board could focus on improving the quality of its mission to define, assess, and foster accomplished teaching.

From one perspective, a closer relationship between the National Educators Association and the National Board is a match made in heaven. For some time now, the union has been criticized for not paying closer attention to issues of quality and instruction. Preoccupied with bread-and-butter issues as defined in contracts, some union leaders are pushing for a "new unionism" that is just as interested in the quality of instruction as it is in the type of benefit packages teachers receive. Without having to reinvent anything, the union could use the Board to represent this pedagogical perspective, while maintaining a keen watch on the rights and benefits of their members.

For the Board, the relationship would offer a well-established network and organization that stretches down to nearly every public school classroom in the country. The ability to mobilize, organize, and inspire teachers to pursue certification would be greatly enhanced with the authority and power of the union behind it. The fact that the union is represented on the NBPTS's board of directors is an encouraging sign that the relationship could evolve into something more meaningful for both parties.

Getting a portion of dues to cover the costs of certification and developing closer ties with the teacher unions are easy tasks compared with the need to convince teachers that NBPTS represents the ideal form of instruction for the entire community. Changing the culture of teaching from one centered on egalitarianism to one of hierarchy based on quality is a tall order. Teachers are not easily put into a single category.

Even though teachers play an important role in the establishment of standards, this has not been a democratic process. Those who work for the Board do not necessarily represent the views of their local colleagues. Participating teachers represent individual professionals selected by the Board for a specific purpose. However, if National Board is to become a soapbox for the profession regarding what constitutes best practice, than there must be a near-complete endorsement from the teaching community.

While most teachers may not want to go through the rigorous assessment process, they should still be able to appreciate its value to the profession and to those colleagues who do complete it—whether successful or not. This is a tough task, akin to herding cats—it's just not part of the teacher psyche to conform. However difficult the challenge might be, NBPTS might not have a choice. It must make the case that the option of NBPTS is beneficial to all teachers, and not just those who succeed at being certified.

This is not a new idea. Back in 1985, Albert Shanker, then president of the American Federation of Teachers said, "We don't have the right to be called professionals—and we will never convince the public that we are—unless we are prepared to decide what constitutes competence in our profession and what constitutes incompetence and apply those definitions to ourselves and our colleagues."[1]

More than twenty-five years later, the community of teachers is still floundering around the same challenge. While the Board is the most mature and meaningful means of expressing a consensus, other less significant attempts are coming online. The American Board for Certified Teaching Excellence, National Institute for Teaching Excellence, and others all hope to speak for the profession regarding how excellence is defined. NBPTS needs to make the case that they are best positioned to represent the values, skills, and knowledge the teaching community should embrace to qualify for accomplished status.

The fate of NBPTS may have very little to do with the Board's direct efforts to become relevant, and more to do with teachers' willingness to embrace a structure that ensures that at least some members of the community are elevated in status, and the rest by proximity.

Teachers face a choice in this work: accept the status quo and remain in an egalitarian occupation where excellence is defined by outsiders, or embrace the idea that some teachers are more effective at engaging learners and fostering understanding than others.

The former choice describes not so much a profession as a trade. In this view, at least everyone could take comfort in each other's misery of being told what to do and how to do it. In the latter choice, teachers retain a say in what constitutes exceptional teaching, and the values and beliefs that define the profession. Just as a rising tide lifts all boats, teachers who achieve National Board certification improve the profession for their colleagues.

If the Board does not address the flawed business model that it currently uses, any further discussion on how to improve the Board's work might be moot. However, in the interest of optimism, a series of ideas are presented next that do not change the nature of the Board's work as much as enhance what it is already trying to do. Suggestions dealing with efficiency, standards revisions, public relations, and potential threats to validity are addressed.

CONVERSION TO ELECTRONIC PORTFOLIOS

One of the biggest steps the Board can take to improve the quality of certification as a professional learning opportunity is to reduce the technical demands of the process. Currently, approximately one-third of a completed portfolio is dedicated to organizational paperwork. Documents to ensure identity, authenticity of evidence, and proper assessment procedures are required throughout the laborious endeavor. With new online technologies available, most, if not all, of these technical requirements could be addressed.

In the era of YouTube and online learning environments, the National Board has yet to embrace the potential of electronic mediums to foster and enhance the complete certification experience.[2] For example, it would not be an insurmountable task to make certification a paperless process. By providing every candidate with a secure website, entries could be uploaded to a virtual portfolio as they are completed. Evidence such as student work, videos, and analysis could all be scanned, transferred, or converted into appropriate file types. The files could then be uploaded and saved in a secure online database. Reliance on paper and overnight services would no longer be necessary.

Of course, an electronic approach would require that teachers have access to and knowledge of computers. For some teachers, this could be an issue. However, in the second decade of the twenty-first century, any teacher not comfortable with computers or web technologies probably has no place teaching the next generation.

Assuming a degree of computer literacy sufficient to complete an electronic portfolio could be something the Board makes clear to any prospective candidate prior to registration. For most teachers, this would not be an issue. For a small minority of educators, the technology requirements of certification might be the necessary stimulus for them to finally join the online revolution.

Converting from an analog to a digital portfolio would have many advantages for the Board. First, by reducing the tedious organization of papers, the certification process could better focus on the issues of teaching and learning according to the standards of accomplished practice. Second, an electronic portfolio would streamline the assessment process and make it more cost-efficient and effective. With electronic files, portfolios would no longer need to be physically deconstructed in one city for evaluation and then reconstructed in another city for tabulation and storage. Electronic portfolios would ensure a more efficient means of assessing candidate work.

Third, with the proper software development, much of the redundancy found in portfolios could be eliminated. In the current form, candidates need to describe repeatedly the context of their school. In an electronic portfolio, they could do it once, and the software could automatically make the information available for assessors evaluating each of the four entries.

Significant challenges are associated with a transition to an electronic portfolio. However, none of these issues represent problems that cannot be solved with careful planning. The upfront costs of converting to a paperless process would be significant, but would pay for themselves over time. If such a conversion could conservatively save 15 percent, this would translate into a $300 savings per candidate on the cost of certification.

With electronic portfolios, assessors could score entries from their living room laptops. While this convenience could save a significant amount in travel costs for the Board, it would come at a price. Evidence suggests that the community of discourse that develops among assessors is vital to the validity of their work. Without the opportunity to discuss assessment (especially during the training phase), assessors' work might not be as effective.

Likewise, online portfolios for candidates might foster further isolation. Where online collaborations might be more possible, the immediacy of colleagues working together on issues of certification may be responsible for the most fertile areas of teacher learning. This aspect of the process could be preserved and even enhanced if the conversion to the electronic portfolio was carefully planned with the input from candidates.

Electronic portfolios would also help address the serious potential problem of academic dishonesty. With the numbers of candidates growing every year, the need to be more diligent with regard to cheating has never been more important. For some entries, teachers might go online and purchase the work of a successful candidate. With a few modifications, the strong entry could be modified to serve the purposes of the new candidate.

Ironically, the same technology that makes this kind of cheating possible also serves to scan for and identify fraudulent efforts. Just as professors routinely scan student papers for plagiarism, the Board could scan all work for evidence of dishonest activity. This can only be done if the portfolio is electronic.

Probably the biggest adjustment for candidates in the electronic system would be the requirements for a digital video. For many candidates, a video recording (analog or digital) is still the preferred medium of their school. Recording, transferring, and uploading digital video files might be a challenge for some. However, if the Board provided some online tutorials for how to execute this process successfully, candidates would probably be able to accomplish this aspect of the work. For those candidates unable to convert to digital video files, the Board might offer the service at an additional charge.

If digital video represents the biggest challenge for the candidates, digital security represents the Board's most pressing requirement for the transition. The database that interfaces, stores, and shares information must be secure enough to prevent unauthorized access. While no system is 100-percent secure, the science of web security has matured enough in the last decade that a system could be developed to meet the needs of the Board. If it works well (for the most part) for banks, hospitals, and businesses, then why not for the National Board?

By converting from an analog to digital portfolio, the National Board could greatly reduce the technical requirements of certification and improve the time and focus candidates spend on issues of teaching and learning. Why this has not happened yet remains a mystery. However, if the Board wants to improve the quality of its services, it is a change that must happen sooner rather than later. In a world where most children routinely record, edit, and upload videos to websites, teachers have no excuses not to make use of this technology for professional purposes.

AN INCLUSIVE VISION OF ACCOMPLISHED TEACHING

The National Board's purpose is to promote a "peer-developed" vision of what accomplished teaching looks like. If that mission is considered a positive message (that teaching is a knowledge-based, complex, reflective practice that focuses on individual student needs in relation to learning objectives), then the Board has been successful in getting a portion of the teaching community to investigate, consider, and even "test drive" practices according to the standards of accomplished teaching. According to the findings from this study, teachers who test drive the standards learn about assessment, reflection, and inquiry—three important dimensions of accomplished teaching.

However, not everyone loves the experience. For some, certification is a tedious and technical task. The Board needs to appreciate the positive impact it has on roughly half the candidates, but also needs to listen to and respect the voices of discontent. The fact that roughly 40 percent of candidates learn about the standards and apply their learning immediately to the classroom would inspire envy in any professional development program.

However, the challenge for the Board is to figure out how best to hear the voices of those teachers who may very well be accomplished in the classroom, but just do not relate to the Board's standards for accomplished teaching. For example, Sam, a candidate from West Virginia who participated in this study, stated: "My practice doesn't match with standards I wanted to do or what I would normally do. I did try to conform the best I could do morally. But I was just not going to make a contrived situation; but I did try to meet their criteria."

Why did Sam not see his values or ideas of accomplished teaching reflected in the Board's vision? Sam described a struggle between conforming to the requirements of the Board and what he believes to be best for his students. On the one hand he wanted to "try to meet their criteria" and on the other, he was "not going to make a contrived situation."

Melinda, another candidate from this study, had an experience similar to Sam's. She stated, "I felt that National Board Certification didn't value the same things that I was really good at. So I had to change my way of teaching to satisfy those requirements."

What does Melinda value that is not reflected in the Board's standards? Could it be that Melinda saw herself as a master of the Socratic method of teaching? Was she the kind of teacher who could present content to students through lecture and presentation in a manner that engaged and educated students? Though Melinda ultimately found the experience to be a positive one, she still believed that her ideas regarding good teaching were not fully represented in the Board's standards.

One possible explanation for Melinda's and Sam's struggles is that they believed in a vision of teaching with fewer complexities, focused more on outcomes than on process. Maybe Sam and Melinda were fantastic lecturers who wove a tale of content that kept their students enthralled with the concepts, personalities, and relevance of science to modern society. Perhaps they had the standardized test scores, parent feedback, and student approval to back up their self-assessment. If true, Board certification would allow little opportunity for these kinds of teachers to showcase and provide evidence for their skills and accomplishments. Should the Board's definition of accomplished teaching be changed to include teachers like Sam and Melinda? If so, what would the changes look like?

If the Board were to revise its definition of accomplished science teaching to include a respect and recognition for the effective use of direct instruction, then maybe Sam would not have felt so caught in a bind. By including language in the standards that supports the effective and selective use of lecture, and a portfolio entry targeting this set of skills and knowledge, the Board would promote a more balanced vision of how accomplished teaching is defined.

While not diminishing the importance of inquiry or whole-class discussion, it is reasonable to include in the standards an aspect of science instruction that nearly all science teachers employ at one time or another. Such an omission is quite conspicuous. Should it be assumed that if a teacher knows and can do everything in the standards, then he or she is necessarily an effective direct instructor? Such an assumption is incorrect. If the Board's standards really are a "broad consensus" of what accomplished teaching looks like, then the voices of teachers like Sam and Melinda need to be included in the standards re-evaluation process.

The Board could take two steps to address this issue. First, the Board could include a specific standard that describes a teacher's communication skills. The standard might read as follows:

> Accomplished teachers communicate in a clear and accessible manner to diverse audiences of learners. Technology can enhance the overall quality and impact of teacher communication by addressing the visual, auditory, and tactile learning needs of students.

To assess this standard, the Board might incorporate a ten- to fifteen-minute video clip into entry 1 (Teaching a Major Idea Over Time) to demonstrate a teacher's communication skills. The video might be a lecture, a technology-enhanced presentation, or demonstration of a scientific concept followed by Socratic-type questions and answers. Multiple ways of addressing communication skills could be used to demonstrate evidence for the standard.

By acknowledging that direct instruction is an equivalent skill to whole-class discussion and scientific inquiry, National Board would take a big step away from being labeled a solely constructivist progressive organization, and move closer to a true reflection of what exceptional teachers do every day in classrooms across the country. By formalizing the vital roles that inquiry, discussion, and lecture each play in a productive learning experience, NBPTS can stop alienating teachers like Sam and Melinda and give them a reason to value the certificate. In addition, a communication standard would allow for the Board to define what effective direct instruction is, and the means by which it is accurately assessed.

It is clear why the Board's standards have a constructivist slant toward student-centered pedagogy—it is a form of teaching that is widely accepted and supported by many powerful voices in the education community. Educational literature has a long history going back to John Dewey's *How We Think* (1910), which details the merits of student-centered approaches to the quality and depth of learning outcomes.

Such a pervasively strong value and belief can be seen in the many national organizations that proselytize such approaches through their websites, reports, publications, and services. Educational organizations such as the Interstate New Teacher Assessment and Support Consortium, National Council for Accreditation of Teacher Education, the National Science Teacher Association, American Association for the Advancement of Science, and the National Research Council are but a few of the big players that push for constructivist approaches to education.

Yet most teachers remain suspicious of these approaches for a variety of reasons. Some see them as too time consuming. Some see student-centered approaches as sacrificing too much control over student behavior. Some see the strategies as ineffective or unreasonable in an era of accountability that values standardized tests as the most important yardstick of success.

However, in its efforts to include more sophisticated forms of pedagogy in the standards for accomplished teaching, the Board seems to have inadvertently forgotten about the important role direct instruction plays in the accomplished teacher's tool box. It could be argued that most teachers rely too heavily on lecturing as the predominant, if not only, form of pedagogy. It could also be argued that most teachers employ a form of lecturing that is both ineffective and uninformed.

Both arguments are reasons to include a communications standard into the definition of accomplished teaching. An effective demonstration of direct instruction is just as indicative of accomplished teaching as an engaging inquiry activity or whole-class discussion. Accomplished teachers should be able to do all three effectively to achieve specific learning outcomes.

Requiring candidates to demonstrate and reflect upon their lecturing abilities according to newly added standards would accomplish two goals:

1. Give candidates who consider themselves primarily student-centered practitioners the opportunity to showcase their skills at communicating content to a class of learners.
2. Attract a greater spectrum of teachers to National Board candidacy who can better see their values, beliefs, and abilities reflected in the standards of accomplished teaching.

If more traditional-type teachers become engaged in National Board certification as a result of a more balanced view of pedagogy, then there is an increased probability that approximately half of those teachers may come to appreciate, learn, and use some student-centered strategies effectively in their classrooms. If National Board claims to be an accurate reflection of what teachers think accomplished teaching entails, than the Board should work to make its consensus more balanced. Just as no one wants to eat the same meal every day, no matter how delicious and exquisitely prepared, students do not want to learn by way of the same approach to teaching every day, whether it be student-centered or traditional.

In education, finding balance and matching strategy to objective is a key challenge if the needs of all students are to be met. Employing only one strategy (even if done well) will not succeed equally with all students. While a few students might enjoy the repetitiveness of an experience every day, most will find it redundant, boring, and disengaging.

Teachers need to be able to call upon a "tool box" of abilities to match a particular learning goal with an appropriate strategy to meet the needs of a specific audience. Just as an inquiry approach can become tired, so can direct instruction. Learners need exposure to an array of teaching strategies to have multiple opportunities to approach and understand specific concepts and skills. While National Board emphasizes the student-centered pedagogies, it should not lose sight of the inherent and practical value of effective direct instruction.

TEST DATA AS A RESOURCE FOR TEACHING

One of the biggest criticisms of the Board is that its standards do not consider the role of standardized test data as a resource for today's teacher. Setting aside the issue of student achievement as a direct reflection of teacher quality, tests offer today's teacher an additional source of information about his or her students that could inform practice. The idea that a teacher should be required to demonstrate in the portfolio the ability to access, analyze, and use this data to shape instruction is something that seems to be a glaring omission.

Part of the problem pertains to the equitable priority of the certification process. Certification should not be a process that favors some over others, especially on issues that do not allow equal access by all. Standardized tests are an example of a resource that is not universally accessible throughout the K–12 education system. While testing has grown in prominence, its use remains spotty at best. Not every subject, for every grade, in every state participates in annual testing. Thus, some teachers have access to the data, and others do not.

For a fifth grade elementary teacher, access is granted pretty much across the board, as this was a grade singled out for mathematics and reading testing by No Child Left Behind. However, teachers of earlier grades may not have access to any equivalent form of student performance data (nor, it could be argued, should they). For the Board, this raises an interesting problem: incorporate test data analysis into certification and favor certain groups of teachers, or ignore test data and ensure an equitable, if incomplete, vision of accomplished teaching.

One possible means of addressing this issue is for the standards to address the use of test scores as a resource for understanding learners and shaping instruction. If "tests" are defined broadly to include both standardized and norm-referenced forms of assessments, more teachers would have access to some form of independent student performance data regarding a specific skill or domain.

As long as teachers employ test data in their analysis of learning, it might be sufficient for the time being to satisfy critics who make a strong argument for data-driven decision making in education. In the meantime, standards for all certificate areas should be revised to include the teacher's role in using test data to shape instructional practices.

PUBLIC RELATIONS

While the Board has done an admirable job of providing a valid and reliable assessment of accomplished teaching, it has utterly failed to communicate its mission to the greater general public. After two decades of work, many areas of the country have no idea what National Board certification is or what it means.

In a society that learns about itself through the efforts of public relation firms, there is no excuse for why the Board cannot also succeed in communicating its message to the general public. If effective, all parents would be clambering for their children to have a Board-certified teacher—or at least for their local school to have a Board-certified teacher among its faculty. Without this kind of pressure, NBPTS has little hope that it can continue to grow and be an influential factor in education.

Any public relations effort must dispel several misconceptions about the work of the National Board. For example, many believe that:

- NBPTS is a left-wing, progressive vision of teaching and learning.
- National Board certification allows any teacher to teach in any state.
- National Board certification replaces state licensing.
- Accomplished teaching is identified through test scores.
- NBPTS is an arm of the government.
- NBPTS is just another attempt to define accomplished teaching.
- National Board–certified teachers are elitist and not elite.
- NBPTS is more expensive than other forms of professional development.

To date, the Board has sponsored one significant effort to spread its message. Teaching America about Accomplished Teaching (TAAT) was a program developed in 2002–2004 that aimed to improve the public profile of National Board certification. TAAT represented an in-house project that aimed to harness the work and expertise of Board-certified teachers to figure out ways to spread the Board's message.[3]

Unfortunately, it was not very successful. In states like New Hampshire, most teachers do not even know what the NBPTS is or what it tries to do. While TAAT did produce a publication, it had little impact on educating the public about the work of the Board.[4] Public relations is not classroom teaching, and should be approached in collaboration with experienced professionals.

For nearly twenty-five years, the NBPTS brand is closely associated with quality teaching and learning. Over this time, the brand has increased in value, but it remains very vulnerable to events that are beyond the control of the Board. For example, if a National Board–certified teacher were to do something offensive or reprehensible, the ensuing media frenzy would seriously tarnish the good reputation that the Board has worked so hard and so long to develop.

One National Board teacher caught having an affair with a student or committing a terrible crime would cast a long shadow over the entire organization, and all other Board-certified teachers. While such events are beyond the control of the Board, the Board should have protocols in place to deal with such an occurrence when, and if, it happens.

One way to deal with such a crisis is to preemptively work with the public to identify what it means to be an accomplished teacher. Like the prior public relations discussion, this depends on the work of experts. If NBPTS has working relationships with such public relations persons, then when the inevitable bad news comes to the attention of the news media, they will be ready to address it quickly and effectively. Investments in public relations need to happen before—not after—the need becomes immediate.

THREATS TO BRAND QUALITY

The other serious threat to the Board's good name and reputation comes from candidates who get caught cheating on the certification requirements. As alluded to earlier, with the advent of communication technology, the World Wide Web, and universal access, desperate candidates will be able to find the work of others and adapt it as their own. If this should happen, and comes to the attention of the public, the Board's image as a professional organization representing the most accomplished teachers would come under significant fire.

A case of cheating made public would not only hurt the Board as a brand, but bring into question the validity of every teacher who ever achieved Board certification. The last thing a Board-certified teacher wants to do is defend himself or herself publicly and say, "I did not cheat on my National Board certification." Yet if such a story were to become public news, then that is precisely what many teachers would feel the need to say.

For its part, the Board can take several important actions prophylactically to address this potential problem. First, it can continue soliciting studies similar to Lloyd Bond and colleagues' validity study (2000). The more investigations that help solidify the validity of the certification process to identify and assess accomplished teachers, the stronger the Board's position will become. The stronger the Board, the better it will be able to weather whatever storms come its way.

Second, the Board can review, revise, and strengthen security protocols associated with certification. As suggested in the section on the electronic portfolio, investments in cyber-security could help to deter plagiarism and other forms of dishonest practice.

Finally, the Board can better emphasize the role of professional integrity before, during, and after the certification process. By being very clear about what types of collaboration are appropriate and what kinds are not, the Board can keep candidates well informed and prepared to participate in an authentic and meaningful manner. In the end, it is up to each and every candidate to provide an honest presentation of one's practice.

THE SIREN'S CALL FOR INCREASING NUMBERS

One of the most appealing aspects of National Board as a reform effort lies in its appreciation of and respect for the classroom teacher. Since the Board's inception, classroom teachers have served on the Board and greatly influenced the standards and assessment practices. The idea that NBPTS would become a vehicle for teachers to define excellence in their specific areas of expertise is and always has been a cornerstone of the organization's work.

What is exceptional teaching? The answer is more meaningful if it comes from those who live with the question every day of their working lives. It is a question left to classroom teachers rather than academics, policy makers, administrators, or politicians. While each of these education stakeholders provides an important and valued perspective, the classroom teacher is best positioned to describe the knowledge, skills, and dispositions necessary to be accomplished.

A few years ago, the National Board instituted the "Take One!" program. Take One allows teachers to complete one of the video entries for National Board certification rather than tackling all four entries in one year. If a teacher wants to investigate what National Board certification is all about, he or she may opt to explore it by participating in the Take One program.

The original hope for Take One was that it would attract a greater pool of teachers to try out the process required for certification. Once teachers experience the process, it was hoped that many would go on to become full-fledged candidates. Unfortunately, the results have been mixed, with fewer teachers than expected deciding to pursue certification. Because Take One is not certification, the learning outcomes identified in this research are not generalizable to the Take One programs.

Assuming that a teacher who constructs a whole-class discussion entry through the Take One program would learn about assessment and reflection to the degree supported by the research in this book would be erroneous. While the two experiences share many similarities, they are not the same. Part of the rigor associated with certification has to do with the complexity of the task and its knack for completely immersing the candidate in work focused on teaching and learning. Without the rigor and pressure to complete the entire process within a given time frame, it is unlikely that teachers will learn anything equivalent with the Take One alternative. However, future research in this area could be helpful in clarifying the relationship.

The Board's latest initiative is to expand its work to include administrators. While standards for administrative leadership are a fine idea, it is unclear if it is the purview of the NBPTS to create them. While it may help to increase the numbers of candidates, it is unclear what effect it will have on the certification of teachers. Will it make administrators more supportive of teachers who are thinking about Board certification? Or, will the resources and time invested in the creation of an administrative certificate distract from the more important work of certifying teachers? Like the Take One initiative, the impact of administrative certification will be interesting to observe.

An unintended consequence of the Take One program is its dilution of the reputation of NBPTS as a professional learning opportunity. Every time the Board develops a program or policy that makes it easier for teachers to complete certification (e.g., Take One or banking scores for up to three years), they run the risk of diminishing the certification's hard-earned reputation for being rigorous and truly challenging to complete successfully. Rather than a candidate being exposed to certification in its entirety, teachers participating in Take One might come away thinking "that was not so difficult" and spread the false idea that Board certification is nothing special.

It is better to offer a service that is effective and rigorous than a policy that aims to increase the number of candidates. Because the Board is so dependent on the certification fees, there is a strong pressure for ever-increasing numbers of participating teachers. While this desire is understandable, it does not help to achieve the long-term mission of the organization.

National Board would be well served to remember its history. Distractions such as securing adequate funding from year to year, attracting more teachers to sample the certification process, and expanding the mission to include administrators may take away from the Board's original and still-relevant mission: to define, assess, and foster accomplished teaching.

Increasing the ranks of National Board–certified teachers has depended heavily on states passing legislation that commits the state to pay successful candidates stipends or bonuses. Some bonuses have been as high as $5,000 per year or $50,000 over the ten-year life of the certificate. While this strategy is very effective at attracting qualified teachers to pursue certification, it does require continuous public approval for the commitment of additional tax dollars. Adding the public compensation dimension outside the traditional labor contract between teachers and districts or states complicates and politicizes the National Board. Ideally, this is a problem that should be addressed within the established framework of collective bargaining, and integrated into teacher contracts.

Teachers are understandably and rightly concerned with issues of compensation. However, other incentives are available that require little to no additional funding by states or schools. Incentives that give teachers greater leadership opportunities to improve in the quality of schooling could be very attractive for many potential candidates. For example, Illinois's use of National Board certifications to identify mentors illustrates a way to incentivize certification by making it a qualification for opportunity.

National Board–certified teachers might also fill leadership roles at the department, school, or district levels. Board-certified teachers could chair personnel, curriculum, or policy committees. They could also serve as school or district liaisons to local organizations and business communities. Some schools might even be able to offer reduced course loads in exchange for more leadership responsibilities.

Most leadership roles already have some form of stipend associated with them, so offering them as an incentive for teachers to pursue certification does not represent additional long-term costs. The arrangement is mutually beneficial for both the teachers and schools. Schools no longer have to depend on experience alone to delegate responsibility. Teachers get an opportunity to become Board-certified and to gain greater control over how their careers develop.

At a time when retaining high-quality teachers in the classrooms is a problem, empowering Board-certified teachers to work closely with administration on important decisions could help to attract and retain the best teachers. The trick is to offer teachers ways to increase their stature, income, and influence in a school without removing them from the classroom. If used strategically, National Board offers a means of promoting teachers while they continue to teach.

After more than two decades of work, the Board finds itself at a crossroads, faced with many significant challenges. Tensions within the organization over how to proceed exist. Is the Board a valuable systemic mechanism for assessing accomplished teaching? Is it an organization determined to be an influential player in Washington politics? Or is it, in the words of Paul Manna, a "policy entrepreneur" that needs ever greater numbers of Board-certified teachers so as to strengthen its voice in policy debates?[5] While the latter may be nice, it is not necessary to the core mission.

Unfortunately, becoming an inside-the-beltway player has become a necessity of the Board. Since the National Board is dependent on government legislation and funding, it needs to lobby the Congress and state-level legislatures to ensure that a constant stream of public funds is channeled toward the support of teachers wishing to pursue Board certification.

While the need for this work is understandable, it can begin to dominate the Board's agenda and increase the inertia that must be overcome to free itself from the confines of the Washington, D.C., trap. From this perspective, the more teachers who become certified, the louder the Board's voice will be in the offices of members of Congress.

In fact, the focus on increasing numbers of candidates in the short term distracts from the more fundamental issue of the organization's sustainability.

It is difficult to think about how one will survive the winter if one is always thinking about the next meal. Maybe if the Board was more focused on the task of defining, assessing, and fostering accomplished teachers, it would be less distracted by the glitz and glamour of education policy and would be a leaner and more effective enterprise.

How this struggle over the Board's future would best be resolved is unknown. While NBPTS addresses issues of survival, it runs the risk of losing sight of its purpose. However, in the final chapter, some important considerations are discussed that deal with reform, teacher quality, and the potential of the Board to contribute to a comprehensive teacher performance system both in the United States and overseas.

NOTES

1. As quoted by Toch and Rothman, *Rush to judgment*, 2008, 15.

2. To the Board's credit, they have made the registration process completely electronic.

3. In 2000, I served on an advisory committee for Teach America about Accomplished Teaching. We met several times in different cities over the course of a year. While it was an interesting opportunity to collaborate with other Board-certified teachers, it was not something that was within our area of expertise. Accomplished classroom teachers are not necessarily very good at public relations. As I have learned since this project, public relations are best left to firms with marketing and communications knowledge and experience.

4. See National Board for Professional Teaching Standards, 2001c.

5. Manna, *School's in*, 2006, 8.

9

The Future of the National Board: Relevancy or Obscurity?

From the beginning, the great promise of the Board has been its potential to cut across state borders and solve the problem of exceptional teaching. If the Board can assess accomplished teaching in a more cost-effective manner than states can do on their own, it has the potential to become a meaningful and sustainable reform. One of the great advantages of a centralized system of teacher assessment is the greater efficiency it offers the education consumer. Rather than develop, test, implement, and maintain fifty different systems of teacher evaluation, the National Board for Professional Teaching Standards (NBPTS) allows for states to outsource this important service in a cost-effective and meaningful way.

More than twenty-three years ago, the Board began discussing the problem of exceptional teaching. Today, a new generation of educators is raising the same issue, but the Board is noticeably absent from the conversation. Just when it appeared that the Board was poised to have its greatest impact, its system of certification for accomplished teaching now seems to be slipping away. The work of the New Teacher Project and the ensuing comments from the Secretary of Education reinforce this unfortunate situation.

Tied closely to the future of the Board is nothing less than the profession's conception of itself. Two different perspectives on teaching are waging battle. There are those represented by NBPTS who embrace teaching as an intellectual endeavor with specific skills and knowledge necessary to foster understanding for diverse learners. The intellectual view sees the standards of accomplished teaching as a work in progress. The standards represent a powerful articulation of what exceptional teaching looks like, and the qualities of learning that emerge from such instruction. It assumes that teachers bring considerable cognitive attention and professional resources to an uncertain classroom setting.

The utilitarian conception of teaching is quite different. In the utilitarian view represented by organizations such as Teach for America and the American Board for Certified Teaching Excellence (ABCTE), teaching is an intuitive activity that depends on a teacher's strong understanding of content as the prime indicator of quality.[1] In the utilitarian view, the emphasis is on student achievement as the valued output. All other outputs represent secondary interests.

The struggle over the nature of exceptional teaching is not limited to the United States. Other countries wrestle with the same problem of exceptional teaching. Scotland, Singapore, Sweden, Chile, and England are all interested in developing a teacher evaluation system that is more effective at identifying and rewarding accomplished teaching. Australia, New Zealand, Poland, Egypt, and Saudi Arabia are examining standards-based career path reforms that would incorporate some kind of professional certification for their best educators.[2] In a new twist to education reform, the National Board could franchise its brand and services to nations looking for ways to both identify and promote exceptional teaching.

While the United States emulates the high-stakes testing and standards of some Asian and European nations who perform better on international measures such as the Trends in International Mathematics and Science Study (TIMSS), some nations are focusing on adapting structures like National Board certification into a comprehensive teacher evaluation system.[3] It is ironic that while the National Board struggles for legitimacy and respect at home, many countries overseas considered it an ideal to be emulated.

Why does a valid and effective system for identifying exceptional teaching need to fight so hard for approval and support from diverse educational stakeholders? This book has made a robust case for the value of National Board certification as a productive and valuable professional learning opportunity. Precious few reforms have received both critical attention from the research community and broad-based approval from teachers. Yet resistance to fully realizing the potential of National Board for solving the problem with exceptional teaching remains strong and persistent. The situation presents a meaningful case study of how a meaningful reform could ultimately fail.

With the future of the Board uncertain, this chapter provides some final thoughts on changes that hint at possible ways to move forward. First, the Board's current status as an education reform is considered. Second, the resistance to Board acceptance is explored. Why is the Board constantly fighting for legitimacy? Finally, ideas are presented regarding how the National Board might contribute in a cost-effective manner to a comprehensive teacher evaluation system.[4]

NBPTS AS A REFORM EFFORT

The New Teacher Project describes the problem with exceptional teaching as the "Widget Effect," in which teachers are thought to be interchangeable in terms of quality. Weisberg and others call for more accountability for teachers and the adoption of a "comprehensive performance evaluation system that fairly, accurately, and credibly differentiates teachers based on their effectiveness in promoting student achievement" (2009, 7).[5]

Unfortunately, Weisberg and colleagues' report never addresses the potential solution offered by the National Board. Instead, it continues to describe a solution that aims to reinvent the proverbial wheel: "Teachers should be evaluated based on their ability to fulfill their core responsibility as professionals—delivering instruction that helps students learn and succeed. This demands clear performance standards" (7).

The report goes on to discuss the relationship between teacher evaluation and professional development. It states that "the core purpose of evaluation must be maximizing teacher growth and effectiveness" (7). The familiarity of the report's recommendation with the language and mission of the National Board is striking—and yet, the New Teacher Project makes no mention of the Board as a possible solution to the problem.

Current Secretary of Education Arne Duncan (2009) raised the issue of exceptional teaching in an address to the National Education Association. Basing his comments on the New Teacher Project, he said that today's educational system "treats all teachers like interchangeable widgets" as evidenced by the fact that "almost all teachers are rated the same." Secretary Duncan used this issue to encourage radical change, suggesting the nation throw out all preconceived notions and "start with a clean slate" (4).

While the New Teacher Project and the Secretary's remarks both emphasize the problem with exceptional teaching, neither considers the solutions
offered by the National Board. There is such a level of frustration with this
issue that the call for a "clean slate" runs the risk of throwing the baby out
with the bath water.

At a time when the work of the Board appears well positioned to offer a
clear solution, why is it ignored? Just when the years of investment in defining, assessing, and promoting accomplished teachers is about to pay off,
educational leaders seem to give little consideration to NBPTS as a possible
solution. Why are there calls to develop clear "performance standards"? Why
do the authors of the New Teacher Project act like an evaluation system that
"fairly, accurately, and credibly differentiates teachers based on their effectiveness" does not exist?

While some seem to ignore National Board, others are busy integrating
it into state education policy. For example, Ohio and Wisconsin currently
require teachers to achieve National Board certification if they wish to qualify
for the top tier in the new licensure system. In Wisconsin, this Master Education License is good for ten years and is renewable through the Board's certification renewal program, known as the Profile of Professional Growth.[6]

Illinois uses National Board certification as a requirement for experienced
teachers to become mentors for new teachers in the state's Teaching Excellence Program.[7] This approach ensures that teachers who have demonstrated
a level of professionalism as reflected by the Board's standards are supporting
new teachers' transition into the profession.

Ohio, Wisconsin, and Illinois represent states that see NBPTS as a valued
resource in achieving very specific goals. NBPTS provides states with a cost-
effective means of identifying teachers based on a performance criteria, and
not only years of experience or graduate credits earned. These states have integrated National Board certification into official policy positions with regard
to teacher status and promotion. Eventually, it is possible that as states wrestle
with the problem of exceptional teaching, more performance-based teacher
evaluation systems linked with teacher salary schedules will use NBPTS as a
reliable and valid measure of teacher quality.

As the Board considers its future, educational leaders debate about the
future of teacher assessment. On one side, policy makers and entrepreneurs
(such as Secretary Duncan and the New Teacher Project respectively) talk

about a system without the National Board. On the other side, state education leaders see the Board as a resource for solving difficult problems associated with teacher quality. Which direction is more indicative of the National Board's future? While the choices are clear, the pathway forward is not. The Board must overcome serious obstacles before it can become a valued institution in the eyes of public education.

RESISTANCE TO NATIONAL BOARD

Over the last decade, National Board certification has been studied, evaluated, and analyzed by a wide array of individuals and organizations. The level of critical attention paid to NBPTS seems far greater than any of its sister reform efforts.[8] Why are educational leaders so resistant to what the Board has to offer? After almost twenty years of operations and more than 80,000 certified teachers, why does the Board still need to fight so hard in the policy arena for legitimacy? Some possible reasons include:

1. Dependence on taxpayer funds to pay for and incentivize certification
2. The system's myopic focus on student achievement as the measure of teacher quality
3. Perception of NBPTS as a threat to the egalitarian model of teaching
4. A view that National Board teachers are elitist, rather than elite
5. A vision of teaching as an intellectual, rather than a utilitarian, endeavor
6. The apparent audacity of teachers to define excellence for themselves

Whether the answer lies with one of these reasons, or with an entirely different explanation, the National Board seems held to a higher standard than other efforts that aim to define, identify, and foster exceptional teaching.[9] For example, are graduate credits worth their cost in terms of improved teaching and learning? Are the significant costs associated with private professional development providers worth the resulting gains to teacher quality? Are conferences, summer workshops, and university research partnerships effective ways of improving the quality of teaching and learning? While these activities do attract research attention, the expectations for success appear much lower than they are for Board certification.

In 2005, the U.S. Congress took up the issue of differentiating between good and great teachers, and asked the National Research Council (NRC) to evaluate the research to date on the National Board. Congress wanted to know if the public was getting its money's worth from years of investing in National Board. The result was the NRC report titled *Assessing Accomplished Teaching,* which concluded that "NBPTS has the potential to make a valuable contribution to efforts to improve teacher quality" (2008, 12). The report goes on to say that the "limited evidence of its impact does not prove that this approach cannot be successful" (13).[10]

The report was cautious but optimistic, using words like *potential.* The latter part of the conclusion is a little more dubious. Why does the report use a double-negative when linking "limited evidence of impact" to success? Why did the authors choose this language, rather than "limited evidence suggests this approach can be successful"? The answer may lie in the need to "prove" the Board's validity in an environment obsessed with accountability.

Proof is in the eye of the beholder. Current educational rhetoric greatly favors the easily accessible—if not misguided—dependence on standardized test scores as the gold standard of objective evidence for proving efficacy. While the standardized test score is a convenient and useful measure of teacher effectiveness, it is only one of many. High-stakes test scores deform curriculum and undermine pedagogical decisions, perverting their usefulness as indicators of quality.

Because education defies a simple cause-and-effect relationship, pretending one exists can be misleading or even destructive. Making positive cause-and-effect statements in education is like saying "sunshine causes happiness." Too many other variables interact with the observed phenomenon to isolate any one as the sole cause.[11]

The business of human improvement is just too complex to be reduced to statements of certainty and fact. If claiming a causal relationship in education is next to impossible, then the opposite must be true. Stating that the "evidence does not prove" validity is an easy conclusion to make. Thus, the report employed the double-negative to acknowledge both those who expect and those who do not expect to find "proof" in education.

If educational research cannot prove anything, then what is its value? For most investigators, research provides tools for understanding possible relationships by making meaning out of the preponderance of evidence. With regard to the NRC's report, the authors suggest that for NBPTS to succeed in changing the landscape of American education, the reform effort needs more time and evidence to guide its continued development.

The preponderance of evidence to date (including the research discussed in this book) strongly suggests that the Board's work offers educational stakeholders a valuable resource worthy of continued attention. NBPTS stands alone as both an assessment process and a professional learning opportunity that, overall, impacts teachers—and ultimately their students—in a positive fashion.

However, the lack of consistent evidence linking Board-certified teachers to improved student achievement scores has nudged the NBPTS into an educational limbo between relevancy and obscurity. Either the obsession with test results begins to morph into more humanistic measures of success, or the Board decides to play the game of high-stakes accountability.

Since the former is unlikely to happen soon, and the latter represents a serious compromise to the educational values represented by the five core propositions, the National Board seems to be stuck between the proverbial rock and a hard place. Is there a compromise or change in policy that could help resolve the Board's predicament?

A WAY FORWARD WITH COMPREHENSIVE ASSESSMENT OF TEACHER QUALITY

NBPTS offers a solution to a common problem. When states and other reform efforts are just beginning to tinker with the idea of evaluating teachers based on a systematic performance review, NBPTS has a long history of addressing the problem effectively. It is understandable that different visions of exceptional teaching might attract some fringe attention. Advocates of extreme constructivist or traditionalist approaches to teaching and learning feel that their agenda is not properly attended to. However, it is puzzling that the National Board is not more central in the work of states.

To date, only a handful of states have integrated the National Board into frameworks for teacher licensure. Significant numbers of teachers are pursuing certification, but not usually as part of any kind of comprehensive state-level evaluative system. It seems states would rather spend precious time, human resources, and money on the creation of their own definitions and protocols for evaluating teacher performance, rather than utilize the proven services and experience the Board provides.

Maybe state departments of education wish to retain sole influence over the quality of their teachers. Maybe NBPTS's omission of student achievement data fails to match the political priorities of government leaders. Or maybe teachers as a group just do not have the consensus and social capital necessary to make their collective voices heard. Whatever the reason, states do have more options than they may realize.

In the current discourse, teacher performance assessment takes on the character of an "either-or" debate. Either a state embraces National Board as the answer to the problem, or it ignores it completely and pursues its own solution.[12] This didactic perspective misses the third option. States could develop assessment systems that compliment the Board's certification process. Parts of a comprehensive system are already in place. Traditional measures of quality based on the work of the individual and administrative observations could work in concert with state and national efforts.

In such an approach, a combination of complex assessments is used to evaluate and foster teacher quality. Measures involving the individual, school, state, and national levels would ensure a well-rounded view of accomplished teaching, while offering teachers a variety of learning opportunities across their careers. Figure 9.1 shows how these pieces could fit together to address the problem with exceptional teaching.

National Board would fulfill the national perspective by evaluating what a teacher knows and is able to do with regard to the standards of accomplished practice. National Board is very good at examining a reflective practitioner's ability to foster a wide array of learning outcomes in students. NBPTS is a national vision of accomplished teaching, but it evaluates at the level of the individual teacher. Individuals are better at reflecting on and addressing the multidimensional issues associated with classroom practice than are districts or states.

States could track the student-achievement dimension of schooling. States, rather than individuals, are well positioned to collect, store, and communicate the results regarding teachers, schools, and achievement. However, unlike most merit-pay schemes, the relationship between practice and value added to student achievement would only count as one-quarter toward the overall identification of excellence. This option saves states money, places a realistic emphasis on the role of testing in the determination of quality, and opens the door for a meaningful and rewarding assessment system.

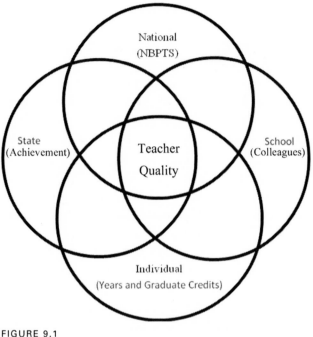

FIGURE 9.1
A Comprehensive System to Evaluating Teacher Quality

School principals, teacher leaders, and administrative specialists could pro-vide a third stream of data that would inform all parties regarding the quality of each teacher's contribution to a school's success. This collegial perspective would serve to balance the overall assessment picture. For example, a teacher might demonstrate accomplished practice at the national level by achieving Board certification, but the state's assessment does not indicate the same level of effectiveness with regard to test scores. Local leadership evaluation could be the deciding factor concerning teacher quality. And if the traditional measures of years of experience and graduate credits are included, the evalu-ative system could be shared among all four measures of quality. By basing the determination of quality on multiple measures, a more refined means of identifying excellence becomes possible.

In such a balanced approach, teacher performance is based on the acqui-sition of all four metrics of expertise. To rise to the top of the quality pool, teachers would work toward achieving defined excellence in each of the four different components. Teachers who demonstrate excellence at all four would receive the most opportunity and compensation for their work. Different degrees of excellence based on these four domains of practice could then be assigned the corresponding and appropriate level of reward. Such an arrangement would reflect a vision of teaching that emphasizes the role of constant and diligent attention to practice and lifelong learning.

Teachers in collaboration with school leadership could organize their long- and short-term professional development plans around these four dimensions of quality. Achieving success with each one over time would become a significant indicator of improving teacher quality over the course of a career. A balanced approach to teacher assessment would make room for different strengths of individual teachers to be acknowledged and respected, while making it feasible to identify the most and least capable within the ranks.

From a practical standpoint, the money that states save by not developing and enforcing standards of teaching could be redirected to support National Board certification or their systems of accountability. This balanced approach might also make spending at the district level more effective. Instead of compensating teachers based only on input indicators of quality (e.g., years experience and graduate credits earned), they could redistribute pay scales based on a formula that includes student achievement (state level indicators), colleague observations (school), and Board certification (the national indicator).

Since traditional measures of quality are already well established, the burden of change would fall on states to redefine their role as evaluators of achievement, rather than definers of practice. Districts would also shoulder the burden of change as union contracts would address this new approach to compensation.

FINDING A WAY FORWARD FOR THE BOARD

In the last part of the interview from the research reported on in part II, candidates were asked to rank fifteen different professional development activities with regard to each item's ability to foster improved teaching. This aspect of the interview allowed assessors to evaluate the level of professional involvement each candidate exhibited. However, the task also served as a survey on what candidates thought about various forms of professional development.

The results were very interesting. National Board candidates ranked certification as the third most effective means of improving a teachers' ability to foster learning in students—just behind developing curriculum with col-leagues and reading content-rich literature. At the bottom of the list, candi-dates ranked traditional in-service professional development as least effective at improving the effectiveness of their teaching.

The findings from this survey bolster the finding that National Board certification is a productive professional learning opportunity. With re-search making a case for the value of National Board certification, it would be shameful to abandon the Board to the garbage heap of reform. Rather, it makes more sense for states, teachers, and teacher unions to recognize the Board's potential, and to figure out ways to integrate it into the fabric of the teaching profession. When a reform actually demonstrates efficacy, it be-comes imperative to respect and utilize its potential.

States and schools should find ways to encourage teachers to pursue NB-PTS with both intrinsic incentives and extrinsic rewards. Committing to NB-PTS as part of the means to identify exceptional teaching sends an important message to the community. It says that this state, district, or school embraces and respects the complexity of teaching as a profession.

National Board represents a vision of teaching where student achieve-ment on standardized tests is but one type of outcome that quality teach-ing fosters. Other outcomes, such as student interest in learning, ability to collaborate, problem solving, making evidence-based arguments, effectively communicating ideas and results, analyzing data, contributing to the local community, engaging with colleagues, and being a critical consumer of information are all outcomes that are just as important as scoring well on a fact- and definition-based test.

The message also states that it takes a village to raise a child. Teaching a child the content and skills necessary to become an informed, capable, and positive member of society depends on teachers, parents, administrators, and community leaders working together to address education issues.

NBPTS represents all of these necessary dimensions of the teaching and learning dynamic. Communities that support NBPTS teachers are saying, "We value a rich and engaging approach to teaching and learning—not just the acquisition of knowledge and skills for the purpose of test performance." While state endorsement of NBPTS would appear to immediately benefit the organization more than the state, in the long run, it's the learners in class-rooms who profit the most.

The issue is bigger than just the future of NBPTS. Nothing less than the country's proclamation of what a quality education means hangs in the balance. Public education can continue to move toward a vision of teaching and learning that is monodimensional and limiting to the most vulnerable in society.

On this path, states would focus singularly on student achievement as the primary indicator of quality. Curriculum would become more regimented, and accountability would become the supreme goal. Meanwhile, the country's most capable individuals would become even less likely to enter the profession. In their place, the least innovative, least passionate, and least skilled individuals will become the only ones left to do the work of schooling. Any person with even a vague notion of education as opportunity would be hard pressed to survive in such a demeaning environment.

Teachers could improve their ability to foster ever greater student achievement, but at a tremendous cost to the quality of the school experience. Students' creativity, engagement, curiosity, and collaborative skills would be consumed by the endless bombardment of worksheets and review exercises. According to this scenario, students would become the victims of a system intent on proving its value to those who are farthest removed from classroom practice. However, public education need not become such a travesty. Opportunities for a different fate are available.

National Board can be part of this alternative future. By building on the Board's accomplishments, states, districts, and schools can recognize the value of a well-rounded learning experience fostered by skillful and knowledgeable professionals. A system that embraces the complexity of education and the entire gamut of worthwhile outcomes benefits not just the learner, but the teaching profession too. In this approach, teaching would become a creative and intellectual act that places a high priority on the ability of the individual teacher to make informed and meaningful judgments. And with a comprehensive teacher performance assessment system, compensation could be matched to quality.

Such values would encourage like-minded individuals to consider a career in teaching. Educated and professionally trained people want opportunities to make a difference in the lives of others, while creating a body of work that is worthy of a career. Of course, they want students to learn the required knowledge and skills deemed important by the community, but they also want the

professional space to try fresh lesson ideas, apply multiple assessment strategies, and pursue collaborative opportunities.

Only a vision of exceptional teaching that acknowledges exquisite and
diversified expertise can attract the best and brightest into such a vital profession. While National Board is not the only means to achieve such an ideal
system, it does accurately represent the possibility. The Board is not a silver
bullet or a perfect approach to assessing teacher quality, but it does offer the
promise of a richer and more meaningful future for teachers and learners.

FINAL THOUGHTS

Ultimately, a comprehensive system of teacher evaluation in which the Board
plays a major role would be a tremendous accomplishment for public education. However, the question remains: Why is there so much resistance to a
reform effort that has more than proven its worth to teachers, students, and
schools? In this final section, a possible explanation may be found at the other
end of the teacher quality spectrum.

While this book has been focused on exceptional teaching, the National
Board's process for evaluating such teachers, and the learning that occurs
for *both those who are identified as accomplished and those who are not,* it has
ignored the problem of incompetent teachers. The irony here is that the problem with exceptional teaching is intimately related to the challenges posed by
teachers who have no business working with young people. In both cases, the
current system has proven inept at differentiating between teachers of dramatically different quality.

A Michigan science teacher describes the situation this way: "Somewhere
along the line, I was told that being a teacher was one of the hardest jobs in the
world to do well and one of the easiest jobs in the world to do poorly—and
still get paid the same."[13] The inability to remove teachers who consistently
fail to improve has produced tremendous frustration outside the ranks of
teachers. How can teachers be trusted to identify the best among their ranks
if they remain impotent to those who give the profession a bad reputation?

A distrust of teachers on issues of quality is understandable. The track
record for teachers to police their own quality is not good. While the unions
have done so much to improve the quality of teachers' lives both inside and
outside the school, they have proven ineffective at helping administrators distinguish between strong and weak educators. Too many school communities

know of teachers who really do not belong in the classroom, but feel helpless to counsel them out of the profession. After years of trying in vain to help them improve, a burgeoning inertia takes over and retirement becomes the solution for these problematic individuals.

These poor-quality teachers take a toll on the entire system. Districts shuffle them around into the least desirable schools. In extreme cases, cities like New York go so far as to put the unwanted teachers into "the rubber room." For teachers deemed incompetent or accused of wrong doing, the rubber room is where they wait for a formal hearing and collect their salary for staying *out* of the classroom.[14]

All professions have their weakest links and different ways of dealing with them. In medicine, the bad doctors become uninsurable. In law, the weakest lawyers get the least desirable cases. However, in education, incompetence has become institutionalized to a much stronger degree. In response, reform efforts dedicated to force change from the outside seem to emerge from an understandable sense of desperation. Reforms such as merit pay and value-added instruction use rewards and punishments to try to leverage "improvements."

While the motivations for such reform schemes are understandable, the consequences are not. Using test scores as the sole means of measuring teacher quality manipulates teachers into providing very limited forms of instruction which stifles creativity and innovation. These approaches see teacher evaluation as something done *to* the workforce for purposes of punishment and reward rather than done *by* the workforce to promote growth, excellence, and progress. The idea that "evaluation" could be synonymous with "learning opportunity" is hard to believe for those who do not see teachers as disciplined professionals.

Some education leaders seem to want teachers that act more like robots who do precisely what they are told, rather than individual practitioners who bring considerable experience, knowledge, and skill to the complex classroom learning environment. For example, some districts offer superintendents an annual bonus based on the percent increase of student achievement scores. For every point of improvement, the superintendent receives $5,000.

In response, some superintendents have been known to implement a "teacher-proof" curriculum that requires all teachers at a particular level to be on the same page every hour of every day. Principals are instructed to monitor teachers for compliance. Every six weeks, the students are tested so as to demonstrate progress and prepare them for the state tests at the end of the year. In response, teachers who can leave go to other districts and those who remain are left to follow the central office directives or suffer the consequences.

Student test scores improve and the superintendent receives a sizable yearly bonus, but the price paid by everyone (except the superintendent) seems to be very high. Reforms such as these that have a shallow conception of learning and a low opinion of teachers often emerge from corporate model of improvement.

From this perspective, learning is a product to be counted, stacked, and sold in the marketplace. To improve the "product," incentives are offered for more production and penalties are handed out for disappointing numbers. Each of these initiatives is imposed on teachers by individuals who live outside the classroom or school. Schools are not factories or sales offices. They are places where dedicated professionals should help learners prepare for a successful life in society, not just perform well on the year-end exam.

National Board represents a very different approach to assessing and improving teacher quality. It represents assessment of teachers by teachers in a rigorous, reliable, and valid manner. While evidence of student learning remains the razor-sharp focus of the assessment, it comes from teachers—not politicians, policy makers, or administrators. Though each of these groups plays an important role in the application of National Board, its policies and practices remain beyond their control. In addition, it is an assessment that actually helps teachers become more effective in the classroom. Teachers learn about their work while developing and sharing the evidence presented in the certification portfolio.

The evidence of student learning required by National Board certification is more difficult to appreciate than a simple 15-percent gain as might be communicated with test scores. However, the test score is only one small part of the picture. The study described in part II of this book reported significant learning gains from the certification process. However, those gains meant very little in terms of teacher quality until they were more qualitatively explored. Only after considerable effort was it discovered that different types of learning could explain the observed gains. The identification of dynamic, technical, and deferred learners would have gone unnoticed had the research stopped at the observed gains in scores.

The same is true for classroom teaching and learning. Does the system really want to encourage teaching that promotes technical student learning for a test? Or should teachers work to foster dynamic learning that means something profound and enduring to the individual learner?

National Board represents an affront to those outsiders who would rather dictate quality from afar than trust teachers to do it from within. It is for this reason that National Board needs to solicit the endorsement and support from the entire teaching community. The stronger the consensus becomes around the National Board's vision of defining and identifying accomplished teaching, the less susceptible it will become to political and economic instabilities. Strong consensus does not necessarily mean ever-growing numbers of candidates. Rather, it means growing support and respect for candidates from their peers and community. If teachers can learn to respect those who demonstrate greater ability to foster learning in the classroom, then they can also learn to be intolerant of incompetence.

If teachers ever want to improve their professional status in society, then they eventually will need to take a more active role in defining quality and identifying who has it and who does not. Otherwise, teachers will continue to be on the receiving end of misguided, ill-informed, and often deleterious reform.

This is no small task. It means teachers engaging in the promotion and dissemination of teacher exceptionalism while identifying and removing incompetent teachers. Teaching is not a right; it is profession that requires a vigilant commitment to professional learning to bring about a richer and more meaningful student learning experience.

In the end, this book has been about exceptional teaching and how the NB-PTS offers an effective and proven solution for differentiating teachers on the basis of quality. Ultimately, for National Board certification to reach its full potential at improving education, teachers will need to answer a fundamental question. Who should be responsible for defining exceptional teaching? If the answer points to everyone but teachers, then the system is sure to be plagued with more short-term, ill-conceived efforts that see education as a linear process with teachers at the receiving end of the carrot and the stick.

However, if the community of teachers can decide for themselves what exceptional teaching means, then they can have a greater voice in how learning is defined, assessed, and measured. National Board stands ready to work with dedicated educators for a future when a quality teaching and learning experience is not the exception for a few, but the rule for all.

NOTES

1. It is difficult to know exactly how many teachers have earned the certificate of excellence offered by the ABCTE. Their website (http://www.abcte.org) does not indicate how many teachers have successfully completed the testing process. According to the website, nine thousand teachers "have started" the program. The website also states that, of those who start, "forty percent of candidates complete the program." It is unclear if completing the program is synonymous with passing the program, but if so, the information suggests that approximately 3,600 ABCTE teachers have been certified since 2005. If a candidate can complete the program and still fail the process, the number of ABCTE teachers would be much lower.

2. See Sclafani, *Evaluating and rewarding,* 2009; and Isoré, "Teacher evaluation," 2009, for analyses of how different countries are working to evaluate and reward accomplished teaching.

3. For further information on the latest TIMSS research, see Gonzales et al., "Highlights from TIMSS 2007," 2008.

4. See Reichardt, *Toward a comprehensive approach,* 2001; and Lieberman, "The future of teacher compensation," 2002, for insightful discussions on comprehensive teacher evaluation and salary systems.

5. It should be noted that the use of the term *achievement* rather than *learning* is a reflection of the New Teacher Project's reliance on student standardized tests scores as the primary indicator of teacher quality.

6. Goertz and Leven, "An analysis of Wisconsin," 2009a.

7. Goertz and Leven, "An analysis of Illinois," 2009b.

8. Some reform efforts such as school choice, vouchers, or alternative certification programs have also been studied quite extensively. However, these efforts are, to some degree, individual and unique depending on the context where they are studied. Specific programs such as Troops to Teachers, Teach for America, The New Teacher Project, ABCTE, the Teacher Advancement Program and others, all make claims about the quality of their work, but do not rival the amount of scholarly attention that NBPTS attracts.

9. The overall effect size of 0.47 identified in this study falls within the moderate to strong range based on several comparative criteria. This effect size would be acceptable within the realm of previous efforts to improve science teacher quality as indicated by Enz (1982), who calculated an average effect size of 0.84 for a different professional development experience. To gain further perspective, corporate training and psychotherapy—which also embrace complex interventions coupled with ambiguous outcome criteria—were also considered. Companies spend billions of dollars annually to improve their employees' ability to lead, produce, solve problems, and collaborate, and some research has examined the effects of corporate training. Morrow and associates (1997) examined eighteen training programs in one very large corporation over a four-year period; it identified effect sizes ranging from .09 to 1.11, with training focused on managerial skills resulting in an effect size of 0.31. Collins and Holton (2004) conducted a meta-analysis of leadership development programs covering eighty-three studies from 1982 to 2001 and found effect sizes for various categories of outcomes ranging from 0.35 to 1.37. Winfred et al. (2003) conducted another meta-analysis that looked at training programs in organizations and found a more consistent result with effect sizes ranging from 0.60 to 0.63. Though the range of results varies, the evidence does suggest that the effects of corporate training generally can be described as "moderate" to "large" based on Cohen's (1977) conventional standard. Research that examines the effects of psychotherapy indicates a similarly large range. For example, a series of meta-analyses examined different approaches to therapy and their impact on patient improvement. Burlingame et al. (2003) found an effect size of 0.58 while Bohlmeijer et al. (2003) found the highest effect size of 0.84. With effect sizes that can be described as "moderate" to "large," these studies provide a fairly consistent picture that psychotherapy, as an intervention, is effective at addressing the short-term needs of patients. These comparisons serve to support the assertion that perhaps NBPTS is held to a higher standard of excellence when compared with other similarly defined efforts. In practices devoted to human improvement, effects of interventions span a broad range, within which the results of this study may be placed.

10. National Research Council, *Assessing accomplished teaching,* 2008.

11. Evidence of the problematic "proof" in education can be found in the Department of Education's "What Works" program. Through the Institute for Education Sciences, reform programs that meet rigorous burdens of evidence are categorized as effective. Since 2002, only a small number of initiatives have met the government's criteria to be labeled as "effective." Most of the five hundred interventions do not meet the criteria, or meet the criteria with reservations. The full list can be accessed at http://ies.ed.gov/ncee/wwc/.

12. It is not uncommon when talking with people who work at the Board to hear phrases like, "That's a National Board state" or "That is not a National Board state." There is a perception supported by levels of state funding that promotes this "'either-or" view of state engagement with NBPTS.

13. Tobias and Baffert, *Science teaching as a profession,* 2009, 66.

14. Medina, "Teachers set deal with city," 2010. It should be noted that the practice of the "rubber room" is to be discontinued and replaced with a more effective means of addressing the problem.

References

American Board for Certification of Teacher Excellence. 2005. *American Board for Certified Teaching Excellence.* Retrieved June 4, 2010, from http://www.abcte.org/.

Adelson, Rachel. 2004. Instruction versus exploration in science learning: Recent psychological research calls "discovery learning" into question. *Monitor On Psychology,* 35(6): 34. Retrieved June 4, 2010, from http://www.apa.org/monitor/jun04/instruct.html.

Anagnostopoulos, D., G. Sykes, R. McCrory, M. Cannata, and K. Frank. 2010. Dollars, distinction, or duty? The meaning of the National Board for Professional Teaching Standards for teachers' work and collegial relations. *American Journal of Education,* 116(3): 337–369.

Areglado, N. 1999. I became convinced. *Journal of Staff Development,* 20(1): 35–37.

Athanases, S. Z. 1994. Teachers' reports of the effects of preparing portfolios of literacy instruction. *The Elementary School Journal,* 94(4): 421–439.

Bailey, D. L. and R. G. Helms. 2000. *The National Board Certified teacher. Fastback 470.* Bloomington, IN: Phi Delta Kappan Education Foundation, 8–47.

Baratz-Snowden, J. 2007. The future of teacher compensation: Déjà vu or something new? Washington, DC: Center for American Progress. Retrieved June 5, 2010, from http://www.americanprogress.org/issues/2007/11/snowden_report.html.

Bellevue School District (N.D.). National Board Certification: High standards for teachers. Bellevue School District, Bellevue, Washington. Retrieved June 1, 2010, from http://www.bsd405.org/Default.aspx?tabid=478.

Benz, J. 1997. Measuring up: A personal journey through National Board certification in art. *Art Education,* 50(5): 20–24, 49–50.

Blank, Rolf, Doreen Langesen, and Adam Petermann. 2007. State indicators of science and mathematics education 2007. Council of Chief State School Officers. Retrieved June 5, 2010, from http://www.ccsso.org/projects/Science_and_Mathematics_Education_Indicators/.

Bohlmeijer E., F. Smit, and P. Cuijpers. 2003. Effects of reminiscence and life review on late-life depression: A meta-analysis. *International Journal of Geriatric Psychiatry,* 18(12): 1088–1094.

Bond, Lloyd, T. Smith, W. Baker, and J. Hattie. 2000. *The certification system of the National Board for Professional Teaching Standards: A construct and consequential validity study.* Greensboro, NC: Center for Educational Research and Evaluation at the University of North Carolina at Greensboro.

Boshier, R. 1994. Initiating research. In *Research Perspectives in Adult Education,* ed. D. R. Garrison, 73–116. Malabar, FL: Krieger Publishing Company.

Boyd, William Lowe, and Jillian P. Reese. 2006. Great expectations: The Impact of the National Board for Professional Teaching Standards. *Education Next* 6(2): 50–57.

Burlingame, Gary M., Addie Fuhriman, and Julie Mosier. 2003. The differential effectiveness of group psychotherapy: A meta-analytic perspective. *Group Dynamics,* 7(1): 3–12.

Burroughs, R., T. A. Schwartz, and M. Hendricks-Lee. 2000. Communities of practice and discourse communities: Negotiating boundaries in NBPTS certification. *Teacher's College Record,* 102(2): 344–374.

Campbell, Donald, and Thelma H. McCormack. 1957. Military experience and attitudes toward authority. *American Journal of Sociology,* 62: 482–490.

Campbell, Donald, and Julian Stanley. 1963. *Experimental and quasi-experimental designs for research.* Hopewell, NJ: Houghton Mifflin Company.

Carnegie Forum on Education and the Economy's Task Force on Teaching as a Profession. 1986. *A nation prepared: Teachers for the 21st century.* New York: Carnegie Corporation of New York.

Chittenden, E., and J. Jones. 1997. An observational study of National Board candidates as they progress through the certification process. Paper presented at the annual meeting of the American Educational Research Association, Chicago, IL.

Clinton, William. 1997. *The State of the Union Address,* Washington, D.C. Retrieved June 4, 2010, from http://clinton2.nara.gov/WH/SOU97/.

Cohen, David. K. 1988. Teaching practice: Plus ça change. In *Contributing to educational change: Perspectives on research and practice,* ed. Philip W. Jackson, 27–84. Berkeley, CA: McCutchan.

Cohen, David. K. 1990. The case of Ms. Oublier. *Educational Evaluation and Policy Analysis,* 12(3): 327–345.

Cohen, J. 1977. *Statistical power analysis for the behavioral sciences.* New York: Academic Press.

Collins, D. B., and E. Holton. 2004. The effectiveness of managerial leadership development programs: A meta-analysis of studies from 1982 to 2001. *Human Resource Development Quarterly,* 15(2): 153–170.

Conroy, James, Scott Spreat, Anita Yuskauskas, and Martin Elks. 2003. The Hissom closure outcomes study: A report on six years of movement to supported living. *Mental Retardation,* 41(4): 263–275.

Cook, Thomas D., and Donald T. Campbell. 1979. *Quasi-experimentation: Design & analysis issues for field settings.* Boston: Houghton Mifflin Company.

Crawford, J., and James Impara. 2001. Critical issues, current trends, and possible futures in quantitative methods. In *Handbook of research on teaching,* ed. V. Richardson, 133–173. Washington, D.C.: American Educational Research Association.

Darling-Hammond, L., and Ida McLaughlin. 1996. Policies that support professional development in an era of reform. *Phi Delta Kappan,* 76(8): 597–604.

Dewey, John. 1910. *How we think.* Boston: D.C. Heath.

Duncan, Arne. 2009. Arne Duncan's speech to RA delegates; delivered on Thursday, July 2. Retrieved September 28, 2010, from http://www.nea.org/grants/33704.htm.

Educational Testing Service. 1999. *Technical analysis report.* Princeton, NJ: National Board for Professional Teaching Standards.

Enz, Judith, W. J. Horak, and B. J. Blecha. 1982. Review and analysis of reports of science inservice projects: Recommendations for the future. Paper presented at the annual Meeting of the National Science Teachers Association, Chicago, IL.

Feynman, R. 1974. Cargo cult science, *Engineering and Science*. Caltech Office of Public Relations, 10–13. Retrieved June 5, 2010, from http://calteches.library .caltech.edu/51/2/CargoCult.pdf.

Floden, Robert E. 2001. Research on effects of teaching: A continuing model for research on teaching. In *Handbook of research on teaching*, ed. V. Richardson, 193–216. Washington, D.C.: American Educational Research Association.

Franke, M., T. Loef, E. Carpenter, E. Fennema, and J. Behrend. 1998. Understanding teachers' self-sustaining, generative change in the context of professional development. *Teaching and Teacher Education*, 14(1): 67–80.

Gallagher, James J. 2000. Teaching for understanding and application of science knowledge. *School Science and Mathematics*, 100(6): 310–318.

Gardiner, S. 2000. I leave with more ideas than I can ever use. *Journal of Staff Development*, 21(4): 14–17.

Goldhaber, Dan, David Perry, and Emily Anthony. 2004. The National Board for Professional Teaching Standards (NBPTS) process: Who applies and what factors are associated with NBPTS certification? *Educational Evaluation and Policy Analysis*, 26(4): 259–280.

Gonzales, P., Williams, T., Jocelyn, L., Roey, S., Kastberg, D., and Brenwald, S. 2008. *Highlights from TIMSS 2007: Mathematics and science achievement of U.S. fourth- and eighth-grade students in an international context*. National Center for Education Statistics, Institute of Education Sciences, U.S. Department of Education. Washington, D.C. Retrieved June 5, 2010, from http://nces.ed.gov/ pubs2009/2009001.pdf.

Goertz, M., and S. Leven. 2009a. *State policies supporting SMHC in education: An analysis of Wisconsin using SMHC state framework*. Consortium for Policy Research in Education's Strategic Management of Human Capital. Retrieved June 5, 2010, from http://www.smhc-cpre.org/download/88/.

Goertz, M., and S. Leven. 2009b. *State policies supporting SMHC in education: An analysis of Illinois using SMHC state framework*. Consortium for Policy Research in Education's Strategic Management of Human Capital. Retrieved June 5, 2010, from http://www.smhc-cpre.org/download/89/.

Haynes, D. D. 1995. One teacher's experience with National Board assessment. *Educational Leadership*, 52: 58–60.

Holmes Group. 1995. *Tomorrow's schools of education.* Holmes Group: East Lansing.

Ingvarson, L., and J. Hattie. eds. 2008. *Assessing teachers for professional certification: The first decade of the National Board for Professional Teaching Standards,* Vol. II. Amsterdam: Elsevier Press.

Ingvarson, L., and K. Rowe. 2008. Conceptualizing and evaluating teacher quality: Substantive and methodological issues. *Australian Journal of Education,* 52(1): 5–35. Retrieved May 20, 2010, from http://www.proquest.com/.

Isoré, Marlène. 2009. Teacher evaluation: Current practices in OECD countries and a literature review. *OECD Education Working Papers,* no. 23. Retrieved June 4, 2010, from http://dx.doi.org/10.1787/223283631428.

Jenkins, K. 2000. Earning Board certification: Making time to grow. *Educational Leadership,* 57: 46–48.

Jimenez, P. M. 1999. Psychosocial intervention with drug addicts in prison: Description and results of programme. *Intervencion Psichosocial,* 8(2): 233–250.

Kennedy, Mary; D. L. Ball, and W. McDiarmid. 1993. *A Study package for examining and tracking changes in teacher's knowledge.* The National Center for Research on Teacher Education: East Lansing, MI.

Koprowicz, Constance L. 1994. What state legislators need to know about the National Board for Professional Teaching Standards. *State Legislative Report,* 19(1): 1–5.

Kowalski, K., E. Chittenden, W., Spicer, J. Jones, and C. Tocci. 1997. Professional development in the context of National Board for Professional Teaching Standards Certification: Implications beyond certification. Paper presented at the Annual Meeting of the American Educational Research Association, Chicago, IL.

Lafferty, Brad Donald. 1998. Investigation of a leadership development program: An empirical investigation of a leadership development program. EdD diss., The George Washington University, Washington, D.C. Retrieved June 5, 2010, from Dissertations & Theses: A&I.(Publication No. AAT 9826782).

Lareau, A. 1989. *Home advantage: Social class and parental intervention in elementary education,* 2nd ed., Lanham, MD: Rowan and Littlefield.

Lave, J., and E. Wenger. 1991. *Situated learning: Legitimate peripheral participation.* Cambridge: Cambridge University Press.

Lieberman, Joyce M. 2002. The future of teacher compensation: Linking salary to National Board certification. Paper presented at the Annual Meeting of the Mid-Western Educational Research Association, Columbus, OH.

Lortie, D. C. 1975. *Schoolteacher: A sociological study*. Chicago: University of Chicago Press.

Lustick, D. 2002. National Board certification as professional development: A study that identifies a framework and findings of teachers learning to manage complexity, uncertainty, and community. Paper presented at the Annual Meeting of the American Educational Research Association, New Orleans, LA.

Lustick, D. 1997. Elemental design. *The Science Teacher,* 64: 47–49.

Lustick, David, and Gary Sykes. 2006. National Board certification as professional development: What are teachers learning? *Education Policy Analysis Archives,* 14(5): 1–43.

Mahaley, D. 1999. One teacher's account. *The Clearing House,* 73: 5.

Manna, P. 2006. *School's in: Federalism and the national education agenda.* Washington, D.C.: Georgetown University Press.

Manouchehehri, A. 2001. Collegial interaction and reflective practice. *The Journal of the Association of Teacher Educators,* 22(Winter): 86–97.

Marriott, D. 2001. Increased insight. *Reading Today,* 18: 7.

Medina, Jennifer. 2010. Teachers set deal with city on discipline process, *New York Times,* April 15, 2010. Retrieved June 5, 2010, from http://www.nytimes.com/2010/04/16/nyregion/16rubber.html.

Merriam, S., and Edwin Simpson. 1995. *A Guide to research for educators and trainers of adults.* Malabar, FL: Krieger.

Miller, Barbara, Brian Lord, and Judith Dorney. 1994. *Staff development for teachers: A study of configurations and costs in four districts.* Newton, MA: Education Development Center.

Morrow, C., Q. Jarrett, and M. Rupinski. 1997. An investigation of the effect and economic utility of corporate-wide training. *Personnel Psychology,* 50(1): 91–119.

Mullens, John E., Mary S. Leighton, Katrina G. Laguarda, and Eileen O'Brien. 1996. *Student learning, teaching quality, and professional development: Theoretical linkages, current measurement, and recommendations for future data collection.* Working Paper Series. Washington, DC: Policy Studies Associates, Inc., 120.

National Board for Professional Teaching Standards. 1991. *Toward high and rigorous standards for the teaching profession,* 3rd ed. Washington, D.C.: National Board for Professional Teaching Standards.

———. 1997. *Instruction manual for adolescent and young adult (AYA) science certification.* Fairfax, VA: National Board for Professional Teaching Standards.

———. 2001a. *The Impact of National Board certification on teachers: Survey results.* Arlington, VA: National Board for Professional Teaching Standards.

———. 2001b. *I am a better teacher. Survey results.* Arlington, VA: National Board for Professional Teaching Standards.

———. 2001c. *Teaching America about accomplished teaching.* Arlington, VA: National Board for Professional Teaching Standards.

———. 2002. *What teachers should know and be able to do.* Arlington, VA: National Board for Professional Teaching Standards. Retrieved June 4, 2010, from http://www.nbpts.org/UserFiles/File/what_teachers.pdf.

———. 2003. *NBPTS adolescence and young adult science standards,* 2nd ed., Arlington, VA: National Board for Professional Teaching Standards. Retrieved June 4, 2010, from http://nbpts.org/userfiles/File/aya_science_standards.pdf.

———. 2009. National Board certification is "critical for nation's schools," says national teacher of the year finalist, April 27, 2009. *Web Feature Releases.* Retrieved June 4, 2010, from http://nbpts.org/about_us/news_media/web_feature_releases?ID=194.

———. 2010a. *2010 Guide to National Board Certification.* Fairfax, VA. Retrieved June 1, 2010, from http://www.nbpts.org/Index.cfm?t=downloader.cfm&id=1225.

———. 2010b. The Portfolio. National Board for Professional Teaching Standards. Retrieved June 1, 2010, from http://www.nbpts.org/for_candidates/the_portfolio#download.

———. 2010c. Become an Assessor. National Board for Professional Teaching Standards. Retrieved June 1, 2010, from http://www.nbpts.org/get_involved/become_an_assessor.

———. 2010. State and local information. Retrieved June 4, 2010, from http://www.
nbpts.org/resources/state_local_information.

National Commission on Excellence in Education. 1983. *A Nation at risk: The
imperative for education reform.* Washington, D.C.: U.S. Government Printing
Office.

National Research Council. 2001. *Testing teacher candidates: The role of licensure tests
in improving teacher quality,* eds. K. Mitchell, D. Robinson, B. Plake, and
K. Knowles, Committee on Assessment and Teacher Quality, Center for
Education, Board on Testing and Assessment, Division on Behavioral and Social
Sciences and Education. Washington, DC: National Academy Press.

———. 2008. *Assessing accomplished teaching: Advanced-level certification programs.*
Committee on Evaluation of Teacher Certification by the National Board
for Professional Teaching Standards, eds. Milton D. Hakel, J. A. Koenig, and
S. W. Elliott, Working Paper 27, Board on Testing and Assessment, Center
for Education, Division of Behavioral and Social Sciences and Education.
Washington, D.C.: The National Academies Press.

Porter, A. Peter Youngs, and Allan Odden. 2001. Advances in teacher assessments
and their uses. In *Handbook of research on teaching,* ed. V. Richardson, 259–297.
Washington, D.C.: American Educational Research Association.

Pratt, D., and J. Collins. 2001. Summary of five perspectives on "good teaching,"
Teaching Perspectives Inventory (TPI). Retrieved June 4, 2010, from http://www
.teachingperspectives.com/tpi_html/tpi_summaries.htm.

Reichardt, R. 2001. *Toward a comprehensive approach to teacher quality.* Policy Brief.
Colorado, Mid-Continent Research for Education and Learning, Aurora, CO: 13.

Roden, Jon-Paul. 1999. Winners and winners: What I learned from not earning
National Board certification. *Teaching and Change,* 6(4): 416–419.

Rosenfeld, E. 2008. Eduholic. *Teacher Magazine,* Blog entry November 21, 2008.
Retrieved June 4, 2010, from http://blogs.edweek.org/teachers/eduholic/2008/11/.

Rotberg, I. C., M. H. Futrell, and J. M. Lieberman. 1998. National Board
certification: Increasing participation and assessing impacts. *Phi Delta Kappan,*
79(Feb.): 462–466.

Sato, Mistilina. 2008. Ethical tensions in mentoring: Introduction. *New Educator,*
4(3): 199–203.

Sclafani, S., ed. 2009. *Evaluating and rewarding the quality of teachers: International practices.* Organisation for Economic Co-operation and Development. Paris.

Schön, D. A. 1983. *The reflective practitioner: How professionals think in action.* London: Temple Smith.

Schwab, J. J. 1962. The teaching of science as inquiry. In *The Teaching of Science,* ed. J. J. Schwab and P. F. Brandwein. Cambridge, MA: Harvard University Press.

Schwab, Joseph. 1978. *Science, curriculum, and liberal education: Selected essays,* eds. Ian Westbury and Neil J. Wilkof. Chicago: The University of Chicago Press.

Sfard, A. 1998. On two metaphors for learning and the dangers of choosing just one. *Educational Researcher,* 27(2): 4–13.

Shavelson, R., N. Webb, and J. Hotta. 1987. The concept of exchangeability in designing telecourse evaluations. *Journal of Distance Education/Revue de l'enseignmement a distance,* 2(1): 27–40.

Shulman, Judith H., and Mistilina Sato, eds. 2006. *Mentoring teachers toward excellence: Supporting and developing highly qualified teachers.* San Francisco: Jossey-Bass, San Francisco, CA.

Shulman, L. 1986. Those who understand: A conception of teacher knowledge. *American Educator,* 10(1): 9–15, 43–44.

———. 1987. Knowledge and teaching: Foundations of the new reform. *Harvard Educational Review,* 57: 1–22.

———. 1991. *An odyssey of teacher assessment: Final report of the Teacher Assessment Project: An overview of the work.* The Carnegie Corporation of New York.

Shulman, L., and G. Sykes. 1986. A National Board for teaching? In search of a bold standard. Paper prepared for the Task Force on Teaching as a Profession, Carnegie Forum on Education and the Economy.

Standerfer, Stephanie L. 2008. Learning from the National Board for Professional teacher certification (NBPTS) in music. *Bulletin of the Council for Research in Music Education,* 176: 77–88.

Strike, Kenneth A., and George J. Posner. 1992. A revisionist theory of conceptual change. In *Philosophy of Science, Cognitive Psychology, and Educational Theory and Practice,* ed. Richard J. Duschl, 147–176. Albany: State University of New York Press.

Tracz, S., J. Daughtry, J. Henderson-Sparks, C. Newman, and S. Sienty. 2005. The impact of NBPTS participation on teacher practice: Learning from teacher perspectives. *Educational Research Quarterly*, 28(3): 36–50.

Tracz, S., S. Sienty, K. Todorov, J. Snyder, B. Takashima, R. Pensabene, B. Olsen, L. Pauls, and J. Sork, 1995. Improvement in teaching skills: Perspectives from National Board for Professional Teaching Standards field test network candidates. Paper presented at the Annual Conference of the American Educational Research Association, San Francisco, CA.

Tobias, S., and A. Baffert. 2009. *Science teaching as a profession: Why it isn't how it could be.* Research Corporation for Science Advancement, Tucson AZ. Retrieved June 5, 2010, from http://www.rescorp.org/gdresources/downloads/Science_Teaching_as_a_Profession2.pdf.

Toch, Thomas, and Robert Rothman. 2008. *Rush to judgment: Teacher evaluation in public education.* Education Sector Report, Washington, D.C. Retrieved June 5, 2010, from http://www.educationsector.org/usr_doc/RushToJudgment_ES_Jan08.pdf.

Tyack, D., and L. Cuban. 1996. *Tinkering towards utopia.* New York: Columbia University Press.

Weisberg, D., S. Sexton, J. Mulhern, and D. Keeling. 2009. *The widget effect: Our national failure to acknowledge and act on teacher differences.* Brooklyn, NY: The New Teacher Project. Retrieved June 3, 2010, from http://widgeteffect.org/.

Wiebke, K. 2000. My journey through National Board certification. *Instructor,* 110: 26–27.

Winfred, A., W. Bennett, P. Edens, and S. Bell. 2003. Effectiveness of training in organizations: A meta-analysis of design and evaluation features. *Journal of Applied Psychology,* 88(2), 234–245.

Yip, J. 2002. Two short notes on statistics. *Porcupine! On line Journal,* no. 25. Retrieved June 4, 2010, from http://www.hku.hk/ecology/porcupine/por25/25-misc-stat.htm.

Appendix A

Structured Interview Protocols

Note: The *italicized* text did not appear in the interviewee's version.

INTERVIEW PROTOCOLS

Before we begin, do you:

1. *Have a copy of the questions?*
2. *Have the videotape and a VCR and television available?*
3. *Have something to write with?*

Before we go to the handout, I have a few introductory questions I would like to ask.

Introduction Questions:

1. *How long have you been teaching?*
2. *What subjects and grade levels do you teach?*
3. *How would you describe the school in which you teach?*
4. *How would you generally describe your students?*
5. *What is your average class size?*
6. *Describe your current status with National Board regarding the portfolio and assessment center exercises.*

I want to remind you again that our conversation is confidential and has no impact on your assessment exercises or the National Board's evaluation of your work. I remind you of this so that you will feel free to speak your mind in response to the questions in the handout.

I. TEACHING AND LEARNING:

Please examine figure A.1 and student responses 1 and 2. This student work is from a two-week science unit on the Kinetic Theory of Matter in a tenth-grade general chemistry class. The teacher conducted preassessment and postassessment exercises. One of the pre- and post-assessments involved distributing the advertisement (figure A.1) and asking students to write an essay that interprets the ad from a molecular point of view. Student A responded to the preassessment with Artifact response #1. At the end of the unit, Student A responded to the postassessment with response #2.

Among the teacher's learning objectives for the unit were:

1. Students will know and understand the Kinetic Theory of Matter.
2. Students will make connections between their background, experiences, and interests and the content material.

FIGURE A.1
Teaching Artifact for Assessing Student Understanding. Used with permission from Ford Motor Company. All rights reserved.

This assignment was used by the teacher to evaluate student learning of a core concept from the unit on the Kinetic Theory of Matter. More specifically, the assignment was constructed to gauge how well a student was able to describe the properties of matter at the macro level of analysis (solidity and liquidity). Furthermore, the students were expected to then explain the observable physical properties of matter from a molecular level of analysis (i.e., kinetic energy, intermolecular forces, and particle proximity).

At this time, please look over and examine figure A.1 and student responses 1 and 2. When you are ready, I will ask you some questions.

Student Response 1 (Preassessment):

The car is sleek and aerodynamic like a drop of water. A drop of water is made of fluid molecules and it has no sharp edges. The car will flow down the road just like a drop of water will flow across a window. The car is not a fluid, however. The car is made of solid materials like steel, plastic, and rubber. These things have sharp edges and are much stronger than liquids. Cars made of solid molecules are safer for the people inside because solid molecules are different than liquid molecules. It would be really hard to build a car out of liquids!

Two weeks later, at the end of the unit on the Kinetic Theory of Matter, the same student responded to the same question with the following response.

Student Response 2 (Postassessment):

The phrase used has much to do with chemistry, and has many little details to make the car sound so unique. First of all, the author of the quote wants the viewer to imagine the car as a liquid. According to the kinetic theory of a liquid, the molecules move faster than in a solid, but not as fast as gas. They are always in constant motion, relating to the car. The attraction between the liquids is greater in a liquid than in a gas. This attraction is known as *intermolecular force*. Since the bonds are weaker than solids, liquids, can take up any shape. If the car is liquid, the wind can go around it depending on how the liquid shapes itself. Liquids have a very low compressibility, giving the viewer security as well. In the event of an accident even though the car moves so fast. Fluidity is a property that a liquid contains. If something flows, it is often seen as smooth and clean. Liquids, by having strong bonds but relatively high molecular movement, move over surfaces like a snake in constant motion. This same idea is thought about the Mercury Sable.

When the author states "yet feels so solid," he is trying to give the viewer comfort since the car looks like it moves so quickly. This relates to the kinetic theory of solids. The intermolecular bonds between the molecules are much greater than in liquids or gases. The molecules have much less kinetic energy and are found extremely close together. Since the car feels so solid, it gives the driver a sense control of what he is doing. Also, a solid has no compressibility and is extremely dense, giving the reader security in the event of a crash. The car will be able to withstand high amounts of impact. If something is solid, it has definite shape to it, therefore luxury. The car flows like a liquid, but is safe and comfortable at the same time.

Questions:
1. *Based on this student's two responses, how would you describe the student's growth in understanding about the kinetic theory of matter?*
2. *What evidence can you identify from the responses that supports your conclusion?*
3. *What does the work tell you about any misconceptions or gaps in understanding this student may be experiencing?*
4. *Based on your comments and Artifacts 1, 2, & 3, describe the feedback or further instruction (if any) that the teacher should provide the student?*
5. *Do you think the car advertisement is an effective instructional resource in establishing a connection between the student's background, experiences, and interests and the content material? Why or why not?*
6. *Based on your comments and the artifacts provided, what advice might you give this teacher to improve this lesson or assignment in the future?*

II. TEACHING AND SCIENTIFIC INQUIRY

A teacher walks around the laboratory as students work in small groups on a lab exercise. The students are working on one of their first activities to explore the evolutionary concept of "adaptation" and Darwin's theory of natural selection. Students are performing a version of the "peppered moth" adaptation lab using three different moth types. In the activity, red, white, and newspaper print moths are all set against a newspaper background. The purpose of the activity is to better understand how a range of characteristics in a species (in this case the color of the peppered moths' wings) plays a role in the survival of the species. Some of the teacher's objectives for this activity include:

1. Students will understand how the environment interacts with a range of characteristics within a population through natural selection.
2. Students will learn to record and analyze data.
3. Students will experience the process of scientific inquiry and scientific reasoning.
4. Students will learn to work collaboratively in groups to solve problems.

The activity can best be described as a modeling of the predator-prey relationship. One student monitors the "environment" (newspaper and cutout moths) while the other students act as predators. In repeated cycles, the monitor adds new moths to the newspaper background and then other students in the group "attack" the environment, snatching the first moth they see. The monitor then replenishes the population with one of each moth type in preparation for the next round of predation. The following table provides the data for the activity after 20 rounds.

In table A.1, you can see the three moth types and how the numbers each of changes.

A teacher listens to the group that recorded the information in the data table have the following conversation regarding a question on the laboratory guide sheet. The question asks:

> If the background for this activity were changed to a colorful type of paper such as the Sunday cartoon section or colorful wrapping paper, how might the population of moths used in this experiment change?

The group is made up of four students: one male—Evan—and three females—Latisha, Yanping, and Alejandra. Alejandra is from Ecuador and new to the class. She says nothing, but is listening and taking notes. Here is

Table A.1.   Student Data Table for Peppered Moth Activity

Predator Attack/ New Generation	Number of White Moths	Number of Red Moths	Number of Newspaper Moths
Before First Attack	33	34	33
After 10th	34	14	43
After 20th	33	1	53

the conversation: *(I can read this passage to you or you may read it yourself. Which would you prefer?)*

> EVAN: I don't think it would have any effect. The red ones would still get eaten the most because they are brightest and the newspaper moths would get eaten least because they blend in the most.

> YANPING: Maybe, but in our experiment, the newspaper moths' population gets bigger because they are harder to see against the black and white newspaper background. But, if the background had lots of colors, then they might stick out and the red ones would be harder to see.

> LATISHA: O.K., but how will the population change? There are so few red ones now that I don't see how they could grow in numbers. And since there are so many newspaper ones now, I think that their population will stay the way it is.

> EVAN: I agree. If we change to the colorful background, the population will stay the way it is. The number of newspaper moths will stop growing and the red moths will stop getting smaller.

> YANPING: Well, the red can't get much smaller. Their population is already at one now. If it gets any smaller, they will disappear. When we started this experiment, there were equal numbers of all three moths. With the colorful background, couldn't the population change back to the way it was?

There is a long pause as the other group members provide no response to this question.

Questions:
1. *How do you think the teacher should respond to this group of students in order to support scientific inquiry? (If the teacher responds by saying "do the experiment," ask what is recommended if time is a limiting factor).*
2. *Do you think your suggestion(s) supports student scientific inquiry? Is there another one that might better promote that goal?*
3. *Another one of the teacher's goals was to help students understand how the environment interacts with a species' population through natural selection. Do you think your suggestion(s) helps achieve that goal?*
4. *Suppose this teacher also said she had a professional goal of ensuring fairness, equity, and access for all students. What steps (if any) should the teacher take to fulfill this objective?*

5. *From their discussion, what aspects of the interaction between the environment and species' characteristics do any or all of the students appear to understand and what misconceptions may still remain?*

6. *Do you see any evidence that any of these students are learning to engage in scientific inquiry? What evidence do you see?*

7. *If you had observed this lesson, and were a mentor to this teacher, what advice or guidance would you give this teacher regarding the planning or teaching of this lesson to this group of students?*

III. Description of a Successful Lesson

Take a moment and think of a recent class that was memorable because of the student learning that you believe took place. It should be a recent occasion from a specific class that you remember well and are comfortable discussing. When you have an example ready in your mind, I will ask you some questions.

1. *Please describe for me the setting for the class you will share. (What was the subject? Length of class? When did this class take place?)*

2. *How many students were in the class and what grade levels were represented?*

3. *What were the student learning goals for this lesson?*

4. *Why were these goals important for these students?*

5. *How did these goals fit into your overall goals for the year?*

6. *What about this particular example of teaching and learning is most significant to you? (What happened in this class that was particularly memorable for you?)*

7. *What specific evidence helped you determine that you were successful at achieving the identified learning goals with your students?*

8. *Were there any ethnic, cultural, or linguistic diversity circumstances you considered in the planning and teaching of this class?*

9. *Did the range of abilities of the students (e.g., exceptional needs, cognitive, social and behavioral, sensory, or physical challenges) and the personality of the class affect your planning? If so, how?*

10. *In the teaching of this lesson, did spontaneity play a role in the success of this class? If so, how?*

11. *What (if anything) would you do differently if you had the opportunity to pursue this lesson in the future? Why?*

IV. EXAMINING A WHOLE-CLASS DISCUSSION IN SCIENCE

The videotape in your packet contains a portion of a whole-class discussion about science. The segment you are about to see is from an advanced placement environmental science class made up of college-bound eleventh and twelfth graders. They are an ethnically and linguistically diverse group of students. Countries from North and South America, Asia, and Europe are represented. English is a second language for most, though nearly all have been studying English since they started going to school.

They have been visiting a local ecosystem approximately once a month for the last six months with their teacher. They have worked in teams and individually to collect both biotic and abiotic data to help them answer the question: "Is this a healthy ecosystem?"

In the clip you are about to see, the teacher has just asked the students, "What is the one most important observation or finding from your individual projects that may shed some light on the health of this ecosystem?" The video clip presents several different students' individual projects focusing on two different species: water cabbages and ripple bugs. Prior to this clip, each of the four teams shared their collective results on different areas of the preserve with the rest of the class. After the clip, each student was to provide a final conclusion regarding the health of the preserve. This is their last visit to the park.

The teacher has set several goals for this discussion:

1. Students will think and reason scientifically.
2. Students will communicate their ideas clearly to the group.
3. Students will demonstrate a sense of ownership over the discussion.
4. Students will come to a better understanding regarding the current status of the ecosystem under investigation.

At this time, I would ask you to please watch the videotape carefully and then I will ask you some questions. Feel free to take notes during the viewing and you may put the phone down if you so desire.

Questions:

1. *How do you describe the academic atmosphere (learning environment) created by the teacher?*

2. *Suppose you were watching this classroom as a representative of an advisory committee focused on a school-wide concern regarding teachers treating their students fairly and equitably. What evidence (if any) can you cite from the tape that indicates that this teacher was, or was not, fair and equitable with learners?*

3. *How would you describe the level of student engagement in this clip?*

4. *According to the National Board's standards, accomplished science teachers facilitate and support meaningful scientific discussion. Do you think the teacher helps students explore and understand important scientific ideas? (What does this teacher do or not do that supports your answer?)*

5. *How would you describe the quality of student-to-student interactions with regard to scientific, analytical, and critical thought?*

6. *Based on the students who participated in this clip, how would you describe the level of student understanding regarding the process of scientific inquiry and content related to environmental sciences?*

7. *If this teacher were a colleague of yours and approached you for some input into this lesson, what advice, guidance, or insights would you offer that might improve the teaching and learning in this class?*

8. *In your opinion, what is the proper role or roles of the teacher in a whole-class discussion about science?*

V. ACCOMPLISHMENTS OUTSIDE OF CLASS: THE IMPACT ON STUDENT LEARNING

The National Board for Professional Teaching Standards has deemed that accomplished teachers contribute to the teaching and learning of their colleagues and the quality of the professional community at large. Figure A.2 provides a list of common professional development activities. For each activity, please indicate whether you have direct experience with the item. Then, on a scale of 1 to 5 where 1 is "no effect" and 5 is "strong effect," rate each activity on its general ability to improve student learning. If you are unsure of the effect, you may enter a "3."

Is there any other activity missing from this list that you think is especially helpful in improving student learning?

The National Board for Professional Teaching Standards has deemed that accomplished teachers know and make good use of all available resources in the community to improve student learning in the classroom. Figure A.3 provides

Figure A.2. List of Professional Activities and Accomplishments

Professional Activity/Accomplishment	Yes	No	Rating
1. Attending educational conferences/workshops			
2. Professional development activities at school			
3. Reading educational literature			
4. Reading scientific literature			
5. Writing educational articles (professional)			
6. Writing scientific articles			
7. Serving on an advisory committee at the school or district level			
8. Serving as a union representative			
9. Developing science curriculum for your class, school, or district			
10. Mentoring a new or student teacher			
11. Leading a professional development workshop for your colleagues			
12. Taking a science course at a local university			
13. Collaborating with colleagues on an interdisciplinary project			
14. Pursuing National Board certification			
15. Taking an educational course at a local university			

a list of common ways teachers interact with the community. For each of the following items, please indicate whether you have direct experience with the item. Then, on a scale of 1 to 5 where 1 is "no effect" and 5 is "strong effect," rate each resource or activity on its general ability to improve student learning. If you are unsure of the effect, you may enter a "3."

1. *Is there any other activity missing from this list that you think is especially helpful in improving student learning?*
2. *Based on both of these lists, which one activity do you think is most important to help a teacher become more effective at improving student learning? Please explain your reasons for making this choice. (If the teacher doesn't choose Board certification, ask about why they rated National Board certification a _____.)*

Figure A.3. List of Community Resources and Accomplishments

Community Resource/Accomplishment	Yes	No	Rating
1. Participating in parent-teacher conferences			
2. Attending open house night			
3. Telephone calls to parents/guardians			
4. Emails communication with parents/guardians			
5. Assisting in scientific research with a local college			
6. Classroom observations from parents			
7. Contacting outside experts by telephone or email			
8. Recruiting guest speakers from the community			
9. Supervising after school activities			
10. Coaching sports			
11. Working with the Parent-Teacher Association			
12. Establishing a partnership with a local teachers' college			
13. Contributing time to local religious or charity groups			
14. Serving as an academic advisor to students			
15. Serving on the local Board of Education			

This concludes our conversation. I want to thank you for your time and participation in this study. Your thoughtful answers are greatly appreciated. I would like to leave you with a few final reminders:

1. *Please fill out the top of page 1 and send the handout and videotape back to me in the self-addressed stamped envelope at your earliest convenience.*
2. *After I receive the handout and videotape, you should expect to receive your $25 gift certificate to Amazon.com in 8 to 12 weeks. I will send you an e-mail heads up when it will arrive.*
3. *Once again, on behalf of the National Board and Michigan State University, I want to thank you for your valuable contributions to this study. Good luck with National Board certification and your teaching!*

Appendix B

Analysis of Population Demographics

To examine the demographic data, three specific questions were asked:

1. How do each of the cohorts (parent populations from which the samples were selected) involved in this study compare with each other?
2. How well do the samples selected from the cohort populations accurately reflect the characteristics of the parent population?
3. How do the samples selected from the cohort populations compare with each other?

To address these questions, the demographic analysis is divided into three distinct comparisons: (1) cohort to cohort, (2) cohort to group, and (3) group to group. The discussion that follows looks at each one of these comparisons in detail.

COHORT-TO-COHORT COMPARISONS

How did each of the three cohorts (2002, 2003, and 2004) compare with each other in their demographic characteristics? To answer this question, the data was analyzed with a combination of paired t-tests, z-statistics, and chi-square tests. Data for each cohort provided by the National Board remained limited to a few basic characteristics. These variables included population size, gender, geographic region, years experience, and (for cohorts 1 and 2) the outcome of certification process for each candidate. Though by no means exhaustive, the information does provide a good basis to compare the basic profile of each year's population. A summary of the cohort-to-cohort comparison is presented in table B.1.

Based on the five vital characteristics available at the cohort level, it is clear from table B.1 that the cohorts do not differ from each other in most categories. Group 3 is a smaller population than the other two groups. One possible reason for this situation may be the availability of funds to support and encourage teachers to pursue National Board certification. The availability of funds for incentive and supportive purposes may fluctuate from year to year depending on the financial status of a district or state.

With regard to candidates' success at the National Board certification process, data was only available for cohorts 1 and 2. (Due to the timing of this study, pass/fail data was not available for cohort 3). For both populations, the rate of passing was very close to 40 percent. This compares as expected with the overall passing rate of 50 percent for all twenty-six certificates combined and in agreement with the historically stable pass rate of nearly 40 percent for Adolescence and Young Adult Science (AYA Science) certification.

Only in years of experience is there a noticeable difference between cohorts. Group 3 appears to have fewer years of experience, which is marginally

Table B.1.   Cohort Comparison of Demographic Variables

Geographical Origin	2001–2002 Cohort 1	2002–2003 Cohort 2	2003–2004 Cohort 3
N	431	434	356
Region	Percent	Percent	Percent
New England	7.19	2.53	3.37
Mid-Atlantic	5.57	7.37	10.39
South	51.51	52.53	46.91
Midwest	18.1	14.29	20.22
Southwest	3.71	2.53	5.06
West	13.92	20.74	14.04
Gender	Percent	Percent	Percent
Female	64.04	61.29	63.2
Male	35.96	38.71	36.8
Years of Experience			
Mean	13.16	12.72	12.09
Standard Deviation	7.89	7.55	7.34

significant at the .05 level. However, Group 3 is not significantly different from Group 2 with regard to this measure.

Where did the teachers in each of these cohorts come from? The answer to this question is not surprising and quite consistent across all three cohorts. Since its inception in 1987, the National Board has found most of its support in the south. This support continues today, followed by the western and midwestern states. The lowest represented regions in all three cohorts are the southwestern and New England states. Only in the mid-Atlantic states does a little inconsistency appear, with cohort 3 having nearly twice the representation as cohort 1. One possible explanation for inconsistencies in regional representation can be traced to fluctuations in state and district support for Board certification. If one year money is available and the next it is not, then it is reasonable that the numbers of teachers opting to pursue Board certification would parallel these changes.

When gender profiles are examined, an even higher level of consistency is observed. For all three cohorts, female candidates outnumber male candidates nearly two to one. In an historically female-dominated profession like teaching, this result is not surprising. However, the study did focus on the level of secondary science that traditionally has a higher percentage of males than other levels of PK–12 education.

With years of experience, cohort 3 is shown to be significantly different (but only marginally at the .05 level with a p value of .051) from cohort 1. With slightly over twelve years of experience, cohort 3 would appear to be less experienced, but not necessarily younger. With more teachers entering the profession as a second career (through Troops to Teachers, for example), it appears that these nontraditional teachers are more willing to delve into National Board certification earlier than traditionally prepared teachers.

However, one could argue that, with all three cohorts averaging more than twelve and less than fourteen years of experience, this difference does not warrant too much concern. After seven years of teaching, it is not unreasonable to think of teachers as experienced. Overall, a dozen years in teaching indicates that most candidates for National Board certification in AYA Science have a wealth of experience that they bring to the process. It is important to note that the National Board requires that teachers have a minimum of three years full-time teaching experience to qualify for certification candidacy. If one cohort

Table B.2.   Summary of Cohort Comparison

Demographic Variable	2001–2002 Cohort 1	2002–2003 Cohort 2	2003–2004 Cohort 3
Region	Different	Different	Different
Gender	Same	Same	Different
Years of Experience	Same	Same	Different
Pass/Fail	Same	Same	Same

had, on average, half the experience of the others, there would be reason for concern. However, with these results, "years of experience" does not appear to be a serious threat to the study.

A summary of the cohort-cohort comparison is provided in table B.2. Differences pertaining to geographic regions among all three cohorts are not unexpected. All in all, the three populations are quite close to each other on the identified variables with the small differences in size and years' experience. This level of homogeneity between cohorts appears to satisfy the recurrent institutional cycle design assumption that from year to year the populations do not significantly change.

CHI SQUARE FOR CATEGORICAL VARIABLES

The same population is defined as an average value of the total divided by the number of cohorts compared. So the deviation is a measure of how different the actual is from the expected. With this analysis it is apparent that most candidates came from the south, west, and midwest and the fewest candidates came from the New England, mid-Atlantic, and southwestern states. The greatest deviation from expected values is found in those areas represented by the smallest sample size, indicating that the most likely explanation for such variability is due to the small number of individuals. Though these differences are consistent across all three populations, differences between groups with respect to region of origin are significant at the .05 level.

Besides availability of supportive funding at the state level, another possible explanation for identified differences is that the total number of teachers seeking AYA Science certification is still relatively small when compared with the total number of secondary science teachers (about 160,000 secondary science teachers according to Blank, Langesen, and Petermann [2007]). In addition, the small numbers of total candidates are being further reduced into six different categories increasing the chances of identifying differences in pairwise comparisons. Regardless of which explanation is more correct, the identified differences should not greatly impact the results of this study since in all likelihood the number of teachers who decide to pursue certification is beyond the realm of control for the researchers.

COHORT-TO-GROUP COMPARISONS

Turning the focus now to the selected groups from the cohort populations, the question becomes, "How do the selected groups compare with their parent cohort populations?" The short answer is that each group is a representative sample of its parent population. An examination of each variable provides even more evidence for this claim. Table B.3 provides a detailed summary of each of the three cohorts and their respective group samples.

With respect to region, all four groups (1, 2A, 2B, and 3) did not differ significantly from the parent population at the .05 level. Only Group 1 was significantly different at the .10 level. When gender is examined, the same condition exists: No group differed from its parent population at the .05 level, with only Group 1 showing a significant difference at the .10 level. For the pass/fail comparison, once again data was only available for Groups 1 and 2, which showed no significant differences at either the .05 or .10 levels.

In the cohort-group analysis, "years of experience" provides the most anomalous results. First of all, Group 1 is significantly different from its parent population at the .01 level, with Group 1 having on average more then three years more experience. Though comparisons with the other three groups were not significantly different, a closer examination reveals some important tendencies. For example, Groups 1, 2A, and 2B all have more years experience than their parent population, though both Group 2A and 2B are not significantly different. Group 3, however, has fewer years experience (just over 1 year difference) than its parent cohort (though this difference was also not significant). Group 3 appears to be less experienced than Groups 1 and 2. This may be due to alterations in the sampling process and one that needs to be addressed if this study is repeated.

When each group is compared with its cohort on the available information, a remarkable level of similarity exists. In summary, each group demonstrates the observed characteristics of region, gender, and pass/fail rates congruous with the parent cohort. Only years of experience showed signs of meaningful difference, though this is probably best explained with inconsistencies in sampling

Table B.3. Cohort-to-Group Comparisons

	2001–2002		2002–2003			2003–2004	
	Cohort 1	Group 1	Cohort 2	Group 2A	Group 2B	Cohort 3	Group 3
N	431	40	434	18	20	356	40
Region	*Percent*	*Percent*	*Percent*	*Percent*	*Percent*	*Percent*	*Percent*
New England	7.19	10.00	2.53	0.00	0.00	3.37	2.50
Mid-Atlantic	5.57	15.00	7.37	5.56	5.00	10.39	10.00
South	51.51	52.50	52.53	50.00	40.00	46.91	45.00
Midwest	18.10	12.50	14.29	5.56	10.00	20.22	20.00
Southwest	3.71	0.00	2.53	5.56	5.00	5.06	2.50
West	13.92	10.00	20.74	33.33	40.00	14.04	20.00
Chi-square		9.46		3.54	5.57		1.65
df		5		5	5		5
p <		0.092		0.617	0.350		0.895
Gender	*Percent*	*Percent*	*Percent*	*Percent*	*Percent*	*Percent*	*Percent*
Female	64.04	77.50	61.29	77.78	60.00	63.20	67.50
Male	35.96	22.50	38.71	22.22	40.00	36.80	32.50
Chi-square*		2.92		1.94	0.01		0.25
df		1		1	1		1
p <		0.088		0.164	0.942		0.618
Years of Experience							
Mean	13.16	16.43	12.72	14.72	14.70	12.09	11.00
Standard Error		1.25		1.78	1.69		1.16
Standard Deviation	7.89	7.57	7.55	9.76	8.96	7.34	7.04
N**	427	40	426	18	20	348	40
z-statistic		2.62		1.13	1.17		-0.94
p <		0.009		0.260	0.240		0.348

*Corrected for discontinuity.

**Excluded cases with missing data.

Table B.4. Summary of Cohort to Group Comparisons for Differences

Demographic Variable	2001–2002 Cohort 1–G1	2002–2003 Cohort 2–G2A	2002–2003 Cohort 2–G2B	2003–2004 Cohort 3–G3
Region	Not Different	Not Different	Not Different	Not Different
Gender	Not Different	Not Different	Not Different	Not Different
Years of Experience	Different	Not Different	Not Different	Not Different
Pass/Fail	Not Different	Not Different	Not Different	Not Different

procedures. There also appears to be a trend toward less experienced teachers applying for certification with each ensuing year. For 2002, the average number of years was 13.16, 2003 was 12.72, and for 2004 it drops to 12.10 years experience. The study also reflects this trend with each consecutive year having fewer years' experience then the prior year. However, where samples for Groups 1 and 2 are higher than the population, sample 3 is lower. A summary of the analysis between cohort and groups is provided in table B.4.

GROUP-TO-GROUP COMPARISON

The last question concerning demographics that needs to be addressed is, "How do the selected samples from each cohort compare with each other on a wider range of characteristics?" The recurrent institutional cycle design rests upon a key assumption that from year to year, the samples selected from the parent populations (cohorts) for the study will not differ greatly from each other.

Even if differences are identified from year to year in the target populations, these differences may or may not become manifest in the selected samples. To facilitate the efficient analysis of the more abundant demographic information on candidates at the group level in this study, variables have been divided into categorical, continuous, and survey-type data.

More detailed and extensive information regarding educational history, institutions attended, certification and preparation program details, standardized test scores for both students and teachers, graduation and drop-out rates in schools, district profiles, and socioeconomic indicators such as rate of free and reduced lunch were not collected. Instead, three brief survey questions were asked at the time of written consent that asked each candidate about (1) how they learned about National Board certification, (2) their motivation for pursuing National Board certification, and (3) the support available and utilized during their efforts toward certification.

The reason for the omission of inquiries into other important candidate and school characteristics was more practical than theoretical. The project was very sensitive to the time demands of the study on teachers who already had a full agenda of work-related responsibilities. It was thought that a more extensive and therefore time-consuming preinterview survey would prove a significant deterrence to participation in the study.

In addition, the interview was already longer than an hour. Every additional question would put more demand on the attention of the participating teacher and thus might lead to a decrease of quality in the responses provided. Though it would have been helpful to collect the omitted data sets, pressures of practicality and time restraints resulted in the current compromise of demographic variables.

CATEGORICAL VARIABLES

Categorical variables communicate information that falls within a series of particular choices (e.g., gender) rather than a range (e.g., age). The additional demographic information for participants in each group was collected both prior to and at the beginning of each interview. The analysis of categorical variables is summarized in table B.5. A chi-square analysis of these variables reveals no significant differences between groups. The distribution of teachers with respect to grades taught, content specialty, school context, geographic location, student type, or gender appears to be the same across all groups.

A special note about "student type": No outside measurements such as standardized assessments, district-wide tests, or any other form of data was collected on the students of the teachers in this study. The data on "student ability" or "student type" results from a teacher's self-report. More specifically, each teacher was asked, "How would you generally describe your students?"

The assignment of a 1, 2, 3, or 4 was based on the teacher's description. If the teacher said that generally speaking his or her students were "below average" ability or "low" achievers, then that was coded as a 1. If the teacher said that his or her students were of "average" ability, then that was coded as a 2. If a teacher said that his or her students were "above average" in ability or "high" achievers, then this was coded as a 3. In some cases the teacher indicated that the students "ran the gamut" of abilities or that their students were a "mix" or "varied" in ability. In the event that a teacher indicated a range of student abilities, the response was coded as a 4.

Table B.5. Group-to-Group Comparisons on Categorical Demographic Variables

	Group 1	Group 2A	Group 2B	Group 3	Chi-Square	df	p <
		Distribution of Teachers (%)					
GRADES					8.63	6	0.1954
9th–10th	30	39	5	23			
11th–12th	25	33	45	28			
9th–12th	45	28	50	50			
CONTENT					6.29	9	0.7110
Biology	43	33	45	40			
Chemistry	30	28	35	38			
Physics	3	11	10	10			
Other	25	28	10	13			
SCHOOL					10.50	9	0.3113
Urban	35	22	15	30			
Suburban	35	44	35	50			
Rural	28	28	50	20			
Other	3	6	0	0			
REGION					18.48	15	0.2382
Mid-Atlantic	15	6	5	10			
Midwest	13	6	10	20			
New England	10	0	0	3			
South	53	50	40	45			
Southwest	0	6	5	3			
West	10	33	40	20			

Rather then a measure of student ability, this information is more of an indication of how teachers perceived their students' abilities. Interestingly, teachers who described their students as high achievers (coded as a 3) were correlated with subjects who rated higher in this study. This tendency was consistent for both the preintervention and postintervention observations. Translated, this might mean that teachers who had greater faith or more optimistic perceptions of their students' abilities were more likely to score higher when compared with those teachers who rated their students less than high. Those who described their students as mixed scored on a par with the group that said their students were average.

This apparent relationship could represent teachers' accurate reflection of student ability and thus teachers with below-average academic performance do not score as well as their peers in this study. Or their perceptions may or may not be an accurate reflection of student ability, but teachers who believe their students are higher-than-average performers (or teachers who have higher expectations of success) are more likely to score better in this study.

Either way, the results do not affect the analysis or results of this study directly, but rather the observation serves as an interesting point for possible future research.

CONTINUOUS VARIABLES

If the continuous variables are included with the group-to-group comparison, some significant differences can be identified with use of t-tests. A detailed summary of these comparisons is provided in table B.6. Though groups did not differ with the average size of their classes or the length of their responses in this study, they were different with respect to years of experience (see table B.7). Each consecutive year saw a decrease in the average number of years taught over the course of this study. Just as with the parent populations, the years of experience decreased from Group 1 to Group 2 to Group 3. More specifically, Group 3 demonstrates a difference at the .05 level.

In addition, not only does Group 3 have fewer years experience than Groups 1 and 2, but it also shows fewer years' experience than its parent population. This relationship is consistent with the cohort-group comparison, which also showed that Group 3 had fewer years experience than the other two preceding cohorts.

SURVEY QUESTIONS

Before a candidate was interviewed, he or she provided a signed consent form in accordance with the University's policy regarding the ethical conduct of research. On this form were four multiple-choice questions aimed at getting a sense of how the candidate (1) learned about National Board certification, (2) what incentives may have been involved in the choice to pursue certification, and (3) what (if any) resources they may have used during the process. The results shown in table B.8 indicate some interesting similarities and differences.

With regard to the first question on how the candidate heard about National Board certification, only Group 2A was different. They heard about the certification process through the media to a higher degree than the rest of the groups. The rest of the groups heard about National Board certification primarily through colleagues (i.e., word of mouth).

Question 2 was potentially a very important question for this study. If enough individuals indicated that they pursued National Board certification with no financial incentive, then a means of comparing learning outcomes between those with intrinsic motivation (no incentives) and those candidates

Table B.6. Group-to-Group Comparisons on Continuous Demographic Variables

	Groups				Comparisons of the Sample Groups				
	Group 1	Group 2A	Group 2B	Group 3	Source	DF	Sum of Squares	Mean Square	F Value
Years Experience									
N	40	18	20	40					
Mean	16.4	15.3	14.7	11.0	Model	3	635.1	211.7	3.24
Std Dev	7.6	10.2	9.0	7.0	Error	114	7452.0	65.4	
Class Size									
Mean	25.5	24.7	25.8	25.1	Model	3	14.2	4.7	0.16
Std Dev	5.4	4.9	5.3	5.8	Error	114	3425.2	30.0	

Table B.7. Orthogonal Contrast Tests Between Groups on Years of Experience

Contrast	df	SS	MS	F Value	Pr > F
Group 3 vs. Others	1	509.41895	509.4189	7.79	**0.0062**
Group 1 vs. Group 2	1	38.595946	38.5959	0.59	0.4438
Group 2A vs. Group 2B	1	3.8	3.8	0.06	0.8099

with extrinsic motivation (incentives) would be possible. Unfortunately, approximately 90 percent of the teachers participating in this study across all groups listed some form of financial incentive. Therefore, an important dimension of linking learning with motivation could not be addressed.

The results do show is that among the 90 percent who had some sort of financial incentive, Group 2B was significantly different than the other groups in that they were more likely to be enticed by salary, step, or rank increase, or with a one-time bonus after successfully completing the process.

With regard to question 3 on support through the process, Group 2A and Group 3 were more likely to expect support from their school or through a district support group, whereas Group 2B utilized support from an e-mail or online resource. Generally speaking, approximately 90 percent of the subjects in this study utilized some form of support to help them through the certification process. To what extent and how valuable this support was to their efforts is unknown. Questions regarding the role of support networks and motivating factors in the quality and quantity of learning from National Board certification must be left to future research projects.

For now and for purposes of this study, the responses to these questions paint a fairly clear picture. First of all, a majority of teachers heard about National Board certification through a colleague. Nearly all the teachers who participated in this study had some form of financial incentive and utilized some form of support through the process.

The significant differences identified with this analysis (i.e., Group 2A hearing about certification through the media or Group 2B's difference with incentive) are most likely due to the small sample size of Group 2A (n = 18) and 2B (n = 20). This explanation is supported by the fact that significant differences were not found in either of the larger Groups 1 and 3. In addition, if the results from Groups 2A and 2B are averaged, their differences from the rest of the study would in all likelihood disappear. Therefore, it is not necessary to place too much importance on how these differences might relate to the observed results.

Table B.8. Group-to-Group Comparisons on Survey Question Responses

Survey Questions 1–3	Group 1	Group 2A	Group 2B	Group 3	Chi-Square (with 3 df)	$p <$
1. How did you first hear about National Board certification?						
a) colleague	47.50	44.44	50.00	65.00	3.395	0.335
b) media	7.50	27.78	20.00	5.00	8.156	**0.043**
c) union	10.00	5.56	5.00	5.00	1.000	0.801
d) school administration	15.00	11.11	20.00	15.00	0.591	0.898
e) other (please specify):	35.00	33.33	20.00	15.00	5.131	0.162
2. What incentives did your district, state, or school offer to encourage teachers to pursue National Board certification?						
a) salary, step, or rank increase	37.50	33.33	**80.00**	32.50	14.184	**0.003**
b) yearly bonus for life of certificate	52.50	27.78	30.00	52.50	5.795	0.122
c) one-time bonus	12.50	27.78	**50.00**	17.50	11.679	**0.009**
d) none	12.50	5.56	5.00	12.50	1.480	0.687
e) other (please specify):	20.00	22.22	30.00	20.00	0.932	0.818
3. In your efforts to complete the certification requirements, which resource(s) do you anticipate using or have used?						
a) school or district support group	50.00	**77.78**	20.00	**65.00**	15.620	**0.001**
b) e-mail group	10.00	11.11	**60.00**	32.50	20.151	**0.000**
c) web	25.00	38.89	20.00	40.00	3.812	0.282
d) none	10.00	11.11	5.00	2.50	2.450	0.484
e) other (please specify):	52.50	22.22	25.00	45.00	7.204	0.066

Appendix C

Portfolio Prompts and Interview Protocols Comparison

NBPTS Portfolio Entry	NBPTS Portfolio Prompt	Interview Prompt	Supported Standard in AYA Science
Context	What are the relevant features of your teaching context (school, class, students, community) that were influential in developing your response to this entry?	What subjects and grade levels do you teach? How would you describe the school in which you teach? What is your average class size?	I. Understanding Students
	What are the number, ages, and grades of the students in the class featured in this entry and the title and subject matter of the class?	How would you generally describe your students? What subjects and grade levels do you teach?	I. Understanding Students
I. Teaching a Major Idea over Time	What are the educationally important characteristics of each of the three pieces of work? What does the work tell you about the students' growth in understanding of the major idea in science?	Based on this student's two responses, how would you describe the student's growth in understanding about the kinetic theory of matter?	X. Assessment
	How successful was the instructional sequence in advancing student understanding of the selected major idea? What worked and what didn't work? What does the work tell you about any challenges or misunderstandings this student is experiencing?	What evidence can you identify from the responses that supports your conclusion?	X. Assessment
		What does the work tell you about any misconceptions or gaps in understanding this student may be experiencing?	II. Knowledge of Science
	Taken together, what does the student work suggest about next steps for your instruction, for the class, or for individual students?	Based upon your comments and artifacts 1, 2, and 3, describe the feedback or further instruction (if any) that the teacher should provide the student?	VIII. Conceptual Understandings

What are specific examples of ways you provided students with a context for the science featured in this sequence by establishing connections to students' backgrounds, experiences, and interests, and to other disciplines and areas of study (e.g., mathematics, history, technology's impact on society, ethics, etc.). In other words, how do you help students make meaning of science and internalize its relevance?

What are specific examples of ways you make good use of instructional resources to support your teaching and extend student learning? Based on your students and your teaching context, why did you select these instructional resources to support your teaching?

What would you do differently, and why, if you were given the opportunity to teach this particular sequence with these students again?

How did you support student inquiry as they analyzed, considered, and evaluated the final results of the investigation?

II. Active Scientific Inquiry

Do you think the car advertisement is an effective instructional resource in establishing a connection between the student's background, experiences, and interests and the content material? Why or why not?

III. Instructional Resources

Based on your comments and the artifacts provided, what advice might you give this teacher to improve this lesson/assignment in the future?

How do you think the teacher should respond to this group of students in order to support scientific inquiry?

XII. Collegiality and Leadership

VII. Science Inquiry
IV. Engagement

NBPTS Portfolio Entry	NBPTS Portfolio Prompt	Interview Prompt	Supported Standard in AYA Science
	How did you support student inquiry in order to conceptualize the primary questions and/or methodology of the investigation?	Do you think your suggestions support student scientific inquiry? Is there another suggestion that further promote that goal?	VII. Science Inquiry XIII. Reflection
	How did you support student inquiry during the collection and processing of data during the investigation?	One of the teacher's goals was to help students understand how the environment interacts with a species' population through natural selection. Do you think your suggestions help achieve that goal?	IX. Contexts of Science II. Knowledge of Science
	How do interactions in the videotape illustrate your ability to help all students explore and understand the scientific concepts being discussed?	Suppose this teacher also said she had a professional goal of ensuring fairness, equity, and access for all students. What steps (if any) should the teacher take to fulfill this objective?	VI. Equitable Participation
	How well were the learning goals for this inquiry investigation achieved?	From their discussion, what aspects of the interaction between the environment and species' characteristics do any or all of the students appear to understand, and what misconceptions may still remain?	X. Assessment
	Cite one interaction on the videotape that shows a student or students learning to engage in scientific inquiry.	Do you see any evidence that any of these students are learning to engage in scientific inquiry? What evidence do you see?	VII. Science Inquiry

III. Whole-Class Discussion		
What parts of the investigation were particularly effective in terms of reaching your goals with this group of students? Why do you think so? What would you do differently if you had the opportunity to pursue this investigation in the future with a different class? Why?	If you had observed this lesson, and were a mentor to this teacher, what advice or guidance would you give this teacher regarding the planning or teaching of this lesson to this group of students?	XIII. Reflection XII. Collegiality and Leadership
As you review the videotape, what parts of the discussion were particularly effective in terms of reaching your goals with this group of students? Why?	How do you describe the academic atmosphere (learning environment) created by the teacher?	V. Learning Environment
Describe a specific example from this lesson as seen on the videotape that shows how you ensure fairness, equity, and access for all students in your class.	Suppose you were watching this classroom as a representative of an advisory committee focused on a schoolwide concern regarding teachers treating their students fairly and equitably. What evidence (if any) can you site from the tape that indicates that this teacher was, or was not, fair and equitable with learners?	VI. Equitable Participation
What interactions on the videotape show a student or students learning to reason and think scientifically and to communicate that reasoning and thinking?	How would you describe the level of student engagement in this clip?	IV. Engagement

NBPTS Portfolio Entry	NBPTS Portfolio Prompt	Interview Prompt	Supported Standard in AYA Science
	What interactions on the videotape show a student or students learning to reason and think scientifically and to communicate that reasoning and thinking?	According to the National Board's standards, accomplished science teachers facilitate and support meaningful scientific discussion. Do you think the teacher helps students explore and understand important scientific ideas? (What does this teacher do or not do that supports your answer?)	VIII. Conceptual Understandings II. Knowledge of Science
IV. Community and Professional Development	In your work outside the classroom, what was most effective in impacting student learning? Why?	5. Based on both of these lists, which one activity do you think is most important to helping a teacher become more effective at improving student learning? Please explain your reasons for making this choice.	XII. Collegiality and Leadership XI. Family and Community Outreach
	Considering the patterns evident in all of your accomplishments taken together, what is your plan to further impact student learning in the future?	4. Is there any other activity missing from this list that you think is especially helpful in improving student learning?	XIII. Reflection III. Instructional Resources

Successful Lesson (Interview Only)	What are the relevant features of your teaching context (school, class, students, community) that were influential in developing your response to this entry?	Please describe for me the setting for the class you will share. (What was the subject? Length of class? When did this class take place?)	I. Understanding Students
	What are the number, ages, and grades of the students in the class featured in this entry and the title and subject matter of the class?	How many students were in the class and what grade levels were represented?	I. Understanding Students
	What are your goals for this lesson, including concepts, attitudes, processes, and skills you want students to develop? Why are these important learning goals for these students?	What were the student learning goals for this lesson?	VIII. Conceptual Understandings
	Why are these important learning goals for these students?	Why were these goals important for these students?	I. Understanding Students
	How do these goals fit into your overall goals for the year?	How did these goals fit into your overall goals for the year?	IX. Contexts of Science

Appendix D

Hypothesis Testing

Table D.1 provides a summary of all hypotheses tested including equivalent, nonequivalent, and the overall comparisons. The discussion addresses the first two in greater detail.

EQUIVALENT HYPOTHESES (H1–H4)

The detailed results of testing the equivalent hypotheses 1–4 are provided in table D.2. Each equivalent hypothesis was analyzed using a two-tailed independent t-test to check for significant differences. The two-tailed test was selected since the means compared could move either up or down. No significant difference was identified in each of the four equivalent hypotheses at the 0.05 level.

Table D.1.   Summary of Hypotheses

Hypothesis	Predicted Relationship	Type of t-Test	Shorthand
1	Group 2A-Post = Group 2B	Independent 2-tailed	O3 = O4
2	Group 2A-Pre = Group 3	Independent 2-tailed	O2 = O5
3	Group 2A-Post = Group 1	Independent 2-tailed	O3 = O1
4	Group 2B = Group 1	Independent 2-tailed	O4 = O1
5	Group 1 > Group 2A-Pre	Independent 1-tailed	O1 > O2
6	Group 1 > Group 3	Independent 1-tailed	O1 > O5
7	Group 2A-Post > Group 2A-Pre	Dependent 1-tailed	O3 > O2
8	Group 2A-Post > Group 3	Independent 1-tailed	O3 > O5
9	Group 2B > Group 3	Independent 1-tailed	O4 > O5
10	Group 2B > Group 2A-Pre	Independent 1-tailed	O4 > O2
Overall	(Groups 1 + 2B) > (Groups 2A-Pre + 3)	Independent 1-tailed	(O1 + O4) > (O2 + O5)

Table D.2. Analysis of Equivalent Hypotheses (H1–H4)

Group Statistics

| | | | Standards Overall Average | | | Independent Samples Test | | | | | |
| | | | | | | | | t-test for Equality of Means | | | |
Hypothesis	Comparison	N	Mean	Std. Dev.	Std. Error	t	df	Sig. 2-tailed	Mean Diff.	Std. Error	Power
H1	O3 (Post)	18	2.723	0.418	0.098	−0.508	36	0.615	−0.070	0.137	0.070
	O4 (Post)	20	2.792	0.425	0.095						
H2	O2 (Pre)	18	2.641	0.559	0.132	0.795	56	0.430	0.101	0.127	0.118
	O5 (Pre)	40	2.540	0.391	0.062						
H3	O3 (Post)	18	2.723	0.418	0.098	−0.703	56	0.485	−0.088	0.126	0.070
	O1 (Post)	40	2.811	0.453	0.072						
H4	O4 (Post)	20	2.792	0.425	0.095	−0.154	58	0.878	−0.019	0.122	0.028
	O1 (Post)	40	2.811	0.453	0.072						

An error-control procedure (i.e., the Bonferroni adjustment) was not used in the analysis of the equivalent hypotheses, since each observation data set involved in a comparison was separate and distinct. Though multiple hypotheses were being tested, each hypothesis compared two different observation points or data sets.

The power for each hypothesis was quite low, indicating a maximum probability of 12 percent for making a type II error, and a minimum probability of 3 percent for making a type II error or failing to see difference when differences really exist. From these results, it can be inferred that the preobservations do not differ from each other, and that the postobservations do not differ from each other. Both inferences work to strengthen the validity of the proposed model on interaction between the dependent variable (candidate scores) and independent variable (certification).

Hypothesis 1 ($O_3 = O_4$) is an especially important test. Hypothesis 1 examines the two postobservations of Group 2. Group 2 was divided into Group 2A and Group 2B in order to investigate the effect of testing. Group 2A was observed prior to the intervention (O_2) and after the intervention (O_3), whereas Group 2B was only observed after the intervention (O_4).

If Group 2A-Post (O_3) was significantly different from Group 2B (O_4), then the act of collecting preintervention data on Group 2A would become a rival explanation to the intervention as the cause of observed differences. In other words, any observed gains in assessed scores could be attributed to either the amazing learning experience of being interviewed for this study prior to the intervention, or the intervention itself. The result of hypothesis 1 indicates that there was no observed effect from being interviewed.

NONEQUIVALENT HYPOTHESES (H5–H10)

The nonequivalent hypotheses are less consistent and more complex in nature. These are the hypotheses that compared the postobservations with the preobservations both within and between groups. In each hypothesis, the postobservation was expected to be higher than the preobservation. Because of the expected direction of difference, a one-tailed t-test was used to compare means.

All t-tests were independent, except for hypothesis 7, which is a dependent t-test and examines the within-group differences. As with the equivalent hypotheses, an error control procedure (i.e., the Bonferroni adjustment) was not employed in the analysis of the nonequivalent hypotheses since each observation data set involved in a comparison was separate and distinct. Detailed results for testing hypotheses 5–10 are presented in table D.3.

All six nonequivalent hypotheses indicate mean differences in the correct or predicted direction as indicated by mean differences that are all positive. Out of the six nonequivalent hypotheses examined, H6 ($O_1 > O_5$) and H9 ($O_4 > O_5$) demonstrated significant improvement at the .01 and .05 levels. H5 ($O_1 > O_2$), H7 ($O_3 > O_2$), H8 ($O_3 > O_5$), and H10 ($O_4 > O_2$) did not demonstrate significant differences. It should be pointed out that three of these comparisons include O_2. This circumstance will be the focus of the discussion later in the chapter when the issue of "status" is explored.

A closer examination of the nonequivalent hypotheses reveals some important details. For example, in two hypotheses that showed significant differences (H6 and H9), the effect size is quite large, at .66 for each. This means that the effect of the intervention on observed changes is equal to 66 percent of a standard deviation. In some educational research literature, an effect size of .15 is considered "fair," making the documented effect size in these two hypotheses relatively outstanding. However, the magnitude of these results is tempered by the other four hypotheses that did not demonstrate a difference.

As a group, the nonequivalent hypotheses show a higher power than the equivalent hypotheses. Greater power indicates a higher probably of committing a type II error (i.e., not seeing differences when differences actually exist). In addition, hypothesis 8 is significant at the .10 level and only marginally significant at the .05 level, with a significance of .056. This is important because hypothesis 8 is the only nonsignificant test that does not include a Group 2 comparison. This observation adds credence to the notion that something may be eschewed with the preobservation for Group 2.

The remaining nonsignificant hypotheses (H5, H7, and H10) all involve the preobservation (O_2) for Group 2. Among these hypotheses, Hypothesis 7 is important because it is the only longitudinal measure in this study examining how Group 2A might change from preobservation to postobservation. Why is it that pre-post comparisons that include O_2 do not show significant differences, while those comparisons that do *not* include O_2 demonstrate meaningful change?

These results provide evidence that something is not right with O_2. Either the model is incorrect, or the procedures used during O_2 were flawed. This issue is explored in the limitations section. For now, the results from testing the validity of the model indicate a fairly good level of confidence in the predicted impact of the intervention. Observation 2 was isolated as the weakest when compared with the other four observations.

Table D.3. Analysis of Non-Equivalent Hypotheses (H1–H6)

Group Statistics

	Comparison	N	Mean	Std. Dev.	Std. Error	t	df	Sig. 2-tailed	Mean Diff.	Std. Error	Effect Size	Power
H5	O1-Post	40	2.811	0.453	0.072	1.229	56	0.224	0.170	0.138		0.331
	O2-Pre	18	2.641	0.559	0.132							
H6	O1-Post	40	2.811	0.453	0.072	2.868	78	0.005**	0.271	0.095	0.662	
	O5-Pre	40	2.540	0.391	0.062							
H7	O3-Post	18	2.723	0.418	0.098	0.867	17	0.398	0.082	0.094		0.202
	O2-Pre	18	2.641	0.559	0.132							
H8	O3-Post	18	2.723	0.418	0.098	1.615	56	0.112	0.183	0.113		0.477
	O5-Pre	40	2.540	0.391	0.062							
H9	O4-Post	20	2.792	0.425	0.095	2.291	58	0.026*	0.253	0.110	0.658	
	O5-Pre	40	2.540	0.391	0.062							
H10	O4-Post	20	2.792	0.425	0.095	0.944	36	0.351	0.151	0.160		0.233
	O2-Pre	18	2.641	0.559	0.132							

Independent t-Test for Equality of Means

*Significant at the p = 0.05 level
**Significant at the p = 0.01 level

Appendix E

Coding and Calculation of Status for Precertifiation Candidates

Example 1   Candidate #301757851   Coded as a 14% Status

INTERVIEWER: Could you please describe your current status with the certification process?

CANDIDATE: Beginning.

INTERVIEWER:—Which means?

CANDIDATE: Beginning means—I've filled out all the paperwork, paid all the fees, and got the box.

INTERVIEWER: Great—okay. Anything else?

CANDIDATE: And well I've read the material a few times, gone to a seminar.

Example 2   Candidate #317870367   Coded as a 52% Status

INTERVIEWER: Could you please describe your current status with the certification process?

CANDIDATE: I'm just finished and am ready to seal the entry envelope 4 with my documented accomplishments. You know, just put it away—I've rewritten it so many times. On entry 2 I think I'm more than half way—I have my introduction and my data analysis and I'm getting the conclusion this week. Hopefully on tape. I'm most of the way through—maybe I'm half way through writing and I will rewrite a lot. So I would say close to 50-percent finished with entry 2.

Table E.1. Estimation of Status for Group 2A

Received Materials	Organize Materials	Read Instructions	Read Standards	Overall Planning	Discussions	Permission Slips	Fill Out Forms	Videotape	Workshops	Entry 1: Idea Over Time				Entry 2: Scientific Inquiry				Entry 3: Discussion				Entry 4: Professional				TOTAL STATUS
										Plan	Collect	Analyze	Write	Plan	Collect	Analyze	Write	Plan	Collect	Analyze	Write	Plan	Collect	Analyze	Write	
2	2	2	2	2	2	2	2	2	2	5	5	5	5	5	5	5	5	5	5	5	5	5	5	5	5	100
2	2	2	2		2		2		2																	14
2																						4				6
2		2				2	2	2		5	5			5	5			5	5			5	5			50
2		2	2				2			5	5											5	5	5	5	38
2	2	2																								6
2										5	5			5	5							5	5			32
2	2	2		2		2		2																		12
2	2	2	2	2		2	2	2														5	5			26
2	2	2	2			2	2	2												5		5	5	5		34
2		2	2																							6
2		2	2	2		2								5	5							5	5			30
2						2		2												5	5	5	5			26
2		2		2		2																5	5	5		23
2	2	2				2	2	2		5				5	5			5				5	5	5	5	52
2	2		2							5												5				16
2										5												5				12
2							2															5	5	5	5	24
2	2		2																							6
2			2																			5	5			14
2						2		2														5	5			16

I'm just getting started on the writing on entry 1—but I have a head full of it. It's jelling and I have my units chosen and my—the pieces of work that I will use for the idea I'm teaching. That one is in process in my head and I expect it to be the most challenging in the writing for me. And the discussion I've just picked a couple of things I think I may use and I haven't even started on that yet except to begin thinking about which topics I think would make good discussion topics and which class. And I haven't given one thought to the assessment center tasks yet.

STATUS CODING EXPLANATION

In order to get the most accurate assessment of a teacher's status with regard to the National Board certification process, a detailed qualitative analysis was performed. This analysis involved coding each participant's response to the question: "Could you please describe your current status with the certification process?" They were asked this question after the introductory questions and before Scenario 1.

The responses provided evidence as to what the teacher had done, completed, worked on, thought about, written, videotaped, and studied. A coding scheme was devised that allocated a certain percentage of the entire portfolio process. For example, receiving materials counted as 2 percent of the total amount of work required to complete the portfolio. The percentages were based on the researcher's experience and familiarity with the certification process and a few basic assumptions. Examples 1 and 2 demonstrate the type of evidence and the resulting coded status.

The first basic assumption is that all four entries are of equal difficulty and require equal amounts of time. This of course is not necessarily true, but it does allow for teachers doing different types of work to be compared. The assumption of equality between entries is not unwarranted. The process is identical for every entry. Each entry requires a candidate to plan his or her activities and response, collect evidence, analyze that evidence, and then write about the experience. For this analysis, completing all four entries accounts for 80 percent of the portfolio construction. The remaining 20 percent includes paperwork, permission slips, preliminary reading, and preparation. The resulting status measure for each candidate is on average within 5 percent of the candidate's own estimation.

About the Author

David Lustick began his teaching career in the New York City public school system nearly twenty-five years ago. He came to secondary science teaching with a bachelor's degree in nutritional biochemistry from Cornell University and earned his master's degree in education from Harvard in 1989. In 1998, while teaching chemistry and environmental science in Brazil, he became one of the first National Board–certified teachers in Adolescence and Young Adult Science. Soon afterward, he earned a doctorate in teaching, curriculum, and policy at Michigan State University. He is the author of numerous articles and publications about education and in 2008 successfully renewed his National Board certification. He is currently an assistant professor of science education at the University of Massachusetts Lowell's Graduate School of Education.